Accelerating the Learning of All Students

Learning of All Students

Cultivating Culture
Change in Schools,
Classrooms, and Individuals

Christine Finnan

Julie D. Swanson

Westview Press
A Member of the Perseus Books Group

Renewing American Schools: The Educational Knowledge Base

All rights reserved. Printed in the United States of America. No part of this publication may be reproduced or transmitted in any form or by any means, electronic or mechanical, including photocopy, recording, or any information storage and retrieval system, without permission in writing from the publisher.

Copyright © 2000 by Westview Press, A Member of the Perseus Books Group

Published in 2000 in the United States of America by Westview Press, 5500 Central Avenue, Boulder, Colorado 80301–2877, and in the United Kingdom by Westview Press, 12 Hid's Copse Road, Cumnor Hill, Oxford OX2 9JJ

Find us on the World Wide Web at www.westviewpress.com

Library of Congress Cataloging-in-Publication Data
Finnan, Christine R.
   Accelerating the learning of all students/ Christine Finnan, Julie D. Swanson
      p.   cm.—(Renewing American Schools)
   Includes bibliographical references and index.
   ISBN 0-8133-9050-8 (pbk.)
   1. Educational acceleration.   2. School improvement programs.   I. Swanson, Julie D.
II. Title.   III. Series.

LB1029.A22 F56 2000
371.2'8—dc21   00-035937

The paper used in this publication meets the requirements of the American National Standard for Permanence of Paper for Printed Library Materials Z39.48–1984.

10   9   8   7   6   5   4   3   2   1

This book is dedicated to Hank Levin in thanks for his support, encouragement, and inspiration.

Contents

Tables and Figures

Foreword

In the early 1980s I undertook a study of why the schooling of children in at-risk situations did not seem to close the gap in academic achievement between them and other students. As part of this study, I visited a very large number of schools with high concentrations of at-risk students. I found most of these students were placed in "remedial" programs that reduced the pace and challenge of instruction and placed great emphasis on "drill and skill" exercises. The notion was that since these children enter school without the developmental experience that would enable them to do "mainstream" work, they must undertake a boot camp of drill to build a foundation of skills before they can entertain more meaningful challenges. Sadly, it is a form of training that most of them never escape as they fall farther and farther behind the mainstream. The remedial classrooms that I observed were characterized by a painfully slow pacing of the curriculum and a reduced challenge of instruction. There was a virtual omission of meaningful applications and problem solving and a derogation of joyful learning experiences and links to the culture of the children. Students and teachers appeared to be disengaged from the educational process, following established routines rather than purposeful and motivating educational paths. It was little wonder that these students got farther and farther behind the academic mainstream the longer that they were in school.

But in many of these schools there were a few classrooms where students were considered to be gifted and talented. In those classes, students were identified by their strengths, not their weaknesses, and provided with activities and projects that built on these strengths. Instead of being stigmatized with labels such as "slow learner," their talents were celebrated. And the learning environment was electric with activity motivating the highly valued and stimulated students to think, reflect, create, and master.

These experiences challenged my own thinking about what was best for students in at-risk situations. Paradoxically, it seemed that the most promising educational route for such students was one that would accelerate their growth and development rather than slowing it through remediation. Academic enrichment seemed to be the prescription for success. Sadly, with the exception of Joseph Renzulli and Sally Reis, there was little recognition in the early eighties that this approach was appropriate for all students. For example, out of hundreds of citations to literature on "acceleration," we could find only a single reference to acceleration for at-risk students. It appeared that the primacy of the sorting and selection function in gifted and talented education had obscured the importance of enrichment approaches for all students including those most at risk of educational failure.

In 1986 we established our first Accelerated Schools as an attempt to use enrichment approaches to meet the needs of all children and to bring at-risk students into the mainstream through acceleration rather than remediation. This work was long and arduous and can best be described as learning how to transform school cultures and practices with limited resources and scarce professional development time. By 1988 we were able to report very promising results, and by 2000 the movement of Accelerated Schools had encompassed over 1,300 schools and 12 regional centers, including some 50 schools in Hong Kong (available: http://www.acceleratedschools.net). One of those regional centers was established in South Carolina along with a Center for Accelerated Learning at the College of Charleston. It is out of the work of this center with its extensive field experiences that Christine Finnan and Julie D. Swanson have written this important volume.

Both authors are extremely talented researchers and practitioners. I have worked closely with Christine Finnan since 1977 in her quest to understand and transform school culture. She has taught me much about this subject. My work with Julie Swanson is more recent and enabled me to connect more closely with the gifted and talented educational community. From Swanson I have learned to validate our accelerated practices in gifted and talented approaches and to connect with the work of Renzulli, Reis, Feldhusen, and other leading researchers in the gifted and talented community. One indirect consequence is the marriage of the National Center for the Accelerated Schools Project with Renzulli's National Research Center on the Gifted and Talented (NRC/GT), which is being consummated in 2000 with the move of Accelerated Schools to the University of Connecticut and the NRC/GT.

Essentially, Finnan and Swanson have written a comprehensive work on accelerating the learning of all students. They have taken the overall concepts of enrichment and acceleration and extended these to all students and all schools, an endeavor that is highly consistent with both our Accelerated Schools Project and the work of Joseph Renzulli and Sally Reis on School-Wide Enrichment. Most notably they have connected the pedagogy of acceleration to the organization and culture of the school, a unique contribution of the Accelerated Schools Project. Much of the literature on school transformation and reform emphasizes what a transformed school and classroom might look like and places little emphasis on the transformational process, how one gets from here to there. Yet, surely the greatest failing of American education is not a dearth of ideas but a failure to take good ideas and incorporate them as regular features of schools and classrooms. The coupling of the concepts and practices of accelerated learning with the cultural and transformational aspects makes this a unique work that should receive the widest readership. It is with great pleasure that I witness the publication of this book.

Henry M. Levin
William Heard Kilpatrick Professor of Economics and Education,
Teachers College, Columbia University, and Founding
Director of the Accelerated Schools Project

Foreword

Equity Plus Excellence: A Very Possible Mission

If there is any single, unifying characteristic of today's schools, that characteristic is surely a resistance, if not an immunity, to change. The ponderous rhetoric about school improvement and the endless lists of mission statements, noble goals, and new paradigms need to be tempered with a little common sense about the purpose of schooling and the essential ingredients needed to make learning enjoyable, efficient, and satisfying for every one of our students. Practice needs to precede policy so that we eventually adopt what works rather than what politicians and others far removed from classrooms try to ram down the throats of the persons who deliver the services. Finally, we need to adopt gentle and evolutionary approaches to change that school personnel can live with and grow with, rather than be threatened by. Within these efforts exists the seemingly impossible pursuit of the marriage of equity and excellence, a pursuit that is essential to maximally effective education but has largely eluded us thus far.

Albert Einstein once said that problems cannot be solved at the same level of consciousness that created them. Transcending these previous levels of consciousness will not be an easy task. For example, the factory model of schooling that gave rise to the clear and present danger now facing our schools cannot be used to overcome the very problems that it has created. We must consider very thoughtfully the idea behind Einstein's words if there is to be any hope whatsoever of turning around a public education system that is slowly but surely deteriorating into a massive warehouse of regimentation, boredom, underachievement, unfulfilled expectations, and broken dreams.

It is difficult to find plans and policies that are qualitatively different from the old top-down patterns of school organization or the traditional linear/sequential models of learning that have dominated our schools. The creative ideas and efforts described in this book provide a plan for bridging the equity and excellence dilemma. The authors, and those with whom they have worked, are setting forth a framework in which opportunities, resources, and encouragement can be provided to support the continuous escalation of student involvement at all levels of achievement in both required and self-selected activities.

This approach seeks to develop multiple potentials for each and every student that we, as educators, are called to instruct and nurture. *Accelerating the Learning of All Students* highlights practices that have been a mainstay of many special programs for "the gifted"—then uses and integrates these best practices into the general education model for the purpose of upgrading the performance of all students. This integration of know-how from programs for the gifted is a favorable development for two reasons. First, the adoption of many of these practices is indicative of their viability and usefulness in total school improvement. Second, all students should have opportunities to develop higher-order thinking skills, to pursue more rigorous content than is typically found in today's "dumbed-down" textbooks, and to undertake firsthand investigations.

Concerns about equity and excellence have framed the dialogue that grew up around the school improvement initiatives that began in the 1960s and that were accelerated in the mid-1980s following publication of the report titled *A Nation at Risk*. Advocates for improving equity in education concentrated their attention on pushing up achievement test scores by developing school reform models and producing materials that focused on highly repetitious basic skill learning. So pervasive was this structured and didactic approach to learning that it earned its own pejorative designation as the "dumbing down of curriculum." This approach, drill and practice in the skills that typically show up on achievement tests, seemed like a logical way of dealing with what was a straightforward problem in learning. If a student was deficient in the basics, give him or her more practice. And if improvements were not forthcoming, simply increase the amount of practice. The only problem is that after almost four decades of investing literally billions of dollars in intensive compensatory approaches, we have found that these approaches simply don't work!

Most educational reform leaders agree that remedial models for school improvement have not been highly successful. Attempts to push up achievement test scores from "the bottom" through highly prescriptive mastery learning models have frustrated low-achieving students and dragged down the performance of average and high-achieving youngsters. These remediation practices have fallen short of accomplishing the gains they purport to foster and the promise of equitably servicing the needs of students at all levels.

With this in mind, accelerated learning approaches take on the challenge of reformulating how we develop the abilities of students who have typically been relegated to remedial practices. The suggestions presented in this book reflect a democratic ideal that accommodates the full range of individual differences in the entire student population and opens the door to programming models that develop the talent potentials of many at-risk students—those often excluded from anything but the most basic of curricular experiences.

No easy method for challenging and accelerating all students' learning exists. The society in which we live, as well as the schools, which are a reflection of this society, are replete with complexity, cultural differences, pressing needs and demands, and perspectives, which bring a variety of assumptions to the mix. And yet we must believe in and strive for the union of equity and excellence as reality and not just as theory.

Perhaps the most impressive and essential idea presented in the text that follows is the mission and commitment to address effectively the vast and individual needs of our diverse student population. The authors wisely recognize the foolishness of utilizing one strategy or model for accomplishing the task at hand. Rather, they offer as an alternative a clear and flexible approach that is broader, incorporating a variety of established and successful strategies for the improved education of all students. Their many practical suggestions just may make the seemingly impossible rapprochement between equity and excellence very possible.

So, regardless of the difficulty, we turn our minds and our eyes forward, working together and with open minds for our kids, and for our collective future.

Joseph S. Renzulli,
Director
The National Research Center on the
Gifted and Talented,
University of Connecticut

Introduction

Imagine a young child you care about deeply. What kind of education do you hope he or she will receive? Most likely you hope for an experience that the child finds stimulating, challenging, engaging, and relevant. Let's imagine this child has been identified as gifted. How likely is it that he or she will receive the kind of educational experience described above? Now imagine the child has trouble learning and has been labeled low achieving. What is the likelihood he or she will receive such an education? What is the likelihood for this kind of an educational experience if he or she is an average student?

Most people would agree that gifted children are more likely than other children to have a stimulating, challenging, engaging, and relevant learning experience. Gifted children are often provided enrichment opportunities that allow them to build on their strengths and use their full potential. Average children's odds of having such a learning experience are greatly reduced. Average children spend a good part of their day working from text books, completing worksheets, and learning isolated facts. Low-achieving children are highly unlikely to have a stimulating learning experience. These children spend the majority of their time drilling on skills they have not mastered or sitting through whole class instruction they do not understand.

Accelerated learning describes learning experiences that stimulate and challenge students. The term "accelerate" can be applied to learning experiences designed for students identified as gifted and for students identified as low achieving. It is most promising when it is applied to the learning of all students. The term "accelerate" can describe efforts to move some students faster than other students through a course of study. We accelerate the learning of gifted students by moving them faster than other students through a course of study, often by having them skip grades. Educators have begun to speak of accelerating the learning of low-achieving students as an alternative to remedial instruction. In this case, the emphasis is on moving students faster through material in order to catch up with other students.

Both of these applications of the term "accelerate" involve labeling some students and separating them from other students. The emphasis on sorting students derives from a desire to meet their individual needs. On the surface this is a laudable goal; everyone wants to meet the individual needs of students. However, such practices exacerbate inequities that have existed in the United States for more than two hundred years. Rather than meeting individual needs, such practices result in middle- and upper-class students predominating in classes or programs for the gifted, while low-income and minority students disproportionately receive remedial or special education services.

When we remove the emphasis on labeling and sorting students, acceleration takes on another meaning. It no longer focuses on identifying students' strengths and weaknesses and grouping them by ability. Rather, it calls for teachers to accept diversity in students' abilities and experiences and to build on students' strengths to provide an educational experience for *all students* that is of high intellectual quality—that is substantive, authentic, and relevant. In addition, accelerated learning for all students is continuous and connected; it encourages students to make connections with prior knowledge and across subjects. Finally, it is a vehicle for all students, whether identified as gifted, low achieving, or average, to meet high standards.

Accelerated learning is a process for achieving the high standards that characterize education reform efforts currently sweeping the nation. As we enter the twenty-first century, nearly all states will have enacted some kind of accountability legislation that is tied to a set of academic content standards. Students across the country are being held accountable to meet challenging content standards, or they will not be promoted to the next grade. It is no longer acceptable for some students to learn challenging material while expectations for others are lower. Moreover, teachers and administrators are being held accountable for improving student achievement. Teacher educators are also being held accountable for the ability of their graduates to challenge all students.

One might ask if the kind of transformation in teaching and learning needed for all students to meet high standards can occur by passing accountability legislation, providing intensive professional development for teachers, or changing teacher preparation. If past efforts to change education through legislation or other outside interventions are any indication, the answer is a resounding no. Transforming schools and classrooms so that all students meet high standards requires deep change in school and classroom culture. For more than a century schools have been labeling and sorting students with the expectation that each group of students will meet different standards; these practices are unlikely to change substantially overnight. These practices are imbedded in school and classroom cultures and support efforts to accelerate learning for well-defined groups of students. Efforts to accelerate the learning of all students require an internal process of culture change that is facilitated through the support of state and district policies.

Schools and classrooms that accelerate learning so that all students can meet high standards do exist, but they are fundamentally different from most schools and classrooms. The key difference is found in the culture of these schools and classrooms. Schools and classrooms bring together individuals who hold sets of assumptions about students (e.g., that students can or cannot learn), adult roles in the school (e.g., that teachers work alone or collaboratively), appropriate educational strategies (e.g., that students are best taught through drill and practice or through active engagement with complex materials), the value of change (e.g., that it is to be avoided or that it is challenging and invigorating), and appropriate communication patterns (e.g., that the teacher directs all communication or that it is communally developed). Individuals' assumptions come together within a school or classroom to form shared cultural assumptions that shape what is valued in the school, the actions individuals are expected to take, and shared expectations about who is responsible for what.

This book moves from a description of the multiple uses of accelerated learning to a discussion of the changes in schools, classrooms, and individuals that must occur for all students to benefit from accelerated learning. Chapter 1 defines accelerated learning and examines the historical and social context that has shaped the evolution of the use of this term. Chapters 2 and 3 provide an in-depth exploration of accelerated learning as applied to students identified as gifted (Chapter 2) and low achieving (Chapter 3). Each of these chapters provides descriptions of the target students and programs that have been developed to accelerate their learning. Chapter 4 provides a description of efforts to accelerate the learning of all students. The examples illustrate a shift from emphasizing the identification of students and moving faster through material to challenging all students to delve deeply into their learning.

Chapter 5 provides a transition from descriptions of students and programs and argues that accelerated learning for all students will not occur without changing school and classroom cultures. The chapter defines culture and highlights the importance of understanding the assumptions held by all people who come together to make up the classroom or school culture. Chapters 6 and 7 identify key components of school and classroom culture that serve to encourage or discourage efforts to accelerate learning. Chapter 8 explores the responsibilities individuals must accept to cultivate school and classroom cultures that encourage the acceleration of all students.

This book synthesizes work both authors have been engaged in through most of our professional careers. We share a commitment to improving education for all students, especially those who come from groups that have historically not received a high-quality education. We have both been involved in efforts to reform schools and classrooms to better serve historically disadvantaged students. I, Christine Finnan, have been the director of the South Carolina Accelerated Schools Project since 1991. I became involved in the Accelerated Schools Project after completing an ethnographic study of the implementation of the project in a California middle school. I, Julie D. Swanson, have directed two federal Jacob Javits demonstration projects. The first was designed to find alternative ways to identify gifted students in rural schools, and the second trains teachers to use materials developed for gifted students with all students in three schools serving low-income students.

We began working together in 1995 when we were awarded a grant from the South Carolina Commission on Higher Education to establish the Center of Excellence in Accelerating Learning at the College of Charleston.[1] At about the same time, Henry M. Levin approached us about the prospect of writing a book for the series *Renewing American Schools,* which he edits along with Jeannie Oakes. This series is designed to create an educational knowledge base of current research on topics of interest to the general public. In keeping with the goals of the series, this book synthesizes research, best practice, and current thought and policy on accelerated learning.

There are many people we want to thank for helping and supporting us through this process. Above all, we want to thank Henry M. Levin for providing us the opportunity to write this book and for trusting us to put into words a commitment to children that has been his passion through most of his career. We also want to acknowledge the special contributions of two colleagues. Chapter 3 was coauthored with Jane F. Zenger and Chapter 8 was coauthored with Diane C. Cudahy. We want to thank our editor, Cathy Murphy, who provided moral support, exhibited great patience, and provided insightful feedback.

Several people provided very useful feedback on the draft of this book. We want to thank Lorin Anderson, Ruth Cohen, Henry Levin, Joe Renzulli, and George Spindler for their comments. We also want to thank all of the teachers, principals, students, and parents in schools where we have worked through the Accelerated Schools Project, Project Search, and Project Breakthrough for their inspiration. Thanks also go out to colleagues at the Accelerated Schools Project national center and satellite centers around the country and to colleagues closer to home who have supported us in our work, especially Russell Sills, Frank Bouknight, Donna Darby, Linda Kirszenbaum, and Fran O'Toole.

Special thanks are extended to colleagues at the College of Charleston, especially to Nancy Sorenson, our dean, for valuing our work and for appreciating the importance of scholarship. We also want to extend special thanks to Ruth Orman for her good humor and careful review of both early and near final versions of the manuscript and to colleagues in the School of Education, especially Diane Cudahy, Ken Bower, and the members of the Center of Excellence Research Group for comments on early versions of several chapters. Special thanks go to Karen Dennis for careful attention to detail and good-humored willingness to help with manuscript preparation and to Natalie Klutz for additional support in manuscript preparation.

We want to thank the South Carolina Commission on Higher Education, especially Nancy Healy-Williams, for providing us the opportunity to establish the Center of Excellence in Accelerating Learning. The commitment of the Commission on Higher Education to disseminating state-of-the-art research provided incentive and financial support for this book.

Finally, we extend our thanks to our families. We thank our parents for instilling in us a love of learning and a work ethic that enabled us to complete this project. We also thank our husbands, George and Tyno, for their patience and support. Finally, special thanks are sent to Holly and Leslie. Not only did they tolerate many weekends and evenings in front of the computer and accept a preoccupation with "The Book," but they also provided inspiration, insightful dinner conversations, and real-life examples of the joy, mystery, and occasional disappointments of school life.

Note

1. The South Carolina Commission on Higher Education funds a Center of Excellence each year at a state college or university to provide state-of-the-art research on a topic of concern in the state. Each center is expected to disseminate research to institutions of higher education and to schools and the general public.

1 The Multiple Meanings of Acceleration

Anna is an attractive, gregarious fifth grader who has been identified as gifted and talented. She lives in a comfortable middle-class neighborhood with her college-educated parents and older sister. Most nights, the family catches up on the girls' activities over dinner. Anna recounts stories from her special class for gifted students, while her sister talks about the demands of Advanced Placement high school courses. Both girls take piano lessons, and Anna is a member of a neighborhood swim team. Anna's parents are proud of her accomplishments, especially the fact that she skipped first grade and tested into the gifted program in her school. Anna's parents are pleased with the schools in their community, as long as their girls are selected for gifted classes or advanced tracks. Knowledgeable parents in the community know that they must be assertive to ensure that their children are well served in the schools.

Richard lives with his extended family in a small bungalow in a neighborhood of light industry and small homes. Richard shares his three-bedroom home with his parents, five siblings, and his mother's sister and mother. Richard's mother finished high school. His father dropped out and has been working since he was seventeen. Richard's older brother recently stopped attending high school, which is causing considerable tension in the home. When Richard is not caring for his younger siblings, he spends most of his time playing baseball and basketball at the local park. Richard began falling behind his peers in the third grade. By fifth grade he was so far behind that his teacher recommended he be retained. The principal of his elementary school thought he might benefit from a special class at the middle school designed to move students through the fifth and sixth grades in one year. Since enrolling in this class, Richard's attitude toward school has improved; he has even begun to talk about attending college.

Sara is a shy and serious fourth grader who lives with her single mother, two younger brothers, and elderly grandmother in a small house near Westview Elementary School. Her mother has worked at the local button factory since she graduated from high school. Sara enjoys singing in the school chorus and the church choir, and she likes to go to school. Although Sara's mother would love to move to a community with better employment options, she stays in her job because she wants Sara and her brothers to graduate from Westview Elementary School. She has been impressed with the innovative and challenging learning experiences Sara and her brothers have had and with the willingness of the teachers and principal to listen to her ideas and concerns. She fears that Sara, not the top student in her class, would not have as engaging or challenging an education experience if she went to another school.

Anna, Richard, and Sara are very different children. They have different home environments and different experiences in school. Anna is considered gifted; Richard, low achieving, and Sara, average. Despite their differences they share one common experience: They are all experiencing accelerated learning. These three children exemplify the three common uses of the term "accelerate." As this chapter and Chapters 2, 3, and 4 describe, educational strategies targeted to very different student populations have all used the label "accelerated." This has led to considerable confusion but also to a cross-fertilization of educational strategies that is potentially beneficial to all students.

Acceleration Defined

Accelerated learning appears easy to define. The *American Heritage Dictionary* defines "accelerate" as "to move or act faster" or "to engage in an academic program that progresses faster than usual." It seems clear from this definition that all accelerated programs involve speed and moving faster through material. As will be evident from the following discussion, this definition lays out only a small part of what is meant by acceleration. The dictionary definition does not address the issues of who is being accelerated or how students are accelerated, or the fact that acceleration has come to mean more than just moving faster through an academic program. It also does not recognize that the term "accelerate" has been associated with school reform initiatives, special curricula, or alternative educational delivery systems. The following discussion is summarized in Table 1.1.

Acceleration for Whom?

When the focus of acceleration is on serving special student populations, it tends to emphasize speed, moving faster. Special programs established for gifted students are described as accelerated because they provide an opportunity for these students to master a traditional curriculum in a shorter time or earlier in their school career than other students. Since

TABLE 1.1   Understanding Acceleration

Core Defining Elements	Target Students	Strategies
Master traditional curriculum in a shorter time or at an earlier age	Gifted students	• Alternative adminis-trative options • Instructional practices
Speed up learning to "catch up" with age peers	Low achievers	• Special classes with special individualized curriculum
Learning that is • of high intellectual quality—substantive, authentic, and relevant • continuous and connected • grounded in high standards	All students	• Instructional practices • School reform initiatives • Use of specific curriculum

gifted students cover the established curriculum in a shorter time, they have the time and opportunity to explore personal interests and go deeper into subject areas. In other words, acceleration for gifted students is based on moving more quickly through an established curriculum, but it also involves providing students an opportunity to work independently with more abstract, complex, open-ended, multifaceted, and ambiguous material (Tomlinson 1996).

The definition of accelerated learning for low-achieving students rests almost exclusively on speeding up learning. These students need to "catch up" with their peers, so they must cover more material in a shorter time. As in the case of gifted students, acceleration for low-achieving students relates to speeding up; unlike gifted students, speeding up for low achievers means catching up. However, programs for gifted and low-achieving students are not based solely on speed. The focus on moving faster is modified for gifted students so that they remain challenged once they have mastered the standard curriculum; for low-achieving students it is modified so that they will not become frustrated by more of the same unsuccessful teaching. Thus, accelerated learning for low-achieving students is based on moving faster through the standard curriculum but in a way that will engage students who lack confidence in their ability.

If moving faster through curriculum is at the center of both of these definitions, where does that leave the average student? The established curriculum is set for the average student, so moving faster through it is not an issue. The issue arises when we focus on the accommodations made for gifted and low-achieving students to make learning more relevant, challenging, and engaging: Shouldn't the same accommodations be made for average students?

How Are Students Accelerated?

The key to understanding accelerated learning is to realize that it does not involve doing more of the same, just faster. It involves a radical change in how and what students are taught and in the context in which they are taught. There is nothing about accelerated learning that makes it inappropriate for any student; as the following chapters illustrate, it describes strategies that are highly effective with all students. Accelerated learning involves holding different assumptions about students, the role of adults in the school and classroom, effective educational practices, the value of change, and appropriate communication and discourse. These assumptions will be discussed in depth in later chapters.

Accelerated learning focuses on the intellectual quality of schoolwork, on the depth and substance of learning (Newmann, Secada, and Wehlage 1995). It builds on students' strengths and intellectual accomplishments and is based on the assumption that all students have strengths (Means, Chelemer, and Knapp 1991; Knapp 1995a). Teachers are primarily responsible for ensuring that students experience accelerated learning. Their teaching must be relevant and integrated, allowing students to engage in challenging and interesting work.

Several school reform initiatives have helped to move the definition of acceleration from a focus on speed to one of depth. The Accelerated Schools Project (ASP) is the most prominent of these initiatives. The Accelerated Schools Project is based on a belief that all students should benefit from the enriched learning experience usually reserved for gifted students. Its concept of "powerful learning" guides all actions taken by accelerated schools (Keller and Huebner 1997; Hopfenberg et al. 1993). Powerful learning is authentic, interactive, inclusive, continuous, and learner centered. Another initiative, Schools for Talent Development (Renzulli 1994b), focuses on accelerating learning for all students through the use of approaches and materials that were formerly reserved for identified gifted students. This initiative provides schools more demanding and challenging instruction, which is based on interdisciplinary, thematic curricula. Its curricula incorporate concept learning, student investigations of relevant problems, and application of student knowledge in order to accelerate learning.

In addition to the influence of school reform initiatives, the definition of acceleration has broadened as schools have adapted curricula developed for gifted students to use in heterogeneous classes. For example, rigorous and challenging curricula in science, social studies, and language arts was designed for high-ability students by the Center for Gifted Education at the College of William and Mary, but they have been successfully used by students of varied ability. The curricula are rich and substantive, based on "big ideas" as the conduit for learning facts, and have numerous models of thinking embedded in the units. These instructional practices, school reform movements, and specific curricula have helped to expand the definition of accelerated learning so that it applies to all students.

Definition of Accelerated Learning for All Students

When accelerated learning is defined as a deep, challenging, and relevant learning experience rather than an opportunity to move faster through an established curriculum, the value of its application to all students is obvious. Accelerated learning is based on the assumption that *all* students have special needs and talents and that it is our responsibility to create a learning environment where all are challenged and engaged. Although the task of nurturing the needs and talents of all students sounds somewhat overwhelming, we argue that real learning is personal and individual and what we want for all students is real, deep, and substantive learning. The concept of accelerated learning is based on the assumption that schools can accomplish both an equitable and excellent education of children. In accelerated learning the emphasis is on challenging all students to think, solve problems, and communicate effectively, not on selecting out the "best" students to experience the best curricula and on training the rest to follow directions. Expectations for all students are high, but they are not the same. When accelerated learning is offered to all students, it is the responsibility of the teacher and other educators to tailor curriculum and instructional strategies to challenge each student. These strategies are discussed in more depth in the following chapters.

The definition of accelerated learning draws from recent research on effective teaching. Whether called gifted and talented teaching strategies (Tomlinson 1996), powerful learning (Keller and Huebner 1997; Hopfenberg et al. 1993), teaching for understanding (McLaughlin and Talbert 1993), authentic academic achievement (Newmann, Secada, and Wehlage 1995), or advanced skills (Means, Chelemer, and Knapp 1991; Knapp 1995a), these practices encourage deep and substantive learning, use student strengths to address weaknesses, and center on active, enthusiastic student participation in learning. Chapter 4 takes an in-depth look at the definition's research base.

Accelerated learning is learning that is of high intellectual quality; it is substantive, authentic, and relevant. Accelerated learning is continuous and connected, it is grounded in high standards. Accelerated learning occurs when students are active and responsible, involved in intellectual pursuits with other students, and turned on to learning. It happens when teachers are highly skilled and knowledgeable; they learn alongside their students and engage in meaningful discussion and dialogue with them. They are reflective in their practice and care about all students.

To summarize, the definition of accelerated learning includes the following:

- Learning that is of high intellectual quality, substantive, authentic and relevant, continuous and connected, and grounded in high standards;
- Students who are active and responsible, involved in intellectual pursuits with other students, and turned on to learning;
- Teachers who are highly skilled and knowledgeable, learn along with their students, engage in meaningful discussion and dialogue with students, are reflective in their practice, and care about all students.

Acceleration for a Few or for All: The Social and Historical Context

Defining accelerated learning has been difficult because it calls attention to tensions that have been part of American education for the past century. Three issues arise when we debate whose education should be accelerated and how we should accelerate. The first is the value of identifying students and labeling them versus serving diverse students. The second involves the consequence of labeling and categorizing students, and the third issue addresses whether we can provide equal educational opportunity without sacrificing access to excellence. Examining the social and historical context that has created and sustained these tensions helps us to understand why they remain unresolved. Key factors influencing the development of accelerated learning are summarized in Table 1.2.

Around the turn of the twentieth century, the United States experienced an influx of immigrants from eastern European countries. These immigrants were different in appearance from earlier immigrants, spoke different languages, and had different cultural practices. At the same time, industrialization was speeding up and the need for factory workers steadily increased. In addition, mandatory school attendance laws and child labor laws were enacted, radically changing the role of public schools (Kliebard 1987). The public schools had focused on educating a democratic citizenry; now they were being called upon to prepare the masses for productive work. Because of the dramatic increase in the number of students in public schools, the pressing issue facing public educators became how to educate large numbers of diverse students. Two competing movements emerged to address the dramatic changes needed in public education: the social efficiency movement and the progressive movement.

TABLE 1.2   Acceleration: Social and Historical Context

Factors	Result
• Influx of Eastern European immigrants • Child labor laws • Mandatory school attendance	• Increasingly large numbers of diverse students
• Social efficiency movement as a solution to meeting the needs of the masses	• Labeling and sorting students based on perceived potential
• Progressive movement as a solution to increased student diversity and promoting democracy	• Focus on equity and preparing diverse students for democratic participation in society
• Remediation as diagnosis and treatment of academic ailments	• Students, not programs, labeled as "remedial" • Diagnosis incorporated into teacher preparation
• Notion of IQ	• Entrenched thinking that intelligence and student potential could be measured with one test
• Sorting students	Development of special programs for special students: • Enrichment and acceleration for gifted and talented • Remediation for low achievers
• High standards for all students	• Change in fundamental education approaches

Creating Efficient Schools: The Social Efficiency Movement

The practice of labeling and sorting students is rooted in the social efficiency movement. Standardization, social control, and efficiency were themes of this movement (Kliebard 1987). Led by Joseph Mayer Rice, Frederick Winslow Taylor, and Franklin Bobbitt (among others), the movement had an effect on the culture of American schooling that is still felt today. The social efficiency movement dramatically altered the organization and management of education in the United States. As many people in the country enjoyed unparalleled prosperity through industrialization, social efficiency proponents sought to apply the principles of scientific management to schools. Students became the raw material, and schools were responsible for shaping the individual according to his capabilities.

Proponents such as Franklin Bobbitt saw social class as the basis of capabilities and advocated the use of different curricula for different classes of people. In his view, teaching students things they would never use was inefficient and wasteful (Kliebard 1987). This view of class as the determinant of the individual's future life role became the foundation for the development of differentiated curricula and led to ability grouping and tracking.

The one-room schoolhouse, which allowed for self-pacing of learning, was no longer the norm. Students were tracked into course sequences that prepared them for a particular role in life: leader, factory worker, or laborer. High-achieving students, primarily from upper- or middle-class homes, were placed in the upper tracks.

Maintaining Democratic Schools: The Progressive Movement

At the same time as social efficiency leaders were advocating scientific management principles as a way to manage a diverse and growing student body, the same social conditions were spawning the development of the progressive movement. Progressives were reformers concerned with a number of social issues:

> Progressive reformers insisted upon government regulation of industry and commerce, as well as the conservation of the nation's natural resources; moreover, progressive reformers insisted that national, state, and local governments become responsive to the welfare of its citizens rather than the welfare of corporations. The progressives had a sweeping agenda, including the secret ballot and universal schooling. Just as reformers, like Horace Mann in the nineteenth century, had looked to schools as a means of addressing social problems, so reformers once again looked to schools as a means of preserving and promoting democracy within the new social order. (Semel 1999: 4)

Whereas the social efficiency movement most visibly influenced how today's schools are organized and managed, the progressives had a profound impact on curriculum and philosophy in American education. As competing movements, the goals of each were quite different. The social efficiency movement's goal was to educate large numbers of diverse students in the most efficient way possible. The progressive educators' goal was to prepare all children for democratic participation in society.

Progressive education was about engaging students in learning. John Dewey, leader of the movement, is often quoted for his description of progressive schools: "What the best and wisest parent wants for his own child, that must the community want for all of its children" (Dewey 1900:

1). Although Lawrence Cremin (1961) notes that progressive education meant different things to different people, Diane Ravitch describes the movement as "an attitude, a belief in experimentation, a commitment to education of all children and to democracy in schools" (in Semel 1999: 11).

Social Efficiency, Intelligence, and Curriculum Differentiation

Throughout most of the twentieth century, concern with efficiency and meeting the demands of employers overwhelmed concern with equity and educating students for informed citizenship. These concerns were bolstered by an assumption that students possessed different levels of innate ability and that some students were better educated to be followers and others to be leaders (Darling-Hammond 1997). Research on intelligence supported the basic underpinnings of the social efficiency movement. The commonly held notion of intelligence as a single-faceted entity justified the accepted practice of providing qualitatively different kinds of education programs and opportunities for some students. The historical roots for curriculum differentiation can be traced to Charles Darwin's *Origin of the Species* (1859) and work that followed soon after by his cousin, Sir Francis Galton (1869; 1892). Galton's research was devoted to eugenics, the improvement of society by breeding out its weaknesses. His belief in eugenics pushed him to advocate for arranged marriages because he believed that the result of such marriages would be superior offspring. He saw "good breeding" and social class as the basis of intelligence, and his research was devoted to providing evidence to support his beliefs.

Alfred Binet's development of the concept of "mental age" was the beginning of entrenched thinking about intelligence as single-faceted. Louis Terman was influenced by the work of Galton and Binet and oversaw the modification of the Binet-Simon tests into the Stanford-Binet Intelligence Scale. Terman believed that intellect was a result of nature, and he saw the Stanford-Binet and other IQ tests as valid and stable measures of ability. Terman viewed a person's abilities as determined at birth and believed that environmental influences on intellect were limited to providing the opportunity to develop those inherited abilities. His views changed over time, but his early work influenced our conception of intelligence.

This notion of intelligence as single-faceted coincided with a search for medical explanations for low achievement. Johnston (1985) suggests that efforts to remediate low-achieving students probably originated from medical interest in children who did not acquire the ability to read due to some innate deficiency such as "word blindness" or some other physiological deficiency. The early programs explained a child's inability to read or thrive in school as some "illness" that could be cured with the proper remedy. Tests to determine a student's reading ability were developed and adapted to help identify the underlying cause. A "treatment" based on this cause could then be "prescribed" by the reading specialist.

Although this concept of diagnosis and treatment of academic ailments was an educational breakthrough in the 1920s, the development of clinics and university programs had little effect on the vast number of disadvantaged children who did not have the opportunity for treatment through some special university-based or private clinic. The early clinics were designed to provide classroom teachers with expert help, but these clinics often ended up in relative isolation from the classroom, classroom instruction, and the classroom curriculum (Johnston 1985).

Schools developed diagnostic, programmatic, and curricular approaches addressing low achievement, usually under the label of "remediation." Remedial education became widespread in the 1960s and 1970s as the federal government increased its involvement in schools through the Title I/Chapter I program. The Elementary and Secondary Education Act of 1965 (ESEA) authorized federal funding to improve the academic success of low-achieving, low-income students. Over the past thirty years, billions of dollars have been used to provide compensatory and remedial programs for so-called disadvantaged students at both the state and federal levels (Stringfield et al. 1994).

Some of the diagnostic/remediation tools popular during the 1960s and 1970s included informal reading inventories that determined a student's reading and listening grade level in oral and silent reading. Relatively easy to administer, these tests could be used by a teacher or aide to assess the student's ability to comprehend text. Teachers in training often took courses requiring them to use a number of diagnostic tools and screening tests and to write diagnostic plans for students who exhibited academic problems. This training stemmed in part from the diagnostic/prescriptive philosophy that began in the 1920s and suggested that once a problem was identified, it could be resolved with the correct treatment. However, the reality was that no matter how many tests one gave a student, teachers in overcrowded and underfunded schools were often not given adequate methods, materials, or time for meeting individual student needs.

While one group of students was found to lack intelligence and to need remediation, intelligence testing led to the identification of another group of students—the gifted and talented. These students were also separated from mainstream students, but in their case, to receive a more challenging education. Interest in challenging gifted students was given a boost in the late 1950s after the Soviet Union launched Sputnik. Special programs for the gifted were designed so that the United States could compete with the Soviets and "win" the race and protect our national interests during the Cold War. The development of giftedness was seen as a social resource (Tannenbaum 1979) and viewed as essential to the national defense of the United States. As a result of fear and competitive nationalism, science and math searches were undertaken to find the "best and brightest," and new and accelerated programs in math and science were developed. Tannenbaum (1979) described the frenzy in American education as a "total talent mobilization." Intense efforts were made to identify bright students and provide them with accelerated academic courses. The reason for increased rigor and advanced courses was to equip bright students to better serve the national interest.

Progressive Education, Intelligence, and Equity

Progressive educators have struggled to build widespread support for a more thoughtful and inclusive education for all students. Progressive education has typically been relegated to small pockets, either in isolated schools or a few school districts (Zilversmit 1993). Although progressive education has not permeated schools and schooling to the same extent as the social efficiency movement, it has remained an influence in American education throughout the twentieth century. This is in part because it embodies several of the tenets that are at the base of American society: democracy and equity in particular. Progressives have held a vision of creating schools that are a mirror of a democratic society, where diversity is valued and openness and learning from others are fundamental (Semel 1999). Democratic society is seen as more than government; it is a way of living without barriers, for example, race and class. It embodies the notion of learning from others, who may be different from yourself (Zilversmit 1993).

The focus of progressives has been to prepare all students to live in a changing world; they focus more on providing all students tools for scientific inquiry and thinking rather than the discrete skills emphasized by social efficiency proponents. Progressives have sought to nurture the development of an open, democratic community welcoming diverse ideas and opinions, a view quite different from those in the social efficiency movement. Dewey and other progressives believed that a democratic society requires an educated populace; not only do citizens have to be literate, but they must also know how to live together.

Intelligence plays a different role in progressive education. With a focus on the civic purpose of education, it is more important to develop critical thinkers and problem solvers to serve as good citizens and community members than to separate students according to their level of intelligence, educating only a few to be leaders. The following highlights the view of progressives:

The debate over curriculum is emotional for progressive educators because they believe that the way students are treated will determine the future of society. If schools respect young people's intelligence and support their ability to think for themselves, then perhaps social and economic injustices, violence, genocide, and environmental degradation that have been so prevalent in the past century can be reduced—even eliminated. It will be helpful in reaching this goal if educators can rid themselves and their students of the mistaken notion that some individuals or groups are better than others. (Weissglass 1999: 47)

Concern for equity has been at the core of progressive education; to progressives, society must encourage excellence in education for all, not just for a few.

Toward Acceleration for All

As we enter the twenty-first century, schools are under intense scrutiny. The weaknesses in the educational system that developed over the past century are evident to most citizens. Ideas to improve schools vary, but some concerns are shared. One concern, as exemplified by the standards and accountability movements, is that we must expect all students to meet the same standards. It is no longer acceptable to hold one set of standards for gifted students and another for other students. In other words, equity in student outcomes is expected. A second concern is that the standards set for all students are high. We are no longer content with minimal standards but are establishing expectations of excellence based on challenging national and international standards. It is becoming increasingly clear that to achieve both equity and excellence many fundamental aspects of our current educational system must change. As Chapters 2, 3, and 4 illustrate, many effective practices already exist that can be used to accelerate all students' learning. As Chapters 5, 6, 7, and 8 illustrate, these practices will not be adequately integrated into schools and classrooms without changing school and classroom cultures and without a deep examination of our assumptions, values, actions, and responsibilities.

2   Accelerate = Serving Gifted and Talented Students

Anna looks forward to going to school. Her fifth-grade accelerated class is challenging and fast-paced. It is a perfect fit for her since she learns rapidly and easily; she quickly comprehends abstract concepts. Anna's teacher worked with Anna and her parents to develop a schedule that allows for growth and challenge. Having skipped one grade already, her parents want her to spend most of her time with classmates, but they also realize that Anna also needs to work independently part of the day. In a typical school day, Anna reports to the library for independent literature study, since her reading has been compacted to allow her to move at a pace and level commensurate with her tenth-grade reading level. She reports back to the classroom for science, where the teacher has incorporated curriculum developed for gifted students. The teacher engages Anna in astronomy through the use of problem-based learning centered around the concept of "systems." Anna works on a sixth-grade level in mathematics. Her identification through the talent search program in her school allows Anna to attend special summer accelerated programs sponsored by Johns Hopkins University for gifted students.

Anna's teacher, a seasoned veteran, is well respected and in demand by the parents of the community. Other teachers in the school also respect her ability but interact little with her. Few of them see the relevance of her teaching methods to the students they teach. Anna's teacher is a member of a network of teachers of gifted and talented students in her state, and through the network, she stays current with curriculum and instructional strategies developed for the gifted. On a regular basis, she engages her students in hands-on learning and uses Socratic teaching strategies. She is passionate about science, in particular astronomy, and many of her students develop a similar passion.

When people hear "accelerate the learning of all students," they may think, "How can you accelerate *all* students' learning? Isn't acceleration an option for bright and able students only?" A student like Anna comes to mind. Many people feel that accelerated learning would be too difficult for an average student like Sara or a low-achieving student like Richard. Because students labeled as gifted and talented can move more rapidly than their peers, many assume that students must be atypically bright in order to accelerate their learning. Indeed, acceleration is often a programming option for gifted students, and much research supports acceleration's effectiveness as an approach for educating gifted and talented students (Gallagher 1985; Van Tassel-Baska 1991; Davis and Rimm 1998).

This chapter examines the application of the term "accelerate" to students identified as gifted and talented. As described in Chapter 1, the emphasis on measuring intelligence, sorting and labeling students for efficient schooling, along with other influences, has resulted in special curricula and educational programs and practices for students identified as gifted and talented. This chapter characterizes the gifted learner and explores how curriculum differentiation led to the development of curricula for gifted and talented students perceived to have special cognitive needs. In addition, it lays out current acceleration practices in gifted education. These practices match the common notion of acceleration as moving more quickly through an established curriculum. This discussion moves to the broadened concept of giftedness–that it is not just faster learning but deeper learning. This broadened definition of acceleration has implications for accelerating the learning of all students, as well as for meeting the special needs of students identified as gifted and talented.

Candidates for Acceleration: Who Is Identified

Because of the nature and needs of gifted learners, acceleration is seen as a productive approach for many bright students. They have the ability to learn rapidly, to process abstract ideas; they are typically developmentally advanced (Schiever and Maker 1991). Some educators argue that content taught to gifted students should be advanced two to three years ahead of regular students (Silverman 1986). Horne and Dupuy (1981) believe acceleration may be a misnomer; "accelerated learning is not really accelerated for the brightest student; it is accelerated only in comparison with average students" (p. 105). They see acceleration as an administrative convenience. Gifted students are accelerated because they have already demonstrated achievement.

In general, most gifted students are identified through the use of traditional IQ and/or achievement or aptitude tests. It logically follows that the students most likely to benefit from the kinds of acceleration approaches described herein are the students already demonstrating their abilities by doing well in their classes and achieving at high levels in school. The noteworthy exceptions are the chronically underidentified gifted minority and low-income students, who, as a result, are often excluded from accelerated learning (Ford 1996).

Within most schools, there is no "talent search," which attempts to match appropriate educational experiences to identified talent. Talent searches are often conducted through external educational agencies and result in accelerated learning opportunities outside of school being offered to identified students. A talent search seeks to identify students who have potential but may not be demonstrating that potential in schoolwork, and the search provides opportunities to students to develop that potential (Stanley and Benbow 1983). In contrast, acceleration options for gifted and talented students within schools rely on some documented achievement and are primarily based on administrative recognition of demonstrated performance and on convenience in accommodating those students (Southern and Jones 1991).

Joyce Van Tassel-Baska (1991) outlines three factors to consider for acceleration: cognitive ability and performance, affective characteristics, and interest and motivation for acceleration. Although cognitive ability and performance, as measured by IQ, achievement, and aptitude tests, often determine eligibility/potential for acceleration, affective characteristics, interest, and motivation are factors that may determine the success of students who are accelerated (Gallagher 1985).

Van Tassel-Baska (1986) argues that not to offer acceleration to students who learn at a rapid pace solely for the purpose of keeping them at grade level is indefensible. Harm occurs when bright students, who learn new material quickly, must wait for other classmates to master the objective that they have already mastered. Affective characteristics indicating a need for acceleration include boredom and frustration and resulting inappropriate emotional and social behaviors.

Critical to determining whether to accelerate a student are individual characteristics and the social aspects of the student's personality. A student's interest, motivation, and desire to move forward are important considerations (Van Tassel-Baska 1991). In order for acceleration to be effective, the student, not his/her parents or teachers, must want to be accelerated. Leaving peers and friends of the same age is difficult, and students must be willing to make what may appear to be social sacrifices for intellectual growth. Careful consideration by the student of the increased challenge and rigor of acceleration combined with the strong possibility of experiencing failure is essential. He/she must clearly understand his/her individual motivations and goals, because the social aspects of acceleration can be problematic for some youngsters.

Why Accelerate Learning for Gifted and Talented Students?

Why should some students' learning be accelerated? As in Anna's case, many students benefit from moving faster through some material (e.g., Anna's individualized reading program) and delving deeper into curricular areas, such as her class's exploration of astronomy. As described in Chapter 1, instructional approaches used to accelerate imply a faster pace in the students' education. When applied to gifted and talented students, the emphasis on speed is evident. For example, in 1949 Pressey defined acceleration as "progress through an educational program at rates faster or ages younger than conventional" (Pressey 1949: 2). More recently, Van Tassel-Baska (1981) states that "acceleration implies no more than allowing students to move at a rate at which they are comfortable and can excel, rather than holding them back to conform to a 'speed limit' set by the average learner" (in Davis and Rimm 1998: 105).

The emphasis on speeding up learning assumes that there is a specific, established set of skills and knowledge through which all students must progress and that there is a "normal" or "average" rate for the typical student to move through this body of knowledge. Since some students like Anna are not average or normal, they have the capability to move more rapidly through this body of knowledge (Southern and Jones 1991). Hence, we see the origin of the link between acceleration (i.e., speeding up) and gifted students.

For many years, educators of the gifted supported acceleration as the best way to meet the special needs of very bright students. Terman and Oden (1947) found that gifted students who were accelerated one or two years made better adjustments than those who were not. Through acceleration, gifted students have been found to "improve in motivation, confidence and scholarship. [They] do not develop habits of mental laziness. [They] complete their professional training earlier. [And, they] reduce the cost of their college education" (in Davis and Rimm 1998: 110). Van Tassel-Baska (1991) states that most gifted students are not well served unless pace of instruction is accelerated. Rogers (1990), in a best evidence synthesis of 314 studies of acceleration, offers two major conclusions: "No form of acceleration led to decreases in any area of performance: academic, social, or emotional. There appear to be generally positive academic effects for most forms of acceleration" (in Davis and Rimm 1998: 107). Stanley (1985) states that "educational non-acceleration is an international tragedy" (in Davis and Rimm 1998: 103). Additional research supports acceleration as an effective method for meeting the educational needs of the gifted and talented (Daurio 1979; Gallagher 1985; Pollins 1983; Robinson 1983).

Models of Acceleration for Gifted and Talented Students

Models of acceleration found in gifted education literature include service delivery models and curriculum models (Schiever and Maker 1991). There is a clear distinction between the two models: The service delivery model is focused on identification and placement of students into already existing courses/programs, whereas the curriculum model is tailored to meet the individual's learning needs.

Service Delivery Models of Acceleration

Service delivery models offer gifted students the same educational experiences offered to all students, but the gifted students have them earlier, either at a younger age or a lower grade level. This model is the one most people think of when they hear the term "acceleration." Students are identified for service delivery programs because they are far beyond their age peers and have demonstrated advanced aptitude. These programs are convenient for schools since they do not require offering alternative programs, but they fail to offer individualized curricula for gifted learners (Schiever and Maker 1991). Service delivery models typically provide a standard curriculum, but provide it earlier. Service delivery models include early entry to school, grade skipping, and subject matter acceleration.

Early Entry to School and Grade Skipping. Early entry to school and grade skipping are well-known acceleration practices. Early school entry is typically an option for students when evidence exists that the student is two or more years beyond his/her age peers. This particular option allows for early entry into kindergarten and/or the elementary grades. With some students, further acceleration is necessary at the middle school level. Considerations for early school entry are the student's chronological age, mental age, attention span, and evidence of advanced language development (Proctor, Black, and Feldhusen 1986).

Grade skipping, sometimes called double promotion (Justman 1959), permits a student to "skip" over a grade. This option allows completion of the "normal" amount of work in less than the "normal" amount of time (Justman 1959). Students considered for grade skipping are generally above average in all academic areas and are able to move on to more advanced learning. Proctor, Black, and Feldhusen (1986) recommend looking at the student's intellectual and social/emotional development as well as academic levels in considering this option.

Acceleration through early entry into first grade or through grade skipping, also known as full acceleration, has little or no effect on school or classroom culture because it occurs as an accommodation for an individual need. The teacher generally takes the initiative in gathering the evidence and calling in the parents, other teachers, and the principal for consultation. Evidence such as achievement test scores, intelligence tests, and demonstration of student abilities, along with interviews with the student and parents, helps to determine whether to accelerate a youngster. Typically, educators take great care in placing the student with a teacher or teachers who will support the intellectual development of the student.

Subject Matter and Content Acceleration.   Subject matter acceleration (also termed partial acceleration), or placing children in an upper grade for one or two subjects based on their specific abilities and needs, is another common practice. For example, a first grade student highly advanced in math and science might take those courses with third grade students. Related to subject matter acceleration is content acceleration. Content acceleration is an approach in which the student works with curriculum beyond that considered age-appropriate (Gallagher 1985). Commonly, this type of acceleration occurs with gifted students who have already mastered the content that age peers are working to learn. For example, early readers or students with an advanced vocabulary at a young age might experience acceleration of their reading and language content study. Some gifted programs at the elementary level use advanced content as the curriculum for their program.

Advanced Placement (AP) Courses.   Advanced Placement (AP) courses are college-level curricula taught within the high school program. Students take AP courses in high school and/or take Advanced Placement examinations. Colleges and universities award credit based on scores received on these examinations. The content of AP courses involves specific, advanced curricula that is learned earlier and at a rapid pace. This acceleration option allows students to remain in a high school setting while gaining college credits. The AP course option is the most open to student enrollment; in many schools, anyone is able to enroll. In some schools, a grade point ratio minimum or some grade as the entrance point may be required, but identification as gifted and talented is not necessary in most high schools.

Curriculum Models of Acceleration

Curriculum models for accelerating the learning of gifted students are more closely aligned with individual student learning needs and characteristics than service delivery models (Schiever and Maker 1991). The regular classroom or a resource room serves as an appropriate setting for curriculum models of acceleration, and the setting makes it possible to incorporate students who may not be identified as gifted. These models speed up the pace at which the curriculum is covered for some students. Examples of curriculum acceleration include the following:

- curriculum compacting, or "buying" time for students to extend their learning;

- continuous progress, or determining readiness level and providing materials appropriate to student's level;
- telescoping, or covering two years of content in one year's time; and
- self-pacing, or providing individual students an opportunity to work through content at their own pace, which, in the case of gifted students, is more rapid than usual.

Curricular strategies in acceleration of gifted and talented students are more diagnostic and shaped to the student's individual characteristics and learning needs. These strategies, which are more difficult to administer and more time consuming, are not employed as often as approaches like grade skipping or subject matter acceleration. Curriculum acceleration models are less well known and less commonly used than service delivery models. The lack of wide application of these strategies to all able students is unfortunate, because these strategies are most likely to benefit students more broadly.

Curriculum compacting adjusts curriculum so that students do not spend time on material they have already mastered (Starko 1986). Students are able to test out of what they already know. The term "compacting" comes from the notion that students have previously mastered material or have mastered it in a very short period of time. The compacting "buys" the student time either to move on through the regular curriculum more quickly or to study particular areas of interest more deeply. This strategy requires that teachers provide some diagnostic testing and plan, along with students, for appropriate learning experiences. On the students' part, this strategy requires independent learning skills, task commitment, and motivation. This strategy works well in a resource room setting and can also be used in regular classroom settings.

Through telescoping curriculum, students complete a year-long course of study in a shorter period of time than normally expected. For example, students may complete a year's algebra course in two or three months, allowing students to move more quickly into advanced mathematics curriculum. This strategy also requires administrative flexibility; students engaged in telescoping do not fit easily into grades and course sections, and they need strong motivation and independent skills to be successful.

Students are often identified for curriculum models of acceleration through their deep interest and aptitude in a subject area; these students benefit from self-pacing opportunities. For example, a teacher might invite a guest speaker from the local historic preservation society to talk about the Revolutionary War battleground near the school. One student's burning interest and insightful questions on this topic reveals his extraordinary knowledge of American history. The student and teacher build on this interest and design a research project using primary and secondary sources to gather and compile more information about the battle site and the effect of the battle on their community. Based on his investigations, the student discovers that the site is threatened by development, and he spearheads an effort to secure a national historic designation for the site. In this model of acceleration, the teacher and student compact his work (i.e., the standard U.S. history curriculum) in order to "buy" time to investigate this area of interest; together, they plan learning experiences that allow him to move forward. The student sets the pace for his own learning (self-pacing), and with the teacher's facilitation, he moves through the learning activities at his own speed. In doing so, his learning is deep and significant.

Programs Combining Service Delivery and Curriculum Models

Talent Search Programs. Founded in 1971 by Julian Stanley, talent search programs identify extremely precocious students through the use of test scores (i.e., the top 1 in 10,000) prior to adolescence (Benbow 1991). Most students involved in talent search programs are in the middle of seventh grade and are not yet thirteen years of age. The students take the Scholastic Aptitude Test (SAT), both the mathematics and verbal sections. Precocious students qualify for educational counseling and extracurricular educational opportunities, primarily through summer programs. The Study of Mathematically Precocious Youth (SMPY), a longitudinal study following students in this program, analyzes the effects of student participation in talent search programs (Benbow 1991).

Talent searches find students who have analytic and verbal abilities but may not have been identified as gifted in their schools. The purpose of the talent search is an obvious one: to find students who have talent and provide opportunities outside of regular schooling, as well as within school, to develop that talent. This talent development has been done through varied approaches to acceleration, from telescoping to radical acceleration (i.e., skipping students two to three years ahead of average), advanced courses, and concurrent course work (Stanley 1977).

Considerable research points to the effectiveness of talent search programs (Cohn 1991). Millions of students have had the opportunity to participate in accelerated options through various talent searches since they began in 1972. SMPY has been following approximately 10,000 of these youth, and that longitudinal research will help educators learn more about the effectiveness of various acceleration practices.

The original program at Johns Hopkins University has been replicated in other universities around the country. One example is Iowa State University, which offers a summer residential program in which twelve to fifteen-year-old students take college-level courses (e.g., biotechnology).

Classes cover the content equivalent to a semester college course in three weeks during the summer. Benbow (1991) makes the argument that this approach to acceleration is an especially good fit with mathematics and science because of the sequential nature of those disciplines.

Residential High Schools and International Baccalaureate Programs. Recognizing that regular high schools cannot offer the number and diversity of advanced courses needed by highly gifted students, several states have established residential high schools. This acceleration option, reserved for highly advanced students, immerses them in a college-like setting with other bright high school students and provides them with advanced content studies. This relatively new option is found in a number of states. Residential high schools include the North Carolina School of Science and Mathematics, the Louisiana School for Math, Science, and the Arts, the Illinois Mathematics and Science Academy, the Texas Academy of Mathematics and Science, Mississippi's School for Math and Science, and the South Carolina Governor's School for Mathematics and Science. These schools' courses progress at a rapid pace and contain advanced, abstract content (Davis and Rimm 1998).

International Baccalaureate (IB) programs are highly selective programs gaining in popularity across the United States. International Baccalaureate programs are usually two-year programs, offered during the junior and senior years of high school. IB students are usually at the ninetieth percentile or above in achievement. The curriculum emphasis is on foreign languages and international concerns beyond the regular high school curriculum. IB programs can now be found at the elementary and middle school levels. The course content is rigorous and accelerated and requires a schoolwide commitment at the lower grade levels (Davis and Rimm 1998).

Table 2.1 lists current approaches to acceleration found in gifted education literature. The table offers approaches and definitions of both service delivery and curriculum models of acceleration. In addition, the table lists examples of programs that use both service delivery and curriculum models of acceleration.

From Identification to Development of Gifts and Talents

What does the current thinking about intelligence mean for accelerating the gifted? Are there implications for changing acceleration approaches for the gifted based on broadened conceptions of intelligence? Treffinger (1991) advocates for a new paradigm to expand our conception of giftedness. The paradigm defines giftedness as a potential to be nurtured rather than a statistical, quantitative entity. Identification in this para-

TABLE 2.1   Approaches Used to Accelerate Gifted and Talented Students
(Southern and Jones 1991, Davis and Rimm 1998)

Service Delivery Models
- **Early entrance to school:** either kindergarten or first grade, middle or high school, or college
- **Grade skipping:** also called full acceleration or double promotion
- **Subject matter acceleration:** also called partial acceleration; student takes a subject or content course ahead of his/her grade level
- **Advanced placement:** high-school courses offering student opportunity to earn college credit

Curriculum Models
- **Curriculum compacting:** student demonstrates mastery through pretesting, "buying time" for acceleration and/or enrichment
- **Continuous progress:** as the student demonstrates readiness, he/she is given material appropriate for achievement level
- **Self-pacing:** student is provided with materials that allow self-pacing; the student moves at her/his own rate.
- **Telescoping:** two years' work accomplished in one year

Programs Combining Service Delivery and Curriculum Models
- **Residential schools:** residential schools where high-school students are offered curriculum beyond the regular high school program
- **International Baccalaureate programs:** highly selective and rigorous programs with international emphasis
- **Talent search programs:** programs that find students with high analytic and verbal abilities and provide opportunities within and outside of regular schooling to develop talent

digm is inclusive, focuses on strengths, and is growth oriented. Programs based on this paradigm encourage gifted behaviors; they are flexible and responsive in design instead of limited in offerings. They have an inclusive curriculum and are a part of the regular curriculum (Treffinger 1991). The models described in this section focus on developing potential giftedness by offering educational opportunities to a wider range of students than those identified as gifted through traditional means.

The Schoolwide Enrichment Model

The Schoolwide Enrichment Model (Renzulli and Reis 1985) applies a broadened conception of giftedness. This model stands apart from other programs for gifted students in that it includes students who may not be identified as gifted by traditional means but who exhibit gifted behavior. It emphasizes the student's behavior and not an IQ score. Although the traditional conception of giftedness is based on an IQ score of 130 or above, educators of the gifted, such as Joseph Renzulli, believe that gifted behavior, not the label of giftedness based on an IQ score, is what educators need to develop and encourage. To Renzulli, gifted behavior includes three basic clusters of traits: above average ability (high IQ and/or aptitude), task commitment (persistence), and creativity. When these three traits come together, the student is said to be exhibiting gifted behavior. The distinction between traditional giftedness and this definition is that ability is demonstrated through performance; his definition focuses on what the student *does*, not what the student *is*, and moves away from labeling students. His Schoolwide Enrichment Model is built on this belief.

This model is based on three types of experiences. Type I experiences enrich and expose students to interesting and exciting topics. Type II experiences include specific skills training based on student interest and need, and Type III activities involve students in real-world problem solving. The model involves many children in the exposure/enrichment phase. Fewer students are involved in Type II, specific skills training, and only those students exhibiting high levels of gifted behavior move on to real-world problem solving, Type III (Renzulli and Reis 1985). Accelerated learning occurs in both Type II and III activities. Students learn skills and content that grow out of their interests and the specific problems they are investigating. Because this model builds on students' interests, their talent and potential giftedness are nurtured.

The Planning Model for Academic and Talent Diversity

Carol Ann Tomlinson (1996), like Joseph Renzulli, is interested in finding the common elements of "good instruction in general and good instruction for highly able learners" (p. 156). She argues that good instruction for the gifted should be good instruction for all students. Because general education has moved more toward constructivist learning, instructional practices mostly used in the past with gifted learners are now widely used with all students. Tomlinson proposes a model, the Planning Model for Academic and Talent Diversity, which includes the elements found in any effective classroom. The model, drawn from an examination of what makes a gifted class different from a regular class, offers principles of content, process, and product that are effective for diverse learners. She also provides a continuum of adaptations that allow all students exposure to challenging curriculum but that accommodate variation in learners' talents and interests. According to Tomlinson,

> there are no environmental modifications; principles of content, process, or product; or instructional strategies uniquely appropriate for gifted learners. Curriculum and instruction for gifted learners will be uniquely appropriate

for those learners when teaching and learning are at a level of transformation, abstractness, complexity, multifacetedness, mental leap, open-ended-
ness, problem ambiguity, independence, or pace suited to advanced learning capacity. (1996: 172–173)

Conclusion

Although acceleration for gifted and talented students has a long history,
it receives little attention and support from most teachers and administrators. Many educators are philosophically opposed to accelerating
bright learners (Southern, Jones, and Fiscus 1989), especially when these
learners merely move more quickly through a course of study. They are
cautious and use acceleration as an option infrequently because they
worry about the pressures on children and the affective and social development of children who are pushed into an age group beyond their age
peers. In addition, most educators assume that socialization with age
peers is best for the youngster (Schiever and Maker 1991).

Although research strongly supports the use of acceleration with individual students (Brody and Benbow 1987; Feldhusen 1989), it is not
widely supported in practice. In *National Excellence: A Case for Developing
America's Talent*, Ross underlines the need to challenge students:

> Reforming American schools depends on challenging students to work
> harder and master more complex material. Few would argue against this for
> students performing at low or average levels. But we must also challenge
> our top-performing students to greater heights if our nation is to achieve a
> world class educational system. (1993: 1)

The reluctance to provide the best possible education to the nation's
brightest students does not fit well with the commitment of public
schools to provide equal educational opportunity to all students. This
tension between excellence and equity has a connection to the demo-
graphics in American schools. Educational practices reserved only for
gifted and talented students are avoided for fear of appearing elitist or
exclusive, particularly when low-income and minority students have
been and continue to be underrepresented in gifted programs (Ford
1996). There is now a focus on inclusion and serving all students well.
The emphasis has shifted from labeling students to exploring how to
challenge all students, including, but not limited to, those labeled as
gifted.

As this chapter illustrates, we may be able to achieve both equity and
excellence in education. Many of the practices once reserved for identified gifted and talented students have now moved into mainstream education (e.g., higher-order thinking, projects, group problem solving,

problem-based learning). In addition, many leaders in gifted education advocate for the development of new approaches and for stronger collaboration with regular education (Renzulli and Reis 1991; Treffinger, Callahan, and Vaughn 1991; Gallagher 1991; Bireley 1992; Tomlinson and Callahan 1992). This kind of collaboration and focus on challenging all students addresses the common lament that our curriculum has been "dumbed down" and that much time in school is wasted, not just for gifted students, but for many students (Renzulli and Reis 1991).

Shouldn't educators consider the benefits of fast-paced, challenging curricula for all of our students? The real and potential benefits for gifted students are evident in the research base on acceleration. If gifted students benefit, isn't it possible that others will, too? In particular, the application of curriculum models of acceleration to all students is promising. Curriculum models, shaped around individual students' learning needs and interests, could help shift the focus from identification and sorting of students into groups that fit into current courses and programs to a focus on reconfiguring courses and programs to better educate all students.

Educators must understand the context of where we have come from to determine where we need to go. The context is clearly different now than at the turn of the past century, and educators need to take a lesson from approaches that were once reserved for "gifted and talented" students and use those approaches to move all students, including gifted students, forward. Gifted education has been and can continue to be a laboratory for experimentation with innovation and challenging curricula. Educators should not discard the acceleration strategies discussed in this chapter as options for gifted students. The strategies clearly work well with bright students. The key is to find ways to open up these approaches to other students.

3 Accelerate = Targeting Low-Achieving Students

Richard used to hate school. At his elementary school he felt stupid because he had trouble reading. He hung out with other boys who were having trouble in school and was beginning to cause problems in class. His fifth grade teacher thought Richard should be retained because of his low reading ability. The elementary principal learned of an innovative class recently created at the middle school designed for students like Richard. A group of students who are behind grade level are taught the fifth and sixth grade curriculum in an intense, individualized, hands-on program. At the end of one year, these students will enter the normal seventh grade.

Richard loves this class. It has made him a better reader because he enjoys the relevant curriculum, the opportunity to use his hands, and learning many things at one time through thematic units of study. In this accelerated class, Richard works with two teachers. One teacher works intensively and individually with Richard on his reading, writing, and communication skills. The other teacher works with individuals and small groups on science and mathematics. The two teachers plan interdisciplinary studies, and the learning activities are often based on real-life situations. Because the class is small, only twelve students, the teachers focus on Richard's specific strengths and academic needs and tailor learning activities to move him quickly through the learning.

Richard exemplifies a new application of acceleration.* Applying the notion of acceleration to low-achieving students is based on the assumption that these students simply need to "catch up" with their peers. In order to catch up with their higher-achieving peers, low achievers must move more quickly through the curriculum they have not mastered. As in the case of gifted students, acceleration for low-achieving students relates to speeding up; unlike gifted students, speeding up in this case is geared to

---

*This chapter is coauthored by Jane F. Zenger and Julie D. Swanson.

catching up. Speed and pace are the key concepts in the application of accelerating low achievers' learning.

What works with low-achieving youngsters to move them forward quickly and enable them to be successful in school? Why, in spite of billions of dollars and over thirty years of effort, have programs geared to educating low-achieving students failed to meet the needs of so many? The earlier discussion in Chapter 1 provides a context for why this particular group of students has been targeted for acceleration and suggests reasons why so many efforts have failed to meet their needs.

In this chapter, we challenge the concept of remediation (i.e., reteaching discrete skills out of context that have not been mastered) and propose a more direct and practical methodology of accelerating low-achieving students. The chapter examines what it means in theory and practice to accelerate low-achieving students, describes students typically labeled as low achievers, and highlights several innovative, successful acceleration programs for low-achieving students.

Remediation or Acceleration?

Remediation, intended to help students labeled as low achieving gain the skills necessary to catch up with their age peers, has unfortunately had the opposite effect. In fact, remediation slows most students' learning down to the point where they rarely catch up. Typical remedial approaches include discrete skills instruction that is linear and sequential, that is, reading instruction emphasizes phonics rules and skills, and mathematics instruction provides drill in operations. Underlying remedial approaches is the premise that learning must move from basic to more advanced skills. Until students master the basics, they cannot move into higher-order skills and advanced curriculum (Means, Chelemer, and Knapp 1991; Knapp 1995a; Jennings 1998).

Since remedial programs were designed to overcome societal inequities, it is ironic that they have failed the very students they were intended to serve. Begun in the 1960s as an effort to address inequity issues highlighted by the Civil Rights Movement, the Title I/Chapter I program has spent billions of dollars providing remedial programs for children in poverty. Although well intentioned, the basic idea behind remediation is flawed; students cannot spend years "catching up" because they are trying to catch up to a moving target—students learning at normal or advanced levels.

At the same time remedial instruction slows down the pace for low-achieving students, average students move ahead in the standard curriculum and gifted students move even faster. While low-achieving students repeat instruction in discrete skills they could not master the first time, gifted students are engaged in group activities, self-selection of books, independent research, creative writing, and inquiry learning. Educators who advocate raising, rather than lowering, the academic expectations for low-achieving students criticize these discrepant approaches for gifted learners and slow learners.

The failure of compensatory and remedial programs to prepare students for academic success is likely one reason some educators are using acceleration as an approach with low-achieving students. Remedial education has proven unsuccessful in upgrading student achievement for a number of reasons. Research conducted by Means, Chelemer, and Knapp (1991) indicates that remedial instruction underestimates students' abilities. It postpones interesting, challenging, and rigorous academic work. Often the more challenging work is put off for so long that low achievers turn off, lose their motivation, and never catch up enough to get the "good, rich stuff." Typical remedial instruction takes learning out of a meaningful and motivating context (Means, Chelemer, and Knapp 1991).

Numerous studies point to increasing evidence that all children, including low-achieving students, respond well to rich and challenging curricula (e.g., Peterson 1989; Pogrow 1990; McLaughlin and Talbert 1993; Russell and Meikamp 1994; Gonzales 1994; Knapp 1995a; Knapp, Shields, and Turnbull 1995; Newmann et al. 1996; Jennings 1998). This growing body of evidence indicates more rigorous, accelerated, and enriched approaches improve student achievement for low-achieving students. In an attempt to raise academic expectations and standards for all students, schools are in transition, implementing and evaluating different types of programs, many of which incorporate the same techniques and concepts developed to motivate and challenge gifted children. The idea of using acceleration rather than remediation with low-achieving students is gaining popularity and support, but the actual implementation may take a number of forms. These forms are described later in this chapter.

Who Are Low Achievers?

Children who do not thrive in our public schools have many labels, and just as many theories are posited to explain their failures in the classroom. Remedial programs developed through the years have been used to both identify low-achieving children and provide diagnostic data to help determine their problems and level of skill in academic areas. The data were in turn used to sort, isolate, and remediate so-called problem students. Programs varied from state to state and school to school. The U.S. Department of Education estimates that almost one-third of the school population has significant learning problems. School or state-sponsored programs serve some students; federal programs such as Title I and the Individuals with Disabilities Education Act (IDEA) serve others.

Identifying Low-Achieving Students

Poor grades and/or poor standardized test scores identify low-achieving students. These tests include norm-referenced tests such as the Metropolitan Achievement Test, the California Test of Basic Skills, and the Stanford Achievement Test, or state-developed basic skills, criterion-referenced, or compensatory tests. Regardless of the method used, most students identified as low achieving come from low socioeconomic backgrounds and may have a high rate of absenteeism and/or retention. Once identified and placed in a remedial program, many students are tested further to determine a reading or skills level; individualized instruction follows based on prescribed tasks. These tasks reteach skills that students seem to have missed in previous grades. Often, teaching in remedial programs consists of rote-type instruction in vocabulary or practice in reading passages and answering questions from a menu of main idea, inference, or detail-based passages. The activities often lack meaning and are repetitive; the literature used in instruction is not inspiring and is described by many students as "boring." Because remedial programs have not been successful in improving student achievement, Levin (1987), Allington (1994), and others advanced persuasive arguments that techniques and concepts developed to motivate and challenge gifted children should be incorporated into remedial programs for low-achieving children.

Labels for Students Identified as Low Achievers

Most often, students who are labeled as low achievers have some problem with reading. Because reading is the basis for learning in other content areas, difficulty with reading can create low achievement in other areas. Louise Spear-Swerling and Robert Sternberg (1996) point out the difficulties of labeling poor readers. They have found that reading problems often result in students being labeled as learning disabled. Their research indicates that special education referral and placement has more to do with the student's gender, race, and classroom behavior than the student's actual abilities (Spear-Swerling and Sternberg 1996: 7). However, they contend that programs for students with generalized reading problems do help students who may have reading disabilities.

Low-achieving students are often labeled "at risk" or "disadvantaged." Poor achievement and performance of students at risk of failure are often attributed to deficits in the students (Means, Chelemer, and Knapp 1991). Many believe these students have the potential to do much better than their performance indicates, but socioeconomic or family problems inhibit learning. Often easy to spot in classrooms, students from impoverished or difficult home environments show poor language and social skills development. Limited experiences outside the home environment may lead to a lack of background schema about the society and world around them. A short attention span, inability to accept authority, and a lack of understanding about how to study and learn include a few of the characteristics attributed to disadvantaged and/or at-risk students.

Although the student might have high academic potential, artistic talent, or charismatic leadership skills, the student's natural abilities may not be realized in many school environments. Excessive absences, disruptive and inappropriate behavior, or avoidance mechanisms often make success for certain students difficult, even when the student is placed in special or remedial classes.

Beyond the label "at risk," students may be further labeled. For example, the reluctant learner is one who can succeed but seems unmotivated. Finding how to change the student's attitude is the often-cited solution for the reluctant learner. Specialists suggest that more innovative classroom procedures and personalized curriculum might stimulate the reluctant learner to become more responsive and involved in the learning process.

The "slow learner" is one whose IQ is below 90, and experts tell educators that expectations for student achievement should be lowered. Reading specialists and special education teachers often state that it is natural for students with a low IQ to perform below chronological expectations and that instruction should be adapted to the student's limited abilities.

Diagnosis of many students as disabled learners is due to an emotional or physiological impairment. The disabled learner includes mentally handicapped students identified for placement in special education classes; these students are required to have Individualized Education Plans (IEPs).

Another type of disabled learner may actually have an above-average intelligence. Their reading and/or math scores may be on grade level or above, but for whatever reason, the student is working below his/her potential. The assumption exists that the disability is not caused by a lack of motivation or intelligence but by some biological cause (Spear-Swerling and Sternberg 1996). Teachers and parents report that learning seems somehow "blocked" and normal classroom procedures are inadequate or inappropriate to help these students achieve. The factors causing the disabilities may be complex and difficult to precisely pinpoint. Severe cases may require extensive psychological and/or medical evaluations, and these students might be confined to self-contained classes or require special tutors or one-on-one instruction.

Spear-Swerling and Sternberg (1996) believe that the use of reading disability as a label is seriously flawed and that educators need to focus more broadly on literacy and literacy acquisition. They make a distinction between reading disability and literacy acquisition by explaining literacy as inclusive of reading comprehension and word recognition and also spelling and written expression.

The underachiever, often described in school settings as one of the most difficult to change or motivate, may be gifted in one or more areas and does not lack the ability to achieve. These students perform below their potential, and as with the reluctant student, a lack of motivation seems to be the primary reason for substandard academic performance in school. These students might score very high on standardized tests and yet have dismal or widely inconsistent grades in content area classes.

Students matching the characteristics of the above profiles are in almost every public school. At one time, these students were allowed to quit or drop out of school, and a sort of "natural selection" determined academic success. As our society becomes more dependent on a trainable, literate workforce, we work to retain these students in our schools and build up their skills so they can be successful in today's modern, technological society.

A Model of Acceleration for Low-Achieving Students

Unlike acceleration of gifted and talented students, it is difficult to find a body of literature that defines and describes models and programs for accelerating low-achieving students. Our definition and model come from an analysis of specific programs that accelerate low achievers. Specific examples range from local, school-based programs to national and international programs. Most of the programs have reading as the focus; some are conducted in early childhood, others in elementary, middle and high schools. The model draws on the common elements of the programs and includes curriculum, instruction, and student learning. In general, accelerating the learning of low achievers means that what students need to know has been boiled down to the essentials, and an intensive, focused program has been developed to push students forward and enable them to master those essentials. The model, illustrated in Figure 3.1, is explained below.

In this proposed model, identification of students is made through a diagnostic process, based on individual need and the match of student need with the program's goal. For example, if the program's goal is to move students out of middle school and into high school, then students included in such a program are at least a year behind, and they are prepared to move forward through intensive, focused efforts. If the acceler-

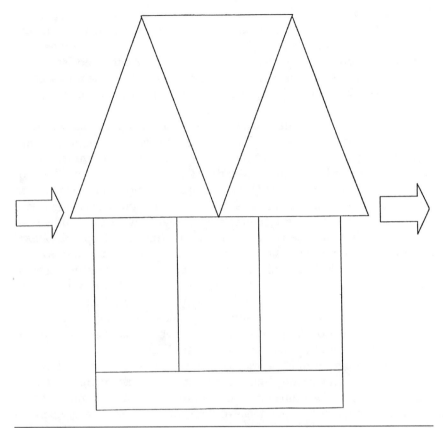

FIGURE 3.1   A Model of Accelerating Learning for Low-Achieving Students

ated program's goal is to prepare students with skills necessary to pass the high school exit exam, then students who have repeatedly failed the exam are included in the program. This type of accelerated program provides students with the skills needed to pass the exit exam, goals that are quite specific and attainable.

Curriculum in accelerated programs for low-achieving students is intensive and focused. It includes interesting, rich, and relevant content. The curriculum's structure allows for individualization and self-pacing. This definition and model of acceleration draws from accelerated programs with the primary purpose of catching students up with their peers in a shortened time period. Assessment in these programs includes traditional paper and pencil tests and quizzes as well as authentic assessment. Students in some accelerated programs have weekly quizzes on specific information; in addition, they build portfolios of written expression used to assess student progress. Self-evaluation is part of assessment for two reasons:

Students' motivation improves with clear goals, and self-evaluation enhances understanding of academic content. Specific academic goals tailored to the student's level help to make goals attainable. Academic successes of students build in small steps and make long-term goals, such as passing the exit exam for high school, attainable. Assessment in accelerated programs for low achievers determines student progress toward established individual goals.

Programs that accelerate low achievers' learning provide a community of learning and support in various ways. Some programs require a commitment from parents and students. In some cases, students must sign an agreement regarding their responsibility and commitment to the program. Other accelerated programs provide support services such as counseling; most work to inspire students' motivation by situating learning in a relevant context. Instructional strategies that allow students to work cooperatively on teams as well as individually, with specific, short-term goals, help to build a sense of community and responsibility, as well as provide opportunity for academic success and achievement. Curriculum is individualized, often self-paced, allowing for choice and personal responsibility. Some programs are primarily skills based; others include skills instruction but are more innovative and focus on construction of knowledge. Most of the programs have aspects of connected, relevant learning and interdisciplinary and/or thematic units.

Whether programs are traditional or more innovative, what separates accelerated programs from others designed for low-achieving students is the rigorous pace, the time on task, the provision for academic success, and the fostering of independence and love of learning. These programs teach students how to learn and often have some aspect of building the student's cultural capital (Mehan, Villanueva, Hubbard, and Lintz 1996).

A variety of instructional strategies are needed to accelerate low achievers' learning. Cooperative grouping and individual research on topics of interest engage learners who have met with limited successes. Basic skills strategies, such as strategies for reading comprehension, vocabulary enrichment, schema building, scaffolding, and test-taking strategies, are integrated with advanced instructional strategies, such as metacognitive skill development, open-ended questioning, Socratic method, graphic organizers, and technology as a tool for learning.

Programs That Accelerate Low-Achieving Students

In his exploratory article "The Schools We Have, The Schools We Need," Richard Allington (1994) reminds educators that expectations are crucial. As long as we continue to believe that some children, usually children with the "wrong parents," cannot learn to read beside their more advantaged peers, there will be little reason to attempt to design instructional programs that ensure all students succeed. If we remain ensnared by unexamined beliefs concerning the limited potential of some children, there will be little reason to work intently to accelerate their literacy development. We must not continue to confuse lack of experience with lack of ability.

The failure of remedial programs to provide opportunities for building background knowledge, reading and discussing high-interest and authentic reading material, or experiencing writing creatively for personal satisfaction deprives the at-risk student of the necessary and critical experiences needed for improvement. The low expectations for these students, combined with a lack of rich and interesting curriculum in their classes, help us understand why unmotivated students placed in these classes do not significantly improve in their scores on achievement tests and often remain in remedial classes year after year.

In response to the ineffectiveness of many remedial programs, educators have looked elsewhere to find program models to positively impact the achievement of students labeled as disadvantaged, at risk, and low achieving. A number of interesting experimental programs being used across the country successfully accelerate those labeled as low achievers in early childhood, elementary school, and secondary school. The programs vary in size; some are small, while others serve entire school districts. In most cases, the program's curricular focus is (or includes) reading. Table 3.1 summarizes general information about these examples of local, regional, national, and international programs that seek to accelerate the learning of low-achieving students.

The Crayton Accelerated Program (CAP)

CAP moves students from the seventh to the ninth grade through an intensive interdisciplinary self-contained program. To qualify for the special class, the students must be fifteen years old or older, be in the seventh grade, have failed at least one grade, and be willing to sign a personal contract along with their parents specifying terms of attendance and behavior. Fifteen students were initially identified and eleven students were selected based on a preliminary student interview involving the program teachers, school guidance counselor, parents/guardian, and in some cases, the school nurse. In the pilot year, ten of the eleven students completed the requirements of the program and entered high school.

CAP combines elements of the Accelerated Schools Project (Levin 1987; Hopfenberg et al. 1993) with an in-school alternative program. In this nine-week, intensive accelerated program, students have guidance and an individualized academic program not possible in the regular classroom. The learning environment includes a key teacher who works col-

TABLE 3.1   Programs That Accelerate Low-Achieving Students

Program	Location	Focus	Students Served
Crayton Accelerated Program (CAP)	Local	Reading, language arts, and social studies	Transition to high school; age 15 or older
Higher-Order Thinking Skills (HOTS)	Nation	Thinking skills	Elementary
Project Success	Local/regional	Reading	Secondary
Ready for School	Local	Reading	Early childhood
Urban Collaborative Accelerated Program (UCAP)	Local/regional	English, math, social studies, science	Transition to high school
Reading Recovery	National/ international	Reading	Early childhood

laboratively with another content area teacher. The self-contained class allows for flexibility in scheduling and enables weekly academic-based field trips that reinforce the interdisciplinary course content. Course materials include seventh and eighth grade texts, authentic materials (e.g., newspapers, magazine articles, maps), videos, guest speakers, field trip guides, personal journals, and portfolios. Students work on cooperative teams and individual research projects in content areas as needed. For example, students might spend two days on a single history project or several entire days perfecting an essay or research report. Emphasis is on students presenting reports, essays, and vocabulary-based creative writing to their classmates for teacher and peer feedback.

Higher-Order Thinking Skills (HOTS)

This program is an intensive thinking skills program designed for at-risk students. The program, part of the National Diffusion Network, is used primarily with Title I students. HOTS's goal is to increase students' basic skills through the use of technology and the Socratic questioning method. Four thinking techniques form the basis of the program: metacognition, inference from context, decontextualization, and synthesis of information to solve a problem. Classes meet four days a week, for thirty-five minutes, over a period of two years. Teachers guide students as they work through difficult, complex problems.

Data from five years of research indicate basic skills achievement gains in math and reading (Pogrow 1990). HOTS program designers believe that at-risk students do not understand "understanding" and that grasping the concept of what it means to understand is a key to learning.

Project Success

Project Success is an academic intervention program used in secondary schools based on systematic and structured reading/writing instruction sequenced from simple to complex. The program includes both reading and writing instruction built into the daily routine. The project's goal is to accelerate reading skills as quickly as possible by helping students learn and apply decoding and comprehension skills. Project Success, fast-paced and intense, takes about thirty to forty minutes a day in addition to balanced classroom instruction; it does not take the place of regular reading and language arts classes.

Reading materials consist of authentic trade books and magazines, sequenced from easy to difficult. The materials contain high-interest content and include cross-cultural and interdisciplinary books and articles. Students write both expository and narrative essays and are required to retell or rewrite the book or story in their own words. Students attend the program for 76–90 days. The goal is to quickly raise students' reading levels and move them out of the program as soon as possible. Teaching strategies include using graphic organizers and reciprocal teaching, an approach in which students read with the teacher as they summarize, clarify, question, and predict (Palincsar and Brown 1984). Scaffolding, building background skills needed to help students become independent, is another emphasized strategy.

Ready for School Program

This program, used successfully since 1994, is an intensive program teaching reading, readiness skills, and world knowledge to low-income pre-first graders during the summer before first grade. The program is designed to provide children with literacy background and base knowledge about the physical world. Approximately twenty-five children from public community housing and boys and girls clubs are identified to participate in the eight-week program. The children attend three classes per week in the summer prior to the first grade. Identified themes that help the young child better understand how the world operates are the basis of the curriculum. The *Reading Rainbow©* Series, a public television production, is used in the program. A *Reading Rainbow©* tape is used for each unit; they can be checked out at most local libraries. The books discussed in each series are also readily available at libraries or can be purchased from bookstores. Volunteers are trained as instructors, and since the *Reading Rainbow©* materials can be checked out, there is no cost for the program resources.

Children are exposed to an estimated two hundred new terms and develop a strong foundation in how to create written language and the structure of grammar. Further, the children learn classroom "etiquette," how to sit and listen to a story and how to appropriately respond. Other areas that help students succeed in first grade are learning how to share, to take turns, and to express ideas in a group.

Urban Collaborative Accelerated Program

The Urban Collaborative Accelerated Program (UCAP) is a publicly funded alternative school serving three participating city school districts in Rhode Island. The UCAP is also an independent, nonprofit entity that receives support from almost two dozen public and private contributors. UCAP provides a small school setting where students who have fallen behind their academic peers can complete three years of requirements in just two years.

All students at UCAP have repeated at least one grade of school. Students may proceed through the seventh, eighth, and ninth grades in two years as long as they meet the predetermined standards for promotion in these grades. The school helps these students return to their regular high schools with the academic and social skills that will enable them to graduate from high school.

Because acceleration in grade is a necessary objective of UCAP, a criterion-referenced grading system allows each student to move forward at his or her own pace. Outcomes for the skills and content expected of a student in each grade of UCAP's four core subjects include the following: English, math, social studies, and science. When students meet their necessary criteria for subject, promotion to the next grade in that subject occurs.

The majority of students' instructional time focuses on work in one of the four core subjects. The school conducts a number of special programs to support student needs. Motivation, a key aspect in programs for low-achieving students, ties to a reward system, of which the most obvious reward is student acceleration and promotion. Recognition of academic successes during school meetings and special presentations to successful students build motivation.

The school social worker provides counseling and uses a case management approach. Local agencies may be part of the case management plan, and family services are provided if needed. Students receive individual and group counseling and may receive follow-up help after leaving the school and returning to high school.

Reading Recovery®

This program addresses reading failure in the early years (first grade). The child who cannot read has academic difficulties and may suffer from low self-esteem. Reading Recovery® is an early intervention program that seeks to prevent years of reading failure. The Reading Recovery® program includes a lesson framework with specified procedures for working with children, a teacher in-service program design that provides continuous monitoring and support, and a cost-effective intervention that reduces the need for future remediation and tutoring. The major investment is in staff development.

To qualify for the program (in the United States), the lowest 15 to 20 percent of a beginning first grade population is identified. Reading Recovery® teachers receive training from a "teacher leader" who has participated in a year-long academic training program at Ohio State University. The Reading Recovery® teacher provides daily one-to-one instruction for fifteen to twenty weeks. The program's goal is to accelerate students to the average level of their classroom peers and to make them independent readers.

Conclusion

Returning to our example at the beginning of the chapter, we know that Richard was on the fast track to dropping out if he had not enrolled in an innovative accelerated learning program. We have learned a lesson from thirty years of remediating students like Richard; they rarely learn and often drop out. As described above, legislation passed in the 1960s provided special remedial classes for low-achieving students, but these programs tended to slow down and simplify instruction. Pull-out remedial classes were initially set up for students not fitting into a special education category. Since these programs have not been as successful as was hoped, researchers and innovators in education have proposed and tested a number of other programs to take the place of ineffective and sometimes even detrimental remedial classes.

Mandates to make changes in remediation abound across the country. The idea of accelerating instruction for low-achieving students rather than slowing it down is consistent with the standards and accountability movements. Although acceleration has been used successfully for many years in the curriculum development of programs for gifted students, the strategies have only recently been expanded into use with low-achieving students, and the results have been positive.

The chapter points to several issues for exploration relative to acceleration of low-achieving students. First is the issue of why so many students are allowed to get so far behind. Why is it that although there has been a clear focus on individual diagnosis and "treatment" of learning problems, the treatments have been unsuccessful in helping students to catch up with their age peers? Why has it taken educators more than thirty years to realize that when approaches are not successful in moving students forward, we need to explore other approaches as possibilities? Is the answer related to our beliefs and values about some students? Have we explained away programmatic failure through a deficit view of at-risk students (i.e., minority, low income, immigrants)?

Next, and related to the issues above, if we know reading is the key to other learning, how do we ensure that all students become strong readers? Most of the programs discussed in this chapter have reading as the central piece of accelerated learning. How might we build on the strengths of students who are not strong readers to provide them with the essential reading skills they need to be successful?

Identifying students' strengths and weaknesses is not the problem. Educators need to know what students know and where they need help. However, labeling students leads to tracking students, and tracking has been detrimental to low-achieving students (Oakes 1985; Wheelock 1992). The discussion in Chapter 1 about remediation illustrates how a program's label can be shifted to the students in the program, and when that shift happens, the student is seen as deficient and the cause of the problem.

Students' opportunity to learn may be blocked because of the prevailing belief that mastery of basic skills must occur before rich and interesting curriculum can be tackled by the low achiever. The widespread belief many hold about the hierarchical nature of learning creates difficulty in convincing educators that not only can basics and advanced learning be combined, but we perform an educational disservice if we do not combine them. Providing access to higher-order thinking and problem solving opportunities enhances student interest and motivation and contributes to learning. Diagnosis and treatment is too simple a solution for the complexity of helping students become successful learners.

4   Accelerate = Challenging *All* Students

Sara can't wait to get to the music practice being held before school. In keeping with the school's theme on cooperation, her class wrote an opera describing cooperation during the journey in James and the Giant Peach. Sara is playing the role of the silkworm, and she wants to be sure she knows all of her lines. Although she is typically shy, she is excited about singing in front of the entire school. Sara's teacher works closely with many of the other teachers in the school, especially the art and music teacher. The art teacher helped the students figure out how to use math to draw large insects to scale. The music teacher taught them about opera as an art form and is working with them to put on their production.

Sara's mother is pleased with the progress Sara has made at Westview Elementary School. She is happy that the school does not separate students by ability because she knows that Sara would not be placed in the advanced class. Sara comes home excited about what she has learned. Sometimes assignments are difficult, but Sara is always able to get help from her teacher or from classmates. Not only have all of Sara's teachers expected a lot from Sara, they have gotten to know her and have helped her to develop more confidence. Sara, her brothers, and her mother all feel like they are part of a family at Westview Elementary School.

Sara is experiencing accelerated learning, but the context in which her learning is accelerated is very different from that of Anna and Richard. Where Anna and Richard are identified as special and separated from other students to receive accelerated learning, students are not separated by ability in Sara's school. Each classroom teacher provides a challenging, learner-centered educational experience to all students. Gifted students, average students, and slower students learn together at Westview Elementary; everyone in the school is committed to finding ways to challenge every student. The primary difference between Sara's school and the schools attended by Anna and Richard is that energy is directed toward identifying the best ways for students to learn rather than identifying differences in students. Sara's school and teacher are not focused on the speed of learning–moving gifted students faster or catching up slower students. It is focused on the depth of learning, on providing a rich, challenging learning environment to all of its students.

Although classrooms like Sara's are unusual, and schools like Westview are quite rare, interest in promoting such classrooms and schools to accelerate the learning of all students is intensifying. Pressure to better serve all students comes from a number of directions. There is great pressure to be more internationally competitive and to better prepare students for a radically different workplace. American students' poor performance within the international arena continues to be a critical issue in today's global economy (Ross 1993; Mathematical Association of America 1998); this concern highlights the need to set high standards for all students.

Schools are also being pressured to minimize the practice of labeling and sorting students by ability. Some educators of the gifted are moving away from a focus on identification of gifted students to building on the potential of all students (Gardner 1983; Renzulli and Reis 1985; Sternberg 1985; Tomlinson 1996). Educators concerned with low-achieving students are finding that acceleration is more effective than remediation in encouraging slower students to learn (Means, Chelemer, and Knapp 1991; Knapp 1995a; Newmann et al. 1996; Spillane and Jennings 1997).

Finally, the accountability movement may constitute the greatest pressure on schools to accelerate the learning of all students. Accountability legislation in states across the country establishes the same high standards for all students. This push encourages schools to find ways that enable all students to reach these standards. Drawing on what we know has worked well to accelerate the learning of select groups of students can help schools identify or design programs that accelerate the learning of all students.

Although pressure to change schools to accelerate all students' learning exists, schools and classrooms are likely to be slow to change. The kind of change required to accelerate all students' learning is deep and systemic. As later chapters describe, accelerated learning requires a change in school and classroom cultures and in the assumptions individuals hold. These assumptions—about students, teachers, and other adults, appropriate educational practices, communication, and change—lie at the center of school and classroom cultures. The bad news for school change is that assumptions are difficult to change; the good news is that once they have changed, assumptions help to sustain and foster continuous improvement. This chapter provides a review of the research supporting accelerated learning for all students as well as examples of programs available to help schools and classrooms accelerate learning.

The Impetus for Acceleration of All

The emphasis at the national and state level on accountability and standards is one impetus for accelerating the learning of all students. Designed to eliminate the practice of setting high standards for some students and low standards for others, accountability policies call for schools to examine how and what students are taught. The standards/accountability movement has increased the emphasis on standardized test scores, but it assumes different ways of teaching and a reconceptualization of the teaching/learning process.

Another impetus for accelerating the learning of all students deals with concern with the mediocrity of educational experiences for many students. For example, *National Excellence: A Case for Developing America's Talent* (Ross 1993), a report commissioned by the U.S. Office of Education, states that "most American students are encouraged to finish high school and earn good grades. But students are not asked to work hard or master a body of challenging knowledge or skills. The message society often sends to students is to aim for academic *adequacy,* not academic *excellence*" (p. 1).

This report suggests steps to improve education for top students, which when implemented, improve education for all students. The recommended steps include setting challenging curriculum standards, providing more challenging opportunities to learn, increasing access to early childhood education, increasing opportunities for disadvantaged and minority children with outstanding talents, broadening the definition of gifted, emphasizing teacher development, and matching world performance (Ross 1993: 2). As the title of the report indicates, determining ways to build on students' strengths and develop their talents is the path to excellence in education.

Although not an impetus to accelerate learning of all students, concern over the quality of teachers is heightened when we think through the ramifications of encouraging accelerated learning for all students. As we reform curriculum, we must also reform how we prepare teachers and sustain their development. The National Commission on Teaching and America's Future (1996) makes a strong case for reform of teacher education and professional development. The commission's research is based on three premises:

> What teachers know and can do is the most important influence on what students learn. Recruiting, preparing, and retaining good teachers is the central strategy for improving our schools. School reform cannot succeed unless it focuses on creating the conditions in which teachers can teach and teach well. (1996: vi)

The commission spells out five recommendations to accomplish the stated goals: take standards for students and teachers seriously, radically change teacher preparation and professional development, recruit and retain enough qualified teachers for every classroom, encourage teachers to be knowledgeable and skillful and reward their efforts, and organize schools to ensure student and teacher success.

The National Commission on Teaching and America's Future and many other researchers and policymakers believe that teachers are the critical element in school reform. Teachers need to learn to teach very differently than in the past since students are expected to learn in different ways. Students need to work productively within groups, to think critically and solve problems. This approach to teaching and learning is very different from transmission teaching (Darling-Hammond 1997) where the teacher knows all and students are passive recipients of knowledge.

A final impetus for accelerating all students' learning is the fear that American students cannot compete internationally and do not have skills needed for today's jobs. The Commission on the Skills of the American Workforce (1990) notes that current employment needs are not being met, and the technology/service orientation of future jobs will require different skills, resulting in a demand for educating young people in different ways. Technological jobs require workers to be able to solve problems and use computers and other advanced technology (Secretary's Commission on Achieving Necessary Skills 1991). These jobs also necessitate higher levels of literacy and critical thinking (Darling-Hammond 1997). Few employers are interested in low-skilled, compliant workers. Most employers want all employees to be able to solve problems, think critically, and communicate clearly. Their demands provide more incentive to move away from sorting students to designing programs that will provide all students an opportunity to be employed, to support family and self, and to live productively.

A Research Framework Supporting Accelerated Learning for All Students

As described above, pressure to improve education for all students is coming from many directions. There are obvious reasons why all students' learning should be accelerated. The United States will become more competitive internationally, the workforce will be better prepared for the future, and educational inequalities will be addressed. Current research on the effectiveness of educational strategies makes it clear that accelerated learning strategies are available (e.g., Means, Chelemer and Knapp 1991; McLaughlin and Talbert 1993; Hopfenberg et al. 1993; Newmann, Secada, and Wehlage 1995; Mehan, Villanueva, Hubbard, and Lintz 1996; Jennings 1998).

These studies provide the framework for our definition of accelerated learning, and they clarify what is and is not a part of accelerated learning.

This research makes it clear that acceleration is not remediation and does not try to compensate for perceived student deficits. The studies provide evidence that accelerated learning builds on students' strengths rather than on their weaknesses. Accelerated learning need not be skill-based drill, and it is definitely not learning disguised as fun, games, and trivia. Accelerated learning assumes high expectations for all students. It includes rich and interesting curriculum that connects and is relevant to the students' world. Accelerated learning embeds basic skills in learning that requires advanced skills and high-level thinking and problem solving.

Acceleration for all applies what we already know about effective teaching:

> Students learn best when new ideas are connected to what they already know and have experienced; when they are actively engaged in applying and testing their knowledge using real-world problems; when their learning is organized around clear, high goals with lots of practice in reaching them; and when they can use their own interests and strengths as springboards for learning. (National Commission on Teaching and America's Future 1996: 6)

Blending what we know about students and how they learn to create a rich learning environment is another critical part of accelerated learning. An accelerated learning environment includes varied learning experiences, continuous learning, motivation, and scaffolding by identifying and building on strengths. Teachers who accelerate learning are highly skilled and knowledgeable about both students and content. "Research confirms that teacher knowledge of subject matter, student learning, and teaching methods are all important elements of teacher effectiveness" (National Commission on Teaching and America's Future 1996: 6). The studies cited above also support raising standards of achievement for all students; higher expectations demand higher achievement. Accelerated learning for all requires that *all* students be held to high standards of learning.

It is from this research base that we developed the definition of accelerated learning presented in Chapter 1:

> Accelerated learning is learning that is of high intellectual quality; it is substantive, authentic, and relevant. Accelerated learning is continuous and connected, and it is grounded in high standards. Accelerated learning occurs when students are active and responsible, involved in intellectual pursuits with other students, and turned on to learning. It happens when teachers are highly skilled and knowledgeable; they learn alongside their students and engage in meaningful discussion and dialogue with students. They are reflective in their practice and care about all students.

The following discussion provides more detail on the studies informing our definition of accelerated learning. The key points from these studies are summarized in Table 4.1.

TABLE 4.1   Research Base for Definition of Accelerating Learning for All Students

---

Gifted and Talented Teaching Strategies (Tomlinson 1996)
- maintain a student-centered classroom
- students engaged in active, participatory learning
- students solve relevant problems
- students make sense of important ideas
- opportunities for high-level thinking
- opportunities to apply learning and understanding
- opportunities for a sense of empowerment through learning

Powerful Learning (Hopfenberg et al. 1993; Keller and Huebner 1997)
- learning that is authentic
- learning that is interactive
- learning that is inclusive
- learning that is continuous
- learning that is centered on the learner
- a learning environment that emphasizes the interplay between curriculum, instruction, and the context of learning

Authentic Academic Achievement (Newmann, Secada, and Wehlage 1995)
- high intellectual quality
- construction of knowledge by students
- disciplined inquiry
- in-depth understanding
- elaborated communication
- value beyond school

Teaching for Understanding (Cohen, McLaughlin, and Talbert 1993)
- students and teachers learn collaboratively
- classroom discourse used to challenge thinking
- conceptual understanding as the goal
- students are explorers, conjecturers, and constructors of their own knowledge
- teachers are guides, coaches, and facilitators of students' learning

Advanced Skills Teaching (Means, Chelemer, and Knapp 1991; Knapp et al. 1995)
- integrated instruction that builds on students' strengths and intellectual accomplishments
- basic skills embedded into more "global, complex tasks"
- challenge, dialogue, and thinking as part of instructional practices

---

Gifted and Talented Teaching Strategies

Researchers interested in gifted and talented students have identified a number of classroom practices that stimulate high-achieving students. Carol Ann Tomlinson (1996) points out that recent research on brain functioning and on the effects of constructivist practices on student learning have attracted regular classroom teachers to strategies formerly used only with students identified as gifted. The strategies traditionally used with gifted and talented students that define and support accelerated learning include the following:

- students work in a student-centered classroom where learning is interactive and collaborative;
- students engage in learning through active, participatory strategies;
- students solve relevant problems that are meaningful in the world outside of the classroom;
- students make sense of important ideas and construct their own understanding;
- students engage in higher-level thinking, including both critical and creative thinking;
- students apply their understanding and skills to deepen learning; and
- students develop a sense of empowerment through learning, which enables students to appreciate and pursue intellectual activities. (Tomlinson 1996: 157)

Powerful Learning

Powerful learning guides the conceptualization of teaching and learning within the Accelerated Schools Project (Hopfenberg et al. 1993; Keller and Huebner 1997). Through research on effective practice, the Accelerated Schools Project identified five characteristics of powerful learning: authentic, interactive, inclusive, continuous, and centered on the learner. Attention to the interplay between curriculum, instruction, and the learning context are also critical in creating powerful learning. Powerful learning is a vehicle for helping students meet internally or externally developed standards (Levin 1998).

Authentic Academic Achievement

Authentic academic achievement focuses on the intellectual quality of schoolwork (Newmann, Secada, and Wehlage 1995; Newmann et al. 1996). Three criteria define authentic academic achievement: construction of knowledge, disciplined inquiry, and value beyond school. Students construct or produce knowledge rather than reproducing it through memorization and rote learning. Just as professionals produce new knowledge or meaning in their work, students learn more and become more engaged in their learning when they have a role in constructing knowledge or meaning. Disciplined inquiry involves the use of students' "prior knowledge base, striving for in-depth understanding rather than superficial awareness, and expressing conclusions through elaborated communication" (Newmann, Secada, and Wehlage 1995: 9). When engaged in disciplined inquiry, students build and develop understanding through spoken and written communication. Students see the value beyond school when they understand the relevance of learning and thinking to the world outside of the classroom.

Teaching for Understanding

Challenge, dialogue, and collaborative learning between teacher and student are critical to teaching for understanding. Teaching for understanding also focuses on conceptual understanding of a discipline. Teaching for understanding assumes that classrooms are places "where students and teachers acquire knowledge collaboratively, where orthodoxies of pedagogy and 'facts' are continually challenged in classroom discourse, and where conceptual (versus rote) understanding of subject matter is the goal." In these classrooms, students are "explorers, conjecturers, and constructors of their own learning," and teachers are "guides, coaches, and facilitators of students' learning through posing questions, challenging students' thinking, and leading them in examining ideas and relationships" (McLaughlin and Talbert 1993: 1). Teaching for understanding assumes that "adventurous teaching" occurs (Wilson, Miller, and Yerkes 1993: 95), teaching that allows teachers and students to take risks and learn together. Students are expected to understand deeply, not merely cover material.

Advanced Skills Teaching

Advanced skills teaching is integrated instruction that builds on students' strengths and intellectual accomplishments (Means, Chelemer, and Knapp 1991; Knapp et al. 1995). Three primary principles guide advanced skills teaching. The first is an attitude toward disadvantaged learners that recognizes, appreciates, and builds on students' existing strengths and that encourages understanding of students' culture.

The second principle focuses on providing curriculum that is based on relevant, meaningful problems that connect learning to what students know and have experienced. Basic skills are embedded into "more global, complex tasks" to help students make connections between new learning and their experiences and culture. Instruction that integrates relevant content enriches learning and allows students to engage in challenging and interesting work.

The third principle describes instructional strategies that explicitly model how to learn, promote open-ended problems with many possible solutions, use scaffolding to permit students to "reach higher places" (Means, Chelemer, and Knapp 1991: 15), and use dialogue and reciprocal teaching to exchange ideas and build understanding.

To summarize, considerable commonality exists between these studies. They call for learning that is substantive and of high intellectual quality. The learning is authentic and relevant, and continuous and connected. Learning experiences for all students are grounded in high standards. These studies describe students who are active, responsible, and involved in intellectual pursuits with other students. In other words, students are turned on to learning. Finally, the studies highlight teachers who are highly skilled and knowledgeable. They learn alongside their students and engage in meaningful discussion and dialogue with students. These teachers are reflective in their practice and care about all students.

This research provides a strong framework supporting the provision of accelerated learning to all students. However, the framework alone will not create change in schools and classrooms. In most cases, school communities and teachers need a structure or process to change their school and classroom culture and to shift their basic assumptions. The following programs, projects, and educational strategies are examples of how accelerated learning can be integrated into schools and classrooms.

Accelerated Learning Programs, Projects, and Educational Strategies

A number of successful programs and projects have been designed to accelerate learning for all students. Most are schoolwide programs, seeking to transform the culture of the entire school. We also provide several examples of programs within schools and programs based on specific curricula and instructional strategies.

Comprehensive School Reform Initiatives

The Accelerated Schools Project. The Accelerated Schools Project (ASP), the brainchild of Dr. Henry M. Levin, is designed to create schools that treat all students as gifted (see Hopfenberg et al. 1993; Finnan, St. John, McCarthy, and Slovacek 1996; Levin 1987). Trained in economics, Levin focused his research on issues of inequity in education. In his studies of schools, he found that in most classrooms students received a deadening routine of worksheets, drill, and memorization; the only bright spot he found in these schools were the classrooms for students identified as gifted. He wondered why all students could not benefit from a similarly engaging and challenging learning environment; from this question the Accelerated Schools Project developed. Levin explains that the "idea was to create a school that would accelerate the development of all of its students by building on their strengths rather than searching for and 'remediating' their weaknesses" (1996: 10). Since its beginning in 1987, the Accelerated Schools Project has been adopted by more than 1,000 schools in thirty-five states and several foreign countries. Schools across the country are served by regional satellite centers established in colleges and universities, state departments of education, and school districts.

The Accelerated Schools Project works with school communities to instill its philosophy, decisionmaking process, and governance structure into their school cultures. The philosophy rests on three principles: unity of purpose, empowerment with responsibility, and building on strengths and nine values (the school as the center of expertise; equity; community; risk taking; experimentation; reflection; participation; trust; and communication). The project's philosophical commitment to teaching and learning, described as powerful learning, was described earlier in this chapter.

Accelerated schools use an inquiry process to make all decisions related to student learning. Keeping the school's vision, the ASP philosophy, and the components of powerful learning at the center of all decisions, cadres of teachers, parents, school staff, and in some cases students engage in a systematic inquiry process. This process is designed to identify root causes of problems, investigate potential solutions, and develop action plans to make the vision a reality. A set curriculum for accelerated schools does not exist; each school determines actions that address its unique needs.

Improving student achievement is the Accelerated Schools Project's primary goal. Levin explains that the Accelerated Schools Project is based on the

> notion of viewing all children as deserving of and benefiting from the same approach that [has] been reserved for gifted students in the past. . . . Acceleration necessitates the remaking of the school in order to advance the academic and social development of *all* children, including those in at-risk situations. This has meant creating a school in which all children are viewed as capable of benefiting from a rich instructional experience rather than relegating some to a watered down one. It means a school that creates powerful learning situations for all children, integrating curriculum, instructional strategies, and context rather than providing piecemeal changes. (1996: 13–14)

Interestingly, much of the philosophical basis of the Accelerated Schools Project has been adopted by the mainstream reform movement calling for challenging and rigorous curriculum for all students.

School Development Program. James Comer's work with schools began in the late 1960s and early 1970s in New Haven, Connecticut (see Comer 1980, 1988; Comer, Haynes, and Joyner 1996). In his work with the Yale Child Study Center, Comer found that schools serving what he calls "underdeveloped children or differently developed children" often punished children because teachers and administrators viewed their behavior as bad. Comer saw the need to build trust between parents and the school because he realized that many parents had a deep mistrust of authority and that they saw the school as "the authority."

The School Development Program (SDP) provides a system to organize and manage the school that is designed to remedy child development and relationship issues. Its purpose is to build a child-centered school with psychological development as the key to students' academic success. SDP focuses on the mental health of students; many SDP schools have mental health teams and crisis rooms for students who are out of control. This mental health focus grows out of Comer's medical background and training as a psychiatrist.

The project has three guiding principles: consensus, collaboration, and no fault. These principles reflect the focus on creating partnerships and trust between parents and schools. Comer includes parents as a critical part of the discussion of developmental and social issues related to schooling of minority and low-income children.

The School Development Program places parents and families at the center of change, encouraging teachers and principals to radically change the way they involve parents in students' education. Actions taken by school communities focus on improving student achievement and are viewed as long-term commitments requiring cooperation and collaboration among school staff and parents. Decisions in SDP schools are made by the School Planning and Management Team, the Parent Team, and the Student and Staff Support Team. The School Planning and Management Team plans and coordinates school activities; the Parent Team works to involve parents at all levels in the school; and the Student and Staff Support Team addresses schoolwide issues and management of individual student cases. They work to develop a comprehensive school plan to guide the improvement efforts of the school. In 1995, there were 550 School Development Project schools across the country.

Coalition of Essential Schools. Founded by Theodore Sizer, the Coalition of Essential Schools provides a set of principles describing an effective school (see Sizer 1992b). Originally oriented toward reforming high schools, the Coalition of Essential Schools has member schools across the country. Their philosophy is articulated through a set of twelve principles:

schools that are small and personalized in size; a unified course of study for all students; a focus on helping young people use their minds well; an in-depth, intra-disciplinary curriculum respectful of the diverse heritages that encompass our society; active learning with student-as-worker/student-as-citizen and teacher-as-coach; student evaluation by performance-based as-sessment methods; a school tone of unanxious expectation, trust, and de-cency; collaborative decision making and governance; choice; racial, ethnic, economic, and intellectual diversity; and budget allocations targeting time for collective planning. (Semel 1999: 19–20)

The Coalition of Essential Schools does not specify a process for schools to follow as they restructure themselves. Each school shapes the principles to their particular setting and faculty. The principles are used to guide the reform effort, not structure it. Coalition schools have had success in improved academic performance of students, but some schools struggle with the lack of structure (Semel 1999).

Central Park East Secondary School (CPESS) in East Harlem, New York City District 4, is an example of a successful Coalition school. Founded in 1985 by Deborah Meier, CPESS uses integrated curriculum, is student centered, has advisory groups for students, and works to de-velop a community of learners in the school. This school is considered a modern progressive school and has been held as an example of an effec-tive school for working-class African American and Latino students.

Programs Using Gifted and Talented Materials and Approaches

Schools for Talent Development.   Schools for Talent Development encour-ages teachers to use both acceleration and enrichment for all students (see Renzulli 1994a). These schools have a focus on concept learning rather than skills learning. Schools involved in Schools for Talent Devel-opment use interdisciplinary curriculum and theme-based studies, stu-dent portfolios, performance assessment, and cross-grade grouping. Schools are encouraged to implement alternative scheduling patterns and to provide "opportunities for students to exchange traditional roles for more demanding and challenging roles that require hands-on learn-ing, firsthand investigations, and the application of knowledge and thinking skills to complex problems" (Renzulli 1994b: 3).

Schools for Talent Development has been effective in stimulating the learning of students considered low or average achievers. For example, in a study investigating enrichment clusters (i.e., students of similar in-terests study together to explore an area and develop an authentic prod-uct), researchers found that quality of student work was similar despite differences in students' achievement levels (Reis, Gentry, and Park 1995). This model takes approaches that have been reserved for gifted and talented students and uses them successfully with students of all achievement levels to accelerate and enrich learning.

Project Breakthrough. This demonstration project, funded in 1998 through the Javits Gifted and Talented Education Act, has as its goal the application of gifted and talented curriculum to all students in three schools serving primarily low-income students (Swanson 1998, 1999). The expected outcome is improved achievement of all students. Three elementary Title I schools are the demonstration sites. Teachers are using problem-based science units and language arts units with all of their students in grades two through five. The curriculum was developed through earlier Javits demonstration projects and has a research base of improving achievement of low-, average-, and high-achieving students. Faculty in the schools applied to participate in the project, so the commitment to accelerating the learning of all students is present at the school level. Classroom observations and teacher logs from the first year of the project indicate that both students' and teachers' responses to the challenging and interesting curriculum has been quite positive (Swanson 1999).

Programs Within a School

Advancement Via Individual Determination (AVID). AVID is a secondary school program focusing on preparation for four-year college for average students (see Mehan, Villanueva, Hubbard, and Lintz 1996). It provides access to college preparatory courses to underachieving average students, most of whom will be first-generation college students. AVID provides a rigorous curriculum for all students who signal an interest in continuing their education after high school and provides increased support for students at risk of failure. These students are taught through a college preparatory curriculum and are provided mentors and tutors to learn about the college experience and to develop study and time management skills. Teachers' professional development focuses on high expectations for themselves and their students and teaches them how to enable students to complete a rigorous academic program. Academic success is built around teaching students writing and language skills and collaborative problem-solving strategies.

AVID is based on the assumption that teachers and students are powerful and capable of changing the pattern of student underachievement. Students and teachers develop new strategies for teaching and learning that focus on success. The teacher becomes as much a student advocate as a teacher, gaining knowledge of students' cultures and special needs. Learning occurs in heterogeneous groups in an academically rigorous environment. Support for student learning includes mentors, often minority college students, who model the academic, social, and cultural knowledge needed to succeed in college. The program is integrated into regular school staffing, curriculum, and funding.

Specific Curricula and Classroom Strategies

The programs described above are either schoolwide or integrated into the total school program. Accelerated learning can also occur in isolated classrooms through the commitment and creativity of individual teachers. Specific curricula and instructional practices are available that show promise in accelerating the learning of all students.

Under the leadership of Joyce Van Tassel-Baska at the Center for Gifted Education in the College of William and Mary, curriculum units have been developed for high-ability learners in science, language arts, and social studies. The curriculum units are not a comprehensive curriculum; they are not meant to include all the content that students should study in a particular discipline. They do, however, include rigorous and challenging models of thinking embedded within the study units: problem-based learning, the need-to-know board, Richard Paul's (1992) wheel of reasoning, the vocabulary web, the literature web, and Hilda Taba's (1962) model of concept development. This curriculum was developed for gifted students but has a research base of evidence that indicates that low-, average-, and high-achieving students show achievement gains (Swanson 1999).

The Keys to Acceleration for All Students

As a student at Westview Elementary School, Sara benefits from accelerated learning in her fourth grade class. She is lucky to be in such a class but even luckier to be in a school committed to accelerated learning. The teachers and principal at Westview Elementary have made a commitment to provide powerful learning to all students. We have profiled her fourth grade class, but she has had similar experiences throughout her years at Westview. Her teachers are committed to providing the best possible education to all students in the school, and the principal ensures that resources are available for them to do so.

Westview Elementary is a rare example of a school that provides accelerated learning to all students. Its teachers hold assumptions and beliefs that motivate and sustain their efforts to meet the needs of all children. They believe that all students, no matter what difficulties they may bring to the classroom, can be challenged to learn.

How did Westview become like this and why are so few schools like Westview? First, Westview joined the Accelerated Schools Project in an effort to improve student learning. The Accelerated Schools Project is not the only vehicle for helping schools improve, but it provides a decision-making process and a structure to involve all members of the school community in decisionmaking. Many schools are unable to sustain efforts to change because they do not have an ongoing decisionmaking and communication structure in place.

Second, Westview's school culture encourages individuals to change. At the core of Westview's culture are a set of assumptions that encourage risk taking, hold high expectations for all students, and promote active involvement in learning. The culture of many schools hinders efforts to change. Deep in the culture are assumptions about students, teachers, and the teaching and learning process that block any efforts to change. Classrooms also have cultures, and these too can be difficult to change. The rest of this book addresses issues of changing school and classroom cultures.

Third, everyone at Westview takes learning very seriously. Teachers engage in professional development, students take responsibility for learning, and parents recognize their responsibilities for encouraging their children to learn and model lifelong learning. Although all teachers claim to take learning seriously, many do not seek substantive learning opportunities. Teachers often lack the pedagogical content knowledge necessary to accelerate learning (Shulman 1987), and their knowledge of the core concepts in the academic areas taught is often limited (Stein, Smith, and Silver 1999). Too often teachers feel comfortable only at the level of superficial teaching, seeking "cute, fun activities" rather than substantive and deep ideas.

Fourth, the teachers at Westview recognize student variation, and they see it as an inevitable part of their job as teachers. They do not spend time labeling students and trying to find other placements for the very students who need them the most. They recognize and build on student differences and create learning experiences that allow students to engage in concepts at different levels of complexity. Although student differences are recognized, all students are held to the same high standards. Few teachers view student diversity in such a positive light. They become overwhelmed by the diverse needs of students, and they lack the skills to create learning environments that challenge students of all ability levels. In some cases, their assumptions about how students learn, about which students are likely to learn, and about effective educational practices prevent them from seeing the strengths in all of their students. The following chapters delve more deeply into these issues.

5 Cultivating Culture Change to Accelerate the Learning of All Students

Anna walks to her school in a comfortable middle-class neighborhood. A small percentage of students (25 percent) receive free or reduced-price lunch and live on the other side of a busy highway. Beginning in fourth grade, students are grouped by ability. Most of the students in Anna's gifted class come from her neighborhood; very few come from across the highway. The faculty and administration have been at the school for years and are comfortable with their teaching practices and knowledge of content.

Richard attends a large middle school in the industrial fringe of a midsize city. Over 90 percent of the students receive free or reduced-price lunch, and most are either Hispanic or African American. Many students come to the middle school behind grade level; discipline and absenteeism are serious problems. Several years ago the district encouraged teaming to address chronic low achievement and poor discipline, but the faculty determined after a few months that it did not work. Two teachers who supported teaming were awarded a grant to develop an "accelerated fifth grade" for students who had been retained. Together, they ensure that a group of twenty students learn the fifth and sixth grade curriculum so that they can join their peers in seventh grade.

Most of the people in Sara's small town work in the local button factory. Approximately 70 percent of the students at her elementary school receive free and reduced-price lunch. In response to an influx of Spanish-speaking migrant workers, the faculty and administration determined that they needed to teach differently to better serve all students. They explored various programs and determined that the Accelerated Schools Project was the best fit for their school. They have been involved with the project since 1995 and are continuously working to refine their teaching so that all students experience powerful learning. All class-

rooms are heterogeneously grouped; Sara's classmates represent a wide range of academic ability and display varied interests and strengths.

Cultivating Acceleration

As described in Chapter 2, many students identified as gifted experience accelerated learning. Anna has the opportunity to move quickly through the typical fifth grade curriculum and delve deeply into her newfound passion for astronomy. A growing number of low-achieving students also experience accelerated learning. Richard is given a chance to learn basic skills while developing higher-order thinking skills in a supportive environment.

Although they represent opposite ends of the achievement continuum, students like Anna and Richard have been given opportunities to move faster through a course of study. Gifted students skip grades and progress through material faster than average students. Increasing numbers of low-achieving students, especially those who have been retained, are provided opportunities to condense two years of work into one in order to attain normal grade level. In these classrooms students are more apt to learn in an environment that is relevant and learner centered than are other students at their school. They understand the importance of what they are learning and have hands-on opportunities as a regular part of their learning. The teacher and students all expect high levels of achievement from everyone in the room.

These classrooms are often isolated from others and have little effect on the rest of the school or on other classrooms. In most schools in which exciting programs exist for gifted students or for low-achieving students, the school and all of the other classrooms remain the same; the culture of the school does not change. Too often these rooms sit aside as islands in a sea of traditional educational practices; the teachers are often viewed as odd and out of touch with the rest of the school.

Sara is fortunate because her school is committed to providing an accelerated learning experience to all students. Such a commitment requires a major change in a school and in all classrooms in the school. For this reason, examples of schools accelerating the learning of all students are rare, especially when we focus on schools serving large numbers of low-income students. However, the rare examples like Sara's school do exist, providing evidence that, under the right conditions, acceleration can occur, even when poverty and cultural and language differences might otherwise make success for all students more difficult. This chapter and the following chapters describe how acceleration for all students can be achieved only through a transformation of school and classroom cultures.

Members of a school or classroom culture must agree to change their culture for it to occur. Mandating change from outside the school, whether from the district or state or through involuntary involvement in a school reform initiative will not result in culture change. Contrary to conclusions drawn by Sarason (1996) and Tyack and Cuban (1995), school cultures are not inherently resistant to change. They can be resistant to externally imposed change, but they are not necessarily resistant to internally initiated change. Most efforts to impose change on schools fail because the change agents fail to realize that changing a school involves changing the culture of the school, which involves changing the assumptions, beliefs, and actions of the individuals involved in the school.

Individuals must engage in an examination of the deeply held assumptions, beliefs, and attitudes that shape their behavior for change to occur in schools and classrooms. In essence, they engage in an examination of culture as it is reflected and manifested in schools and classrooms and in themselves. Change in school and classroom culture is complicated by the fact that culture at these levels reflects the assumptions, beliefs, and attitudes that shape behavior in the surrounding community and the larger society. The following discussion of culture further explores the importance of identifying and examining the influence of assumptions on initiating and sustaining change. Chapters 6 and 7 further examine how assumptions encourage or discourage efforts to accelerate the learning of all students at both the school and classroom level. Chapter 8 draws on the preceding chapters and describes how individuals, both those inside and outside of the school, can act on their assumptions and ultimately assume responsibility to promote acceleration for all students.

What Is Culture?

The concept of culture, whether used to describe schools or larger societies, is not easy to define. It is something that surrounds us, gives meaning to our world, and is constantly being constructed both through our interactions with others and through our reflections on life and our world. Culture is so implicit in what we do that we really do not know it is there. Clyde Kluckhohn (1949: 11) said of culture that it is like fish and water—fish will be the last creatures to discover water. We do not know it is there, but it is the lubricant of our lives. Cultures have six characteristics that have an impact on schools and classrooms.

First, although culture is essential to making meaning, it also restricts our objectivity and shapes our preferences. Culture is not neutral; by valuing certain attributes (e.g., thin figures over full figures) and behaviors (e.g., spontaneity over deliberate action) over others we limit our exposure to and appreciation of our world (Spindler and Spindler 1987; McDermott and Varenne 1995; McQuillan 1998: 3). Culture serves a restrictive role in society by making some behaviors, ideas, and interactions natural and seemingly right, thus making other ways of doing things and seeing the world seem strange and wrong. Just as culture allows us to make meaning in an otherwise chaotic world, it also constricts us by condoning limited and often repressive perceptions of others and ourselves. In schools this characteristic of culture is evident when we value students' analytic and verbal ability and overlook their artistic and kinesthetic ability. It is also evident in people's insistence that students learn best when placed in homogeneous ability groups.

Second, culture is both conservative and ever changing. As a conservative force, culture protects people from the unknown, providing often very limited answers to what would otherwise be unanswerable questions. As Schëin writes, culture reflects "our human need for stability, consistency, and meaning" (1992: 11). At the same time that it plays a conservative function, culture is also ever changing (Wax 1993: 109); it is "a 'contested' phenomenon (Clifford 1986) that individuals can use to their strategic betterment, not an unwavering prescription for behavior" (McQuillan 1998: 214). It adapts to influences from other cultures and from changes in the physical, social, and political environment. We see this characteristic in classrooms when we visit one teacher's room over the course of several years. Her room always looks and feels the same even though it reflects the influence of different students and new teaching strategies.

Third, boundaries between cultures are usually very permeable. Multiple cultures are always interacting; although some are relatively bounded, such as the Amish, others are rather amorphous, such as "American culture." Cultures are nested within each other, mutually influencing each other. At times they are permeable and open to change from outside; at other times, they are closed and resistant to change. Schools contain and are influenced by multiple cultures. Each classroom has a culture that is nested in a school culture. The classroom cultures influence each other as teachers interact, as students pass from one class to another, and as the whole school makes decisions about appropriate educational practices. In addition, each school has a culture that is at once influenced by the multiple classroom cultures and also by the cultures that exist in the local community and in the wider society.

Fourth, individuals experience the culture through their role or position within it (Spindler and Spindler 1993). A teacher's experience of school culture is different than that of the principal or from that of students. Overlap in expectations and assumptions occur, but the school becomes a social system and has a culture through an orchestration of differences and similarities of individuals with distinct roles (Spindler 1999). School change usually necessitates role change, which is not always easy for everyone to accept. For example, the principal's role changes dramatically when schools implement reforms such as the Accelerated Schools Project. Rather than making all decisions, the principal facilitates group decisionmaking. From a teacher's position this change can be invigorating, or it may appear that the principal is abdicating responsibility for decisions.

Fifth, culture is transmitted, shaped, and maintained through language and dialogue (Hymes 1974). Within schools and classrooms, culture is created and maintained by what is talked about and what topics are avoided, by how language is used, by whose language is encouraged, and by who has control of the discourse (Hymes 1972; Phillips 1983; Florio-Ruane 1989).

Finally, the most important characteristic of culture for the purpose of this book is that it manifests itself in both tangible and intangible ways. Culture at its most fundamental is intangible; it is the assumptions people of a culture share. Assumptions are those things we take for granted, that we accept as true without proof. We assume that the sun will rise in the east and set in the west. We assume that our hearts will beat and our lungs will fill with air. We do not spend a lot of time thinking about these things; we just take them for granted. We also make assumptions about people, about learning, and about schools that go unchallenged. These assumptions shape our values, which in turn shape our behavior (Evans 1996). For example, if a teacher assumes that university professors are too theoretical and removed from day-to-day challenges in the classroom, he or she will not value advice given by university professors. The teacher acts on this belief by sitting sullenly through mandatory in-service sessions offered through the local university.

The relationship between these components of culture (assumptions, values, beliefs, and actions) is not clearly understood to most people. As Patrick McQuillan writes, "Culture is something of a paradox: People create culture, but their cultural values predispose them to perceive the world in particular ways. Culture does not determine social action, nor is it predictive; but it defines the possible, the logical" (1998: 3). It is assumptions that define the possible and the logical.

These assumptions are made manifest in the belief systems evident in schools and in the tangible, visible signs of a culture. The school culture supports the teachers' and principal's decisions on how to set up classrooms, how to schedule classes, how to group children, what to display and where to display it, and many other aspects of the school that are easily seen by a casual observer. It also influences less tangible features of school life such as what is considered beautiful, what is considered functional, and what is considered worthwhile. The school culture also influences the processes, rules, and procedures that guide work, play, and social interactions of adults and students both within the school and, to some extent, beyond the school.

Societal Assumptions Influencing School and Classroom Culture

Culture in the context of schools does not exist in a vacuum; schools, classrooms, and the individuals involved in schools reflect and influence the society around them. Assumptions held by people in the immediate communities surrounding the school and the larger society influence the culture found in schools. Some of these assumptions change (albeit slowly and unevenly) as economic and demographic shifts cause society to change. Others are more resistant to change because they are embedded in our national culture, in who we are as citizens of the United States. Tensions arise when assumptions held by some individuals do not reflect changes in society; tensions often escalate because they largely go unspoken and unexamined. The following are six commonly held societal assumptions that, depending on how they are acted upon, support or hinder efforts to accelerate learning. These assumptions are summarized in Table 5.1.

Assumption: All People Need Skills for
Productive Work and Active Citizenship

For generations schools have taken a lead in providing young people necessary skills to work and to participate in society. In the past, it was assumed that schools functioned to provide *basic skills* to those destined to work in factories and on farms, reserving more advanced skills for the few who would engage in more managerial or professional work (Tyack 1974; Darling-Hammond 1997). It is only recently that we have begun to realize that all people need a mix of basic and higher-order skills to function productively in today's more complex technical and service-oriented society. When members of local communities and the nation agree that for all people to lead productive lives students must develop strong communication skills as well as basic and higher-order thinking skills, efforts of individuals within schools to challenge all students will be enhanced. Shared assumptions that we need a workforce and a citizenry that can solve problems, communicate effectively, work collaboratively, and take initiative will translate into decisions at the school level that all students must have opportunities to learn and practice these skills in school (Secretary's Commission on Achieving Necessary Skills 1991; Rumberger, Darrah, Levin, and Finnan 1994).

TABLE 5.1 Assumptions That Support Efforts to Change Schools and Classrooms

Commonly Held Societal Assumptions	Assumptions That Support Acceleration in School and Classrooms
• All people need skills for productive work and active citizenship.	• All students are capable of leading productive lives and consequently need basic and higher-order thinking skills.
• Groups of people share certain innate characteristics and abilities.	• Students are judged by their accomplishments, not by their race, ethnicity, social class, gender, etc.
• Equal opportunity extends to all citizens.	• All students need access to a challenging and engaging learning environment.
• Success is a limited commodity.	• All students can be successful.
• There are simple answers to complex questions.	• Multiple perspectives and thorough inquiry are more apt to provide effective solutions to problems.
• Divesity and unity are mutually exclusive.	• Diversity is a strength when it is channeled toward a goal or vision.

Assumption: Groups of People Share Certain Innate Characteristics and Abilities

As described above, culture provides meaning to our world but it also restricts our objectivity. This is exemplified by our tendency to assign attributes to people based on their ethnicity, race, social class, gender, or other characteristics. For example, a lost tourist may not approach an Asian American for directions because he assumes that the Asian American does not speak English. These stereotypes hinder everyone. The tourist remains lost, and the Asian American has to repeatedly prove that he is as American as anyone else.

Despite a preponderance of evidence to the contrary, the assumption that certain groups of people are capable of contributing more to the community and the nation than others still exists. Stereotypes of the ability and behavior of people of different ethnic, racial, social class, and gender groups have perpetuated inequities and have limited opportunities for generations of students. These assumptions are manifest in decisions regarding which students are provided access to advanced courses and to challenging curriculum. They are also evident in the allocation of financial resources and teaching staff and in the condition of school facilities. For too long, people have justified inequity by saying that inferior teachers, buildings, or curriculum are "good enough for *those* students." For school communities to successfully accelerate all students' learning, we must continue to challenge these assumptions and encourage people within schools to judge all members of the school community by their accomplishments, not by group affiliations (e.g., race, ethnicity, gender, social class) and to actually provide equal educational opportunities.

Assumption: Equal Opportunity Extends to All Citizens

For a country founded on the belief that "all men are created equal," able to advance through hard work and determination, the chronic economic disparities between social classes, races, and ethnic groups are difficult to justify. It is clear that advancement because of merit appears to be easier for some than for others. Although certain segments of society have historically benefited from social and economic connections that ease admissions into elite schools and pave the way into good jobs, efforts to open such paths to other groups are seen as unfair. For instance, affirmative action efforts designed to increase access to work and higher education for racial and ethnic minorities and women have been challenged as unconstitutional. States such as California have eliminated affirmative action admissions to higher education and minority/female set-asides in business, and racial quotas are rarely used in school admissions decisions.

Few middle-class Americans attribute their success to the social connections and cultural knowledge they acquired at birth or see them as a form of privilege or capital.[1] They argue that their success was achieved through hard work. When asked why other people who also work hard find it harder to advance economically and socially, they are reluctant to credit the advantages that came from how and where they grew up. On the one hand, they know that their path to success was made easier by parents who knew the value of a good school system (Metz 1998), who exposed them to cultural, economic, and artistic experiences, and who knew people who could help them on their way to success. On the other hand, this recognition goes against our belief that we succeed through hard work and initiative.

Schools are assumed to be social equalizers and avenues to advancement. Many tales are told about the poor child who became successful through hard work in school and with the help of caring, dedicated teachers. However, it is more common for the children of well-educated, middle-class parents to be successful, whereas the students from low-income, working-class families are more apt to either accept the inferior education provided them or to rebel against a social system that tolerates inadequate schools. We are lulled into an acceptance of the fallacy of equal opportunity by structuring schools so that on the surface they look like they offer equal academic opportunity. As Mary Metz (1998) points out, middle-class parents recognize that this is a case of "smoke and mirrors"; they carefully choose schools or districts for their children where academic excellence is likely. Low-income families often lack the resources or expertise to make such choices, leaving them to send their children to schools that on the surface offer similar programs but in reality fall short of academic excellence.

Assumption: Success Is a Limited Commodity

As a society, we have assumed that for some people to succeed, others must fail (Spindler and Spindler 1989; McDermott 1997, 1989). American society values individual competition; we strive to be on the top. In the workplace, we compete to advance as individuals even if much of our work is collective. Parents want their children to attend the best schools and to be at the top of the class in these schools. Inherent in this striving is an acceptance of the fact that for one person to "win," many others have to "lose." We assume that students will fail in school, and rather than setting up school so that all students will succeed, we pit students against each other in a competition to be "above average" (Spindler and Spindler 1989; McDermott 1997, 1989).

Individualism and competition are central to who we are as a nation. Rather than build on collective strengths and pull all members of a group up, we hold to old adages such as "pull yourself up by your bootstraps," "one rotten apple spoils the barrel," and "may the best man win." This is not to say that individual pursuit of excellence and all competition is bad; as a nation these assumptions have led to great prosperity for many. However, the basic assumption that education of children is a win/lose proposition is destructive. Failure is institutionalized in our society; it is expected that some will "not make the cut." The devastating consequences of this assumption are that students' future opportunities are severely limited if they fail in school. A more supportive assumption is that all students can be successful and that it is the responsibility of everyone to find ways for all students to succeed.

Assumption: There Are Simple Answers to Complex Problems

How often do we hear opinions and read letters to the editor proposing simple solutions to complex problems? People are very quick to shake their heads and say, "If only they would . . . ." With a little distance from a situation people are able to offer very clear, very easy, and usually very inadequate solutions to problems. Knee-jerk reactions and "new" quick-fix reforms abound on the policymaking level and in the minds of the public. Poorly performing schools and low-achieving students are part of a complex problem that does not have a simple answer (Finnan and Swanson, forthcoming). To turn schools around so that students' learning is accelerated involves a process of culture change, which by its nature requires listening to multiple voices. It also involves engaging in thorough inquiry into the causes of problems and an in-depth examination of potential solutions. This kind of inquiry takes time and focus. It rarely results in one solution; rather, many actions by many people contribute to the ensuing change.

Assumption: Diversity and Unity Are Mutually Exclusive

Diversity is both the strength and the challenge of our society. We are a richer society because of the diverse artistic and intellectual expressions that abound in this country. Our culture has benefited from diverse perspectives on the issues and challenges we face as a nation. However, diversity can be destructive if it splinters any society, community, or organization. Diversity becomes a powerful strength when it is allowed to flourish in pursuit of a shared goal or vision. By seeking unity we do not mean conformity to one way of thinking and doing; rather, we look to developing unity through setting shared goals. Multiple approaches to achieving these goals are encouraged, explored, and implemented. For schools, the shared goal becomes to accelerate the learning of all students; it is accomplished by listening to many voices and incorporating many perspectives in pursuit of the goal.

These societal assumptions exist in all school and classroom cultures, although how they are manifested differs for each school. They remain relatively unchecked in schools like Anna's and Richard's. We cannot create schools that accelerate the learning of all students without addressing how these assumptions influence the values and actions of everyone in the school community. We revisit them in Chapter 8 when we examine the actions individuals must take to make acceleration for all students a reality.

Cultivating Culture Change

The remaining chapters in this book focus on changing school and classroom cultures by changing assumptions, expectations, and behaviors of key individuals in schools. As described above, culture, when thought of as the assumptions, beliefs, values, and expected behaviors of a group of people, is conservative even though cultures continuously change. Changing cultures to accelerate the learning of all students requires purposeful, not reactionary, change. It requires nurturing change from within, not imposing change from outside. To understand purposeful culture change, it is productive to think of the term culture not only as a noun (as described above) but also as a verb, as in to culture or cultivate. Murray Wax introduced this distinction between "a culture" (noun) and "to culture" (verb) to refine the use of the term culture as applied to multiculturalism (Wax 1993).

Scientists, horticulturists, botanists, and medical and agricultural researchers design experiments to culture change in living things. Experiments may take place in petri dishes in a laboratory or on experimental plots in laboratory farms. Wherever the culturing takes place, the outcomes and procedures are clear, the experiments are carefully tended, the environment is controlled, and experiments are replicated to assure research reliability and validity.

What do such experiments have to do with school change? We suggest that schools, classrooms, and individuals that accelerate the learning of all students engage in purposeful change by essentially "cultivating" change toward clear goals. For change to be purposeful and lasting, the outcomes or desired goals of the change are clear and the process used to reach these goals is well defined. Once the change process is underway, it is carefully tended. Widespread support for the change must exist in the school, and resources (both human and material) must be available. Careful tending involves more than providing a rich soil for growth; it involves constant attention to the change effort so that the change goes beyond surface change to deep change in assumptions. Essentially, the change must be watered, fed, and protected from adverse forces in the environment. Change imposed from outside of a school is rarely closely nurtured; isolated training sessions and mandates to change do not provide the needed attention and support.

Unlike laboratory experiments, it is difficult to control change efforts in schools and to replicate change efforts that were successful in other schools. Schools do their best to control their environment by building support in the community for change (Mathews 1996; Schlechty 1997) and aligning their goals with state and local initiatives. However, external factors often complicate change processes. Similarly, successful experiments with school, classroom, or individual change are rarely replicated. Teachers and principals frequently borrow ideas from others, but efforts to transplant successful practices typically fail (Wehlage, Smith, and Lipman 1992; Tyack and Cuban 1995), largely because they do not account for the influence of the existing school or classroom culture and because they are not nurtured and supported. This is analogous to agricultural researchers attempting to replicate an experiment without ensuring that the characteristics of the soil in the two experiments are the same and without ensuring that crops are watered.

Culturing change in schools and classrooms requires a clear understanding of the desired outcomes and careful attention to the change process—essentially the tending and nurturing of the change and a thorough understanding of the context in which the change occurs. The following chapters describe differences between schools and classrooms in which a culture supporting the acceleration of all students has been cultivated and those in which it has not been cultivated. Chapter 6 explains why the school Sara attends is so different from Anna's and Richard's schools. Chapter 7 illustrates that although all three students' classrooms are accelerated, classroom culture isolates Anna's and Richard's classrooms from others in the school, while it is nurturing and supportive in Sara's school.

Note

1. The concept of social and cultural capital derives from the work of Bourdieu and Passeron (1977) and MacLeod (1987). They argue that knowledge–both social and cultural–is a valuable resource, just as economic capital is a resource.

6 Cultivating Acceleration Within School Cultures

Sara attends Westview Elementary School located in a small Midwestern community. For years Westview's student population was stable, mostly children of farm families and the few families who worked at the local button factory. Student achievement levels were about average for the state, and Westview students were generally seen as ready for middle school when they graduated.

Beginning around 1990, Spanish-speaking families began moving into the community to work on farms and in the button factory. Westview's faculty felt unprepared to teach limited-English-speaking students and to blend the Spanish-speaking families into the close, caring community that already existed at Westview. Although some faculty longed for the "good old days" when all children were known in the community and communication was easy, a commitment to teaching all children pervaded the school culture.

The administration and faculty began to research strategies to better work with the new children. Through their research they came upon the Accelerated Schools Project and found its philosophy of holding high expectations for all students and involving all members of the school community in decisions compatible with their school culture. In 1995 they joined the Accelerated Schools Project and have used it as a vehicle to examine their existing school culture and to make changes in the school to support accelerated learning for all students.

Today Westview Elementary is an inviting school. It is clear from a walk through the building and from conversations with faculty, students, and parents that children's learning is valued, that adults are active learners, and that the school supports teachers' efforts to improve what and how children learn and the context in which they learn. For the last three years, student performance on standardized tests has improved, and several Westview teachers have taken l eadership roles in providing professional development to other teachers in the region.

Change is welcome at Westview because they have control over the direction change takes, and they are confident that all proposals for change are well researched through the Accelerated Schools inquiry process.

As described in Chapter 5, efforts to accelerate learning of all students occur within school and classroom cultures.* These cultures are a complex mix of assumptions, beliefs, and actions of key individuals in the schools. Changing school culture involves deep change, not just change at the level of displaying student work or adding processes of site-based management (Elmore, Peterson, and McCarthey 1996). This change has to be nurtured internally; a school community cannot be told to change its school culture. To create a culture that fosters and encourages the acceleration of all students, the basic beliefs and assumptions of all school community members (e.g., teachers, parents, administration, students, staff, and community members) must be examined and potentially changed. These changes occur as individuals reflect on their basic assumptions, as they engage in discussion with each other, and as they take actions to improve learning opportunities of all students. Ultimately all members of the school community assume that it is their responsibility to challenge all students. Once this process has begun, lasting change in the more visible manifestations of culture (e.g., display of student work, classroom schedules, student placement decisions, ceremonies and rituals) change as an expression of the deeper change.

School culture describes both the sameness and uniqueness of each school. When you walk into almost any school you are struck by how familiar it is. There is something about the place that just says "school." The function of the school—to provide a site for teaching and learning—can be felt as soon as you walk through the door. Most schools share a similar design for classrooms and common areas, organize the day in predictable ways, and develop recognizable patterns for relationships among the students and adults.

Despite these similarities, it is also easy to recognize the differences and uniqueness of each school. Even the casual observer will recognize that each school feels, looks, sounds, and smells different from any other school. The culture of a school can change radically when a principal leaves and is replaced by someone with a different philosophy and leadership style. It changes when demographic changes in the community change the student population. It changes when the state or district dictates radically different approaches to teaching.

School culture functions at its most important, deepest level in framing individuals' basic assumptions, even as it shapes everything else in a

---

*Portions of this chapter appear in C. Finnan and H. M. Levin (2000).

school, from what is seen and heard (e.g., the way physical space is used, the use of language in the school, the dress and deportment of the people) to what is valued as "the way we do things" (Evans 1996: 42). As Evans states, the basic assumptions are "fundamental, underlying shared convictions that guide behavior and shape the way group members perceive, think, and feel" (1996: 43). These assumptions are rarely stated explicitly, but they underlie all actions and interactions in a school. For example, individuals in an inner-city school may assume that the students cannot learn challenging material because they live in poverty. Teachers give students a steady diet of uninteresting worksheets and textbooks and proceed to allow students to slide through to the next grade level having mastered neither basic nor higher-order skills. When asked why these students have not learned what they need, these teachers assume no responsibility, passing the blame to the students themselves or to their families.

An important determinant of school culture is the history of the school—both real and perceived. Most schools have a history that molds both the structure and culture of the school (Schlechty 1990). Westview Elementary School's history as a mainstay in a small rural community had to be considered and respected before initiating changes to accommodate new students. The origins of the school, the population it has served, its unique claims and accomplishments all constitute this background. From this history come heroes and villains, ceremonies, rituals, legends, and stories (Deal and Peterson 1998). These are very important links to the community and can give children the feeling that they are attending school in an important place and that by being a part of this school, they too will "make history." Private schools, elite public schools, and special schools such as magnet schools and charter schools proudly display artifacts from their past and cultivate continued involvement in the school of successful alumni (Conway 1995). Schools with strong continuity to the past quickly acculturate new teachers, parents, and children to the culture of the school (unless the student population changes radically).

Alternatively, many inner-city and rural schools find it difficult to shake off the ill effects of their history. Many schools attempting to improve are burdened by conventional wisdom in the community that the school is inadequate, that it is a school for "losers." This historical legacy takes its toll on teachers, parents, and students attempting to improve the learning environment. Efforts to improve these schools are often seen as little more than attempts to look like "real schools" (Metz 1998). It is impossible to understand the culture of a school without examining the past.

Another aspect of school culture's historical dimension relates not to the collective school culture but to the experiences each individual brings to the school, whether as staff, parents, or students. Teachers' expectations of students, of their role in the school, and their comfort with different educational practices derive from their experience as students, as teachers in preparation, and as practicing teachers (O'Laughlin 1990). Parents bring to the school experiences from their past, both when they were students and more recently as parents concerned about their children's learning. Students also bring expectations learned from other school experiences (e.g., preschool or other schools) and from encounters with their peers and older children.

Basic Assumptions Shaping School Culture

A school's culture is a composite of a culture that existed in the past, the cultural assumptions brought to the school by members of the school community, and the cultural forces in the larger community. These cultural forces come together within the context of the school and shape, and are shaped by, the school culture. Westview Elementary School's culture is a composite of past and present influences. It includes memories of what the school was like in the past and assumptions brought to the school by longtime residents of the community, by teachers who commute to the school from other communities, and from parents and other family members of the Spanish-speaking students. It is at the level of assumptions, beliefs, and values that culture has its most profound influence, and it is this level where change must occur in most schools to accelerate the learning of all children. The assumptions, beliefs, and values that shape school cultures can be grouped into five components of school culture. They include the following:

- Assumptions related to expectations for children
- Assumptions held by children about themselves and their future
- Assumptions related to expectations for adults (teachers, principals, and parents)
- Assumptions about educational practices that are considered "acceptable"
- Assumptions about the value of change

This chapter delineates each of these components and describes how assumptions related to each component can discourage or encourage efforts to accelerate learning. As each component is described, a contrast is made between how the assumptions related to a component of school culture function to create an environment that discourages or encourages the acceleration of all students. For most descriptions, we have focused on research on schools serving low-income students. Table 6.1 summarizes assumptions that encourage or discourage acceleration of all students.

TABLE 6.1   Cultural Assumptions: School Level

Discourage Acceleration	*Encourage Acceleration*
Assumptions Adults Hold for Children	
• Some students cannot attempt advanced material because they have not mastered basic skills.	• High academic expectations for all students are shared by community members.
• Low-income students come to school with deficits.	• Build on strengths students bring to school.
• Students lack self-control.	• Students are expected to learn, not be controlled.
Assumptions Students Hold About Themselves and Their Future	
• Students feel disconnected from school and society.	• All students can learn from each other.
• School is important only to meet friends or participate in sports.	• All students can acquire the social and cultural capital needed to succeed in wider society.
• Students feel that no one cares about them.	• Students expect adults to care.
Assumptions Related to Expectations for Adults (teachers, principals, and parents)	
• Only ineffective teachers work in schools serving low-income students.	• Teachers are highly effective in the classroom and in making decisions for all students.
• Administrators' role is to keep order.	• Administrators facilitate a learning community.
• Parents do not provide adequate support for their children.	• Families love their children and will do what they think best for them.
Assumptions About Acceptable Educational Practices	
• Schools are structured to maintain order and provide "appropriate" education to all.	• The school structure gives all students access to challenging learning environments.
• Students and subjects are sorted and separated.	• Teaching results in understanding, not acquisition of facts.
• Teaching is an act of transmission of knowledge from teacher to student.	
Assumptions About the Value of Change	
• Resist all change.	• Change will lead to improved achievement for all students.
• Systematic change is impossible.	• Positive changes are possible when they are supported internally and externally.
• Student achievement would improve if other people changed.	• Personal change is challenging and invigorating.

Assumptions Adults Hold for Children

Adults expect all children to receive an education at school, but do they expect all students to receive equal access to stimulating education? Each school's culture shapes the answer to that question. Adults at Westview expect all students to receive a stimulating education, but this expectation is not the same at Anna's school where only students identified as gifted are expected to be challenged. Adults have a powerful influence on the expectations all school community members have for children. Adults' expectations of children shape the curriculum and instruction offered, the school's organization, and the climate in the halls and the classrooms.

Assumptions That Discourage Acceleration

Some students cannot attempt advanced material because they have not mastered basic skills.   In many schools people share an assumption that some students (primarily white, middle-class students) benefit from engagement with advanced material, ideas, and concepts, whereas others (primarily low-income students, often students of color) must spend time in school mastering basic skills. Chapter 1, in tracing the historical origins of both gifted and talented education and remedial education, illustrates that this sorting of students by perceived ability has been common since the turn of the twentieth century.

In addition, a linear conception of learning (i.e., that basic skills must be mastered before advancing to higher-order skills) has shaped curriculum since the early 1900s. Although there have been dissenters (e.g., W.E.B. DuBois, John Dewey), this belief in a progression from basics to advanced material has prevailed. For an agricultural and industrial economy the assumption seemed to work. The elite were educated for thinking occupations and the poor (especially indigenous minorities and immigrants) were taught basic math and reading and were prepared for vocations (Tyack 1974; Darling-Hammond 1997: 7). This was a convenient belief since the factories of the north and the farms of the south needed a large submissive workforce that could follow orders but would not question the social order.

Although our economy now requires more advanced skills from almost all workers, children are still drilled on basic skills, and many are denied an opportunity to develop more advanced skills. This practice has been prevalent despite research that indicates that low-achieving students benefit from opportunities to work with advanced, higher-order materials (Knapp 1995a; Jennings and Spillane 1996; Newmann 1996).

Low-income students come to school with deficits.   A related assumption that permeates the culture of many schools is that low-income students come to school with deficits that must be remediated. The label "at risk" is applied to almost any student who comes to school with a background different than that enjoyed by a shrinking number of middle-class, white children who come from two-parent/one-income families (Swadener and Lubeck 1995). Too many teachers and administrators assume that all students should enter school with the same type of language, fine motor, and social skill development that most middle-class children possess. These schools are ill prepared to accommodate cultural, language, and social class differences (Ladson-Billings 1994; Darling-Hammond 1997). Rather than accommodate these differences, the students are labeled as "at risk," and many will eventually be further labeled as having a learning disability (Franklin 1994; Spear-Swerling and Sternberg 1996).

This labeling of children results from an underlying assumption that the skills and cultural knowledge low-income and minority students bring to school are not valuable (Swadener and Lubeck 1995; Fine 1995; Arnold 1995; Payne 1998). From the day children are born they are surrounded by a social network of family and community that provides them with a cultural lens through which to see the world. Pierre Bourdieu refers to this knowledge as cultural capital (1986) because it exists as a valuable commodity in a multicultural world. The cultural capital acquired by low-income and minority children is quite different from that acquired by middle-class children. It is the cultural capital of the middle class that is valued in most schools (Mehan, Villanueva, Hubbard, and Lintz 1996; Bourdieu and Passeron 1977); students with different cultural capital find that they have knowledge that is valued in their community but not in school (Payne 1998). That low-income and minority students come to school with strengths is rarely given more than lip service.

Students lack self-control.   Finally, many school cultures perpetuate a belief that low-income children must be carefully controlled and disciplined. They maintain that students lack the self-control needed to be successful and that "if you give them an inch, they will take a mile." In an attempt to appear culturally sensitive, people will justify punitive discipline and a quasi-military emphasis on order by saying that students come from cultures where punishment is not only acceptable but "the only thing they respond to" (Hale 1994).

In case studies of urban high schools, Fine (1991), McQuillan (1998), and McNeil (1986) found that urban, low-income, minority students were silenced in school in an effort to maintain order and discipline. McQuillan and McNeil also found that the quest for control usually led to lowered expectations for students. Rather than threaten the social order by providing students challenging work, teachers assign them work they

know the students can already do so that students will not become disruptive. Administrators condone this practice, discourage teachers from
taking risks, and limit time and opportunities for students to develop a
sense of community because taking risks and creating community threat-
ens the delicate order they find so precious (McQuillan 1998: 66).

Assumptions That Encourage Acceleration

*All school community members share high academic expectations for all stu-
dents.*   A first step to creating a culture that holds high expectations for
all students is to engage all members of the school community in developing a shared vision for the school, one that includes setting high standards for all students (Finnan and Levin 1998). By engaging everyone in
this process (e.g., parents, community members, students, teachers, staff,
building and district administration, higher education representatives,
politicians), school community members begin to make their assumptions public and openly discuss what they value and assume about student learning. Those who might not truly believe that all students can
learn through challenging, engaging curriculum and instruction have
these assumptions questioned by their colleagues and by the success of
other schools that have adopted a similar philosophy. As the school community embraces the vision, it becomes a living part of the school, not
just a page in an accreditation report. Discussion and dialogue are key to
this process.

In addition, school cultures that support acceleration expect that all
students will be successful with materials that demand higher-order
thinking, are rich in language, and have relevance beyond school (Newmann 1996). These schools provide challenging curriculum to all students, support teachers' efforts to teach for meaning, and provide organizational support and adequate resources (Knapp, Shields, and Padilla
1995). It is easy to *ask* members of a school community to expect that all
students can learn through challenging, relevant curriculum and to *expect* teachers to teach for understanding. However, it is difficult to accomplish this without adequate resources for materials, professional
development, and flexible use of time and resources (Darling-Hammond 1997).

Build on the strengths students bring to school.   Rather than dwelling on
what students do not bring to school (e.g., an extensive vocabulary in
Standard English, well-developed fine motor skills, pre-reading skills),
schools that accelerate the learning of students identify strengths in all of
the students and build on these strengths to develop the skills required
for successful engagement in school (Hopfenberg et al. 1993). From elementary schools to high schools, teachers, administrators, and staff mem-

bers build activities and programs around the developmental level of the students (Comer 1988). Early childhood teachers build on young children's natural energy, imagination, inquisitiveness, and playfulness (Piaget 1970; Darling-Hammond 1997). Middle and high school teachers build on students' growing social awareness, energy, need of affiliation and autonomy, and peer orientation (Carnegie Council on Adolescent Development 1989; Phelan, Davidson, and Yu 1998). Effective middle and high schools build on the social and cultural capital the students have acquired, and they provide access to the social and cultural capital needed for skilled jobs and higher education (Mehan, Villanueva, Hubbard, and Lintz 1996).

Schools that accelerate learning also view diversity as a strength. Rather than limiting their focus to a narrow set of skills, these schools recognize the complex mix of intelligence students bring to the educational experience (Gardner 1983; Sternberg 1986; Darling-Hammond 1997). In addition to recognizing the importance of individual diversity, schools that accelerate learning celebrate the diversity of thinking brought about by the interaction of people from different cultures, social classes, and geographic areas. This emphasis on cultural diversity is not only important to make members of minority groups feel valued, it also encourages the valuing of multiple perspectives (Darling-Hammond 1997; Banks 1998) and of culture as a nurturing process, not a division between people (Wax 1993).

Students are expected to learn, not to be controlled. Visitors to schools in which students are involved in an active, engaging learning environment often comment on the hum of activity, the enthusiasm students exhibit for their work, the lack of any visible discipline rules, and the happy demeanor of the students (Finnan and Swanson, forthcoming). This kind of school environment exists not because students' behavior is tightly controlled but because students feel a sense of control over what and how they learn. They do not need to engage in a battle with the teacher or the administration over who controls the school. Everyone in the school knows students are at school to learn and that they are responsible for their own learning and for maintaining a climate in the school in which all students can learn (Wasley, Hampel, and Clark 1997).

In addition to providing students an engaging learning environment, adult members of the school community make it clear to students that they care about them as individuals (Noddings 1984; Phelan, Davidson, and Cao 1992; Phelan, Davidson, and Yu 1998). In addition, they demonstrate to students that they understand and appreciate their culture (Solomon 1992; Ladson-Billings 1994). Racial and ethnic minority students are less apt to resist learning if they feel that teachers and administrators understand their culture and are not afraid of their community

(Foster 1974; Solomon 1992; Ladson-Billings 1994). These students attend schools that have close connections with the community and create an "extended family" for students so that the high expectations held by the school are supported by the rest of the community.

Assumptions Students Hold About Themselves and Their Future

Students actively participate in shaping school culture, both individually and collectively. As individuals, students may want to succeed in school, but as members of a peer group, they may accept, even applaud, failure. As a culture that encourages and rewards individualism and individual accomplishment, most Americans ignore the fact that people act in terms of the meaning that is made through social interaction (McQuillan 1998: 85).

Assumptions That Discourage Acceleration

Students feel disconnected from school and society.   Many low-income and minority students determine that they do not fit into either the school environment or mainstream society. Students who find themselves in remedial tracks or low-ability groups and students who attend schools that fail to educate large numbers of students feel that they are not really a part of the school and are unlikely to be accepted within the economic mainstream. Students in low tracks are often restricted from participating in extracurricular activities (McQuillan 1998), and they form a sense of community with other students who are not destined to do well in school. Rather than behave as the rugged individualists that we idolize in the United States and pull themselves up by their bootstraps, most of the students choose to participate as minimally as possible in this system they believe will not help or work for them.

Through tracking, low-achieving students are isolated from the influence of higher-achieving students. Those who make obvious their disengagement from school cut themselves off from adults who might help them meet higher academic goals (Mehan, Villanueva, Hubbard, and Lintz 1996; McQuillan 1998). Overtly resistant students attempt to exert power over the system by sending the message, "You may not want us, but we don't want you either" (Solomon 1992; Ogbu 1987; Ogbu and Simons 1998). By actively resisting the rules and beliefs of the system, these students disrupt the order that is so important to most teachers and administrators.

School is important only to meet friends or participate in sports.   For many students, school is a social institution, not an academic one. Ted Sizer bluntly states, "School's residual attraction for many kids is simple; it is where their friends are" (1992b: 126). In many schools, students find the curriculum dull and meaningless, the adults indifferent or remote, the structure oppressive, and the assignments meaningless. The only engaging aspect of school involves the social interactions students create. Social interaction often leads to disengagement from academic pursuits and creation of subcultures that mock academic achievement and further alienate low-achieving students from adults and higher-achieving peers (Solomon 1992; Sizer 1992b; Lee 1994; McQuillan 1998). Students, especially in middle and high school, usually form tight friendship circles that are not highly porous (Varenne 1982; Phelan, Davidson, and Cao 1992; Lee 1994, 1996). These groups are usually very homogeneous; students of the same racial and ethnic groups stay together; students of similar academic ability stay together. This social grouping further limits access to alternative views on academic achievement for low-achieving students.

In addition to being a social institution, many students find athletics to be the only source of positive engagement in school. Poor academic performance and overt resistance to the academic courses by athletes is often tolerated because of their importance on the playing fields (Solomon 1992). Given the limited likelihood of anyone making a career in athletics, this is a poor choice. The 1994 documentary *Hoop Dreams* (James 1994) vividly illustrates the fragile hope athletics gives to low-income minority students. It follows the daily life of two inner-city high school students who hope that basketball will be their route out of poverty. Neither boy made it close to a professional basketball career. Both suffered from inattention to their academic work, but they did use basketball to leave the inner city. The film leaves the viewer asking, if even a fraction of the time spent on the basketball court was applied to academics, would these boys, like many other athletes, have benefited?

Students feel that no one cares about them. Many students believe that no one in their school cares about them, and many of them assume the lack of caring is because they are not good enough or smart enough. Caring adults are prime motivators for many students to take learning in school seriously (Darling-Hammond 1997: 173). Both high- and low-achieving students desire caring relationships with teachers, but these students define "caring" differently (Phelan, Davidson, and Cao 1992: 698). Whereas high-achieving students describe teachers as caring when they provide assistance in academic matters (e.g., suggestions to improve a paper, help solving difficult math problems), low-achieving students express a desire for direct, person-to-person interaction with teachers (e.g., engagement in conversations, expressions of interest in family and friends).

Although most teachers choose a teaching career because they care about students, many students find teachers uncaring. Unfortunately, the press of too many students, too little time, too little support, added to the numbing effect of losing students to apathy, cynicism, and to other negative influences takes its toll on even the most compassionate teachers. Schools, especially middle and high schools, are not structured to encourage the development of close, caring relationships between adults and students. Most urban high school teachers see between 120 and 150 students a day (McQuillan 1998: 192), and teachers feel lucky to even know the names of all of their students. They are more apt to develop a relationship with a class than with individual students, contributing to students' beliefs that they do not matter as individuals. Just as children are quick to assume that they are at fault when their parents divorce, students assume that teachers do not want to know them because they are not good enough or smart enough for teachers to take time with them.

Assumptions That Encourage Acceleration

All students can learn from each other.   For all students to hold high expectations for themselves and others, they must all be given equal access to challenging learning environments. This involves eliminating tracking and making ability grouping more fluid while supporting teachers and students as they better understand the strengths of all students.

Students are also more likely to develop high expectations for themselves and others when schools provide avenues to break down the social barriers between students. Phelan, Davidson, and Yu (1998) and Wasley, Hampel, and Clark (1997) present case studies of adolescents that illustrate how barriers develop between students that are related to cultural, linguistic, and class differences; these barriers are exacerbated by the structure of schools. Schools that accelerate the learning of all students provide avenues for students to interact with a diverse set of peers in ways that promote a positive exchange of beliefs and opinions. As Stanton-Salazar writes, "For minority children and youth, the ability to cross borders, overcome barriers, and resist the violent effects of exclusionary forces has much to do with developing resiliency through *supportive ties with protective agents within the home and community* (1997: 26, italics added). In these schools, teachers and administrators become protective agents, and the considerable energy that is spent crossing and maintaining borders is channeled toward understanding and building on strengths of diversity.

All students can acquire the social and cultural capital needed to succeed in the wider society.   Many students not only need access to challenging academic content but also to the cultural and social capital they will need to make use of what they have learned. Recognizing that some students need help translating the academic content knowledge into productive work or further study, some high schools augment college preparatory courses with special supports so that students will have the social and cultural capital needed to make best use of this opportunity. The AVID (Advancement Via Individual Determination) program works with high schools to provide such support. Schools participating in AVID make college preparatory courses available to students who demonstrate potential to succeed even though by traditional measures they would not be eligible for the college preparatory track. In addition to enrolling in college preparatory courses, students enroll in an AVID class that teaches them study skills, skills for entry to college, and conflict resolution strategies (Mehan, Villanueva, Hubbard, and Lintz 1996: 84–88). The AVID program also provides a network of resources (social capital), such as tutors from local colleges, visits from college recruiters, and interaction with former AVID students who are currently enrolled in college. With access to both cultural and social capital, student acceptance rates at colleges have been high, and students are completing college (Mehan, Villanueva, Hubbard, and Lintz 1996). Programs such as the AVID program diminish the sense of dislocation experienced by many minority students who attempt to cross cultural and class borders (Stanton-Salazar 1997).

Students expect adults to care. Possibly the most important way that school culture helps students develop high expectations for themselves is by structuring the school to show students that adults care. In these schools, caring is not coddling; it is caring enough to hold all students to high standards (Noblit 1993; Wasley, Hampel, and Clark 1997). In these schools, students are given a voice (Fine 1991; Mahiri 1998) and are treated as subjects (i.e., people who act) rather than objects (i.e., people who are acted upon) (Freire 1970, in Mahiri 1998). Students develop high expectations for themselves by having teachers who care enough to challenge them to work for the intrinsic reward of learning rather than rewarding work that the students know is mediocre (Kohn 1993).

Schools that accelerate learning develop structures that encourage the development of caring relationships among students and between students and teachers. Teams, tutorials, and "family" groupings all provide opportunities for people to know each other as individuals rather than as faces in a crowd (Carnegie Council on Adolescent Development 1989; Sizer 1992b; Wasley, Hampel, and Clark 1997). These efforts have the effect of reducing the size of otherwise large and impersonal schools (Sizer 1992b; Lee, Smith, and Croninger 1995), thus allowing students to have an identity, to be known by everyone. When adults in small schools hold high expectations for students, students cannot escape these expectations.

Assumptions Related to Expectations for Adults (Teachers, Principals, and Parents)

Adults play an important role in shaping a school's culture, and the school culture shapes the expectations held for adults. Students are direct beneficiaries when their teachers, administrators, staff members, and parents are held to high standards and are seen as positive influences in their lives. Many adults are connected with schools, but the most important adults for this discussion are teachers, principals, and parents.

Assumptions That Discourage Acceleration

Only ineffective teachers work in schools serving low-income students.   What is the image of the average teacher working in a school serving primarily low-income or minority students? Unfortunately, most people do not think of the best and the brightest. Descriptions such as "burned out," "uninspiring," "unmotivated," and "ill-prepared" come to mind. Teacher expertise and experience have been found to be the most important determinants of student achievement (Ferguson 1991, in Darling-Hammond 1997). Therefore, if student achievement is low, it is assumed that their teachers are inferior to teachers of high-achieving students.

Excellent teachers can be found in nearly all schools serving low-income and minority students, but these teachers work side by side with mediocre to poor teachers. The school culture in many of these schools assumes that mediocrity is the norm, and it helps provide a rationale for low achievement of students and poor performance by teachers. The collective culture works to maintain pride in teachers, assuring them that if it were not for "these kids," we would be effective teachers (Metz 1989).

State and district policies and procedures do little to encourage excellent teachers to teach in schools in which they are most needed. Efforts to control educational practices from the state or district level (e.g., accountability, mandated reform, centralized curriculum) often alienate teachers, especially in schools where teachers feel helpless to meet the mandates because of chronic low student achievement and highly politicized environments (Cedoline 1982, in LeCompte and Dworkin 1991: 99). In addition, schools are employing increasingly large numbers of teachers who are ill prepared to teach (National Commission on Teaching and America's Future 1996). Since the 1980s there have been few incentives to recruit teachers, so many states and districts hire uncertified teachers through "temporary" or "emergency" designations (Darling-Hammond

1997). Schools also find it difficult to find teachers qualified to teach certain content, especially math and science, and many teachers have limited understanding of child development and how to teach children with special needs. These conditions are worse in urban and rural schools because of poor working conditions and lower pay (National Commission on Teaching and America's Future 1996).

What are the expectations of teachers who work in many of our schools serving low-income, minority students? Unfortunately, teachers are often expected to do little more than fill time, keep order, drill students on skills that will be tested on standardized tests, and not "rock the boat" (McQuillan 1998). In too many schools, teachers are not expected to take responsibility, be lifelong learners, or reach out to their students. As William Ayers writes, "The structure of schooling combines with a defeatist and cynical school culture to render teachers silent, passive, and powerless" (1992: 15). Teacher burnout is more prevalent in schools serving low-income and minority students because many of these schools have cultures that exacerbate the stress, sense of inefficacy, and normlessness that can be a part of working in schools (LeCompte and Dworkin 1991). In an effort to be considered "real" schools, teachers, especially at the high school level, engage in what they know is a charade. They offer courses with the same titles as those offered in more affluent schools, but the material covered in the courses is not nearly as challenging (Metz 1998).

The expectations for students held by adults and students also rub off on teachers. As Metz reports from a study of three magnet middle schools, the characteristics of students are often transferred to their teachers. She writes, "Always unspoken was the assumption that if some teachers were 'gifted and talented' by association with their students, others were 'inner city teachers' by association with theirs" (1989: 215). This association, coupled with low pay and often poor working conditions, works against even the most dedicated teachers. As LeCompte and Dworkin state in their book *Giving Up on School: Student Dropouts and Teacher Burnouts*, "these phenomena [dropping out and burning out] are generated by identical socio-cultural and structural forces. Factors that lead teachers to quit teaching also cause students to drop out of school" (1991: 2). They find that alienation triggers both dropping out and burning out.

Administrators' role is to keep order. If expectations for teachers are to maintain order, fill time, and prepare students to perform adequately on standardized tests, what are the expectations for principals and other building-level administrators? It is no surprise that the creation of an environment that fosters student learning is not high on the list. Many principals behave as compliance officers, enforcing mandates and policies from outside of the school (Christensen 1996) and as managers, not leaders (Evans 1996). Principals are also expected to serve as policemen, ensuring a quiet, orderly, and highly disciplined school (McQuillan 1998; Fine 1991). McQuillan (1998) provides a vivid description of the orientation of many principals:

> If one never knew that Russell High was a school and you happened into the building you might think the school's administrators were actually a squad of police detectives. Wearing coats and ties, they walked the school's corridors, stopping students to question them, usually asking for passes. During lunch, one principal worked the lunchroom, another patrolled school grounds, the third remained in the main office. So they could communicate instantly with one another, they all carried walkie-talkies. . . . In brief, controlling students and keeping the building orderly were high priorities for Russell's administrators. (p. 62)

The traditional principalship is a product of a bureaucratic hierarchy that leaves principals in the role of middle manager. Most principals are expected to carry out decisions made at the state and local level and to make all other school-level decisions (Murphy and Hallinger 1992; Christensen 1996). They are not expected to facilitate collaborative decisionmaking among their staff and parents, and few are expected to have expertise in curricular and instructional areas. With pressure from the state or district to respond to disparate directives (e.g., accountability, increased student achievement, safe schools, better transition to the workplace, drug-free schools, etc.), principals often grab a potpourri of curricular, instructional, and student behavior reforms and inform their faculty that they need to implement the reforms. Often just as initiatives are beginning to take hold, a new set of initiatives is proposed from on high and the principal responds.

In many schools, principals make little effort to engage the entire faculty in making decisions. Many principals are not trained to facilitate shared decisionmaking, and they have little confidence in their teachers' ability to work collaboratively and plan effectively (often because the teachers also lack training in effective collaborative planning) (Christensen 1996). Principals often inform teachers of decisions made in private (or with a small cadre of loyal supporters) and are surprised at how powerless they feel when the teachers' implementation of the plan is not as they expected (Evans 1996: 150).

Parents do not provide adequate support for their children.   If expectations for teachers and administrators are low in many schools, it is no surprise that they are especially low for parents. Generations of parents have been blamed for the poor school performance of their children. Labels have changed, but "culturally deprived," "disadvantaged," and "at risk" imply that students' homes are lacking because their families, mothers in particular (Lubeck 1995), do not provide the skills needed to do well in school (Moles 1993; Chavkin 1993; Swadener and Lubeck 1995).

Low student achievement is linked to poverty, single parenting, culture, and parental employment. In a survey conducted by Lubeck and Garrett, school superintendents and principals summarized their perceptions of the causes of poor student performance:

> We have large numbers of children who come from homes with no emphasis on education. . . . Large numbers of youngsters come into school with absolutely no background, either academic or social. . . . Many of our five-year-olds come to kindergarten with minimal experiences and marginal skills, partially due to poor parenting skills. Many parents are "drop-outs" and lack the know-how and ability to provide quality preschool experiences for their children. . . . Many of our homes do not offer children the support needed to develop emotionally, socially, and academically. (Lubeck and Garrett 1990: 336–337, in Lubeck 1995: 55)

This focus on student weaknesses precludes understanding the strengths of their families and their cultures (Billingsley 1968; Cook and Fine 1995; Arnold 1995) and places the blame for the ill effects of poverty and inequity on the victims (Fine 1995; Levin 1986). Families living in poverty bring to school a relationship to many aspects of life (i.e., material possessions, social interactions, time orientation, and language) that differs from that held by middle-class families (Payne 1998).

A lack of parent involvement in their children's school is a common lament of teachers and principals. This concern is supported by research linking student achievement with parent involvement (Henderson 1987; Dornbusch and Ritter 1988). Henderson found that gains are especially significant when minority and low-income students' parents are involved in their schooling (1987). Teachers and principals in many schools grudgingly accept low levels of parental involvement because they understand that work schedules, transportation, limited educational level, limited English ability, and an aversion to schools prevent many parents from being involved at the school. They rarely examine their definition of parent involvement to consider if a different definition consistent with the culture and lifestyle of low-income minority parents might bring more involvement.

Assumptions That Encourage Acceleration

Teachers are highly effective in the classroom and in making decisions for all students. The portrait painted of teachers in schools that discourage acceleration is rather bleak. Fortunately, this is not the situation in all schools.

In schools that accelerate learning everyone makes their high expectations for teachers clear during the hiring process, and the school provides a structure and environment that encourages strong teachers to remain at the school and to continue to grow as professionals (Darling-Hammond 1997; Finnan and Swanson, forthcoming). Mediocrity is not acceptable. These schools use their resources to hire the best teachers possible and to structure the school to encourage innovative teaching (e.g., reducing class size, teaming, providing mentor teachers, creating alternate scheduling and student grouping arrangements, etc.) (Darling-Hammond 1997). In other words, teacher excellence is expected and supported in the school culture.

In schools that accelerate learning everyone expects all teachers to make decisions that influence every child in the school and to take responsibility for these decisions. These schools generally have a governance structure in place that involves all teachers in making decisions affecting all students. School reform models such as the Accelerated Schools Project (Hopfenberg et al. 1993; Finnan, St. John, McCarthy, and Slovacek 1996) and the Coalition of Essential Schools (Sizer 1992b) stress the importance of involving all teachers (as well as family, community, students, and other school staff members) in making decisions. Teachers find that this level of involvement in decisionmaking is time consuming, but it builds a sense of collegiality, cohesiveness, and professionalism that is missing in many other schools (Finnan and Swanson, forthcoming).

Teachers in schools that accelerate learning remain active, lifelong learners. Through engagement in inquiry, reflection, and research, teachers are able to influence curriculum and act as professionals in determining what is best for their students (Calhoun 1994; St. John, Meza, Allen-Haynes, and Davidson 1996). The enthusiasm teachers exhibit for their learning rubs off on their students, and students understand that learning continues throughout life.

Possibly the most important assumption held for teachers is that they are expected to care for students. As described above, students are more apt to have high expectations for themselves when they are taught in a caring environment. The expectations for teachers in such schools are not only to care for students but to care enough to expect high achievement from all of them (Noblit 1993; Ladson-Billings 1994). Tracy Kidder (1989) summarizes the expectation that keeps excellent teachers in the profession:

> Teachers usually have no way of knowing that they have made a difference in a child's life, even when they have made a dramatic one. But for children who are used to thinking of themselves as stupid or not worth talking to or deserving rape and beatings, a good teacher can provide an astonishing revelation. A good teacher can give a child at least a chance to feel *"She* thinks I'm worth something, maybe I am." Good teachers put snags in the river of children passing by, and over the years, they redirect hundreds of lives. (pp. 312–313)

Administrators facilitate a learning community.   High expectations for administrators no longer equate to maintaining a quiet, efficient school but to cultivating a school culture of high expectations for all. Recent research is clear that school administrators play an important role in shaping school cultures (Evans 1996; Deal and Peterson 1998; Peterson and Deal 1998) and that such cultures call upon different characteristics than traditional managerial administrators (Christensen 1996; Mims 1996; Evans 1996). The top-down managerial model of the past is clearly not effective in schools committed to holding all members of the school community to high standards and to involving everyone in decisionmaking (Christensen 1996; Evans 1996). Evans states that "authentic leaders build their practice outward from their core commitments rather than inward from a management text" (1996: 193). They have both integrity and savvy, using their personal integrity to engage in practical problem solving.

Deal and Peterson (1998) suggest several actions principals can take to shape successful school culture. One includes understanding the school, both past and present. To understand the school, they suggest that the principal become both a historian to understand the important rituals, stories, heroes, and villains of the past and an anthropologist to understand the beliefs, values, and assumptions of the present. They also suggest making everyone in the school a leader, which involves recognizing a wide range of leadership roles, some of which are visible while others are symbolic.

Families love their children and will do what they think is best for them. Schools that accelerate learning are open and accepting of all family members. Members of the school community understand the hardships many families endure due to poverty and inequity, but they do not assume that poverty and hardship create dysfunctionality (Payne 1998). As the chapters in Swadener and Lubeck's *Children and Families "At Promise"* (1995) describe, the assumption that poverty, single parenting, maternal employment, and minority status automatically lead to failure blames the victim and potentially harms more than it helps. Schools that treat poor, minority families as "at promise" build on an assumption that the family members love their children and want the best for them. Cultural differences, fear of letting children go, and suspicion of the white middle class often lead to adversarial relationships (Cook and Fine 1995). These relationships can be turned around through better understanding of the communities in which families live and of the cultures families bring to the school and through demonstration of true caring for all children (Ladson-Billings 1994).

Schools that accelerate the learning of all students include students and family members in determining what "family involvement" entails. As parents, teachers, and students work together to develop an understanding of how, when, and where families are best involved in their children's schooling, the circle of blame for poor achievement can be broken. This understanding of involvement includes knowing that in some cultures it is disrespectful for parents to "challenge the authority" of the teacher (Yao 1993). In addition, in some communities parents do not attend evening meetings because they fear for their own or their children's safety if they leave home (Cook and Fine 1995). In other situations, language differences, lack of formal education, and lack of comfort in schools must be overcome (Moles 1993). Schools that accelerate learning find ways for family members to be involved in their children's learning that are within the limits of their available time and resources and that build on family members' strengths.

Assumptions About Educational Practices That Are Considered "Acceptable"

Although the bulk of all teaching occurs in individual classrooms, the school culture shapes the assumptions held by teachers, parents, administrators, and students about what is acceptable classroom practice. The school structure, both in terms of how time is used and how classrooms and grade levels are grouped and organized, directly influences each child's educational experience. The school culture also indirectly influences what teachers do in their classrooms. Chapter 7 discusses in depth the characteristics of classroom culture that make each classroom unique. Despite considerable differences between classrooms, the school culture determines if classrooms fit into a unified whole or if they stand alone as isolated islands. In all schools a few teachers do not share the basic assumptions about the educational practices that are considered acceptable, but the majority do, and they find comfort and support in the school culture for their beliefs.

Assumptions That Discourage Acceleration

Schools are structured to maintain order and provide "appropriate" education to all.   Many schools are structured to provide little more than minimal learning to large numbers of students, reserving more stimulating learning environments for those students identified as gifted and talented. By sorting, labeling, and grouping students, the school is structured to provide a wide variety of educational experiences, from very stimulating (reserved for those identified as gifted and talented) to uninspired repetition of basic skills (reserved for those identified as slow learners) (Tomlinson 1996).

Often those students who are sorted into the lower-track courses continue to fail. Their failures are rarely attributed to the educational practices used to teach them but to their lack of ability. With the "medicalization" of low achievement (Franklin 1994), most low-achieving students are eventually tested for learning disabilities. Those who are found to possess these disabilities carry the label of reading or learning disabled through their school career (Spear-Swerling and Sternberg 1996). Students benefit from special education placements when the placements help overcome their disability. However, researchers have found that special education teachers hold much lower expectations for students' growth in reading than do remedial reading teachers (Allington and Li 1990; McGill-Franzen and James 1990; McGill-Franzen 1994, in Spear-Swerling and Sternberg 1996: 11). Because of low expectations, students often develop "learned helplessness" because they lower their expectations for themselves (Diener and Dweck 1978; Wong 1991, in Spear-Swerling and Sternberg 1996: 10).

This practice of sorting students by ability not only denies many students an opportunity to learn in a stimulating environment but also sorts students by race, ethnicity, and social class. In many schools, sorting students effectively segregates students within a school. Wheelock uses data from the National Educational Longitudinal Survey of 1988 (NELS 1988) to show that "African-American, Latino, Native American, and low-income eighth graders are twice as likely as white or upper-income eighth graders to be in remedial math courses" (1992: 9).

The structure of the school day also influences educational practices. In many schools, especially middle and high schools, the bell determines instructional practices. Students see five to ten teachers in set blocks of approximately forty minutes. Within this time period there is little opportunity to engage in extended dialogue or deep exploration of subjects (Sizer 1992a; McQuillan 1998). Teachers are concerned about "coverage," and students become increasingly passive. Students move through a sea of divergent topics and teaching styles and find that their only anchor is a locker located in a hallway teeming with other students (Darling-Hammond 1997). Knapp, Shields, and Padilla found that "teaching for meaning" was least likely to happen in elementary schools with a great deal of student movement throughout the day and in districts that emphasized the learning of discrete skills (1995: 164).

State and district policies that shape the size of schools and classes have a direct influence on educational practices. Driven more by budgetary concerns than by research on effective practice, districts create large schools, processing as many as 3,000 students a day. In these schools, teachers see as many as 150 students a day and feel fortunate to at least know the names of all of their students (Darling-Hammond 1997). We have already discussed the effect of large schools on students' expectations for themselves, but large schools and classes also lead to educational practices that are unlikely to stimulate students. It is difficult for teachers to engage large numbers of students in discussion, inquiry, and exploration and for these teachers to work as members of teams with other teachers to plan for meaningful instruction.

Top-down governance and autocratic decisionmaking influence what is considered acceptable educational practice. In many schools, decisions about curriculum and instruction are made at the district or state level. Principals are expected to oversee implementation of these decisions (Knapp 1997). Teachers have little say in what they teach, relying on the closed door to exert their influence over curriculum and instruction. Students and parents have even less influence.

Students and subjects are sorted and separated.   Most educators assume that learning is an orderly progression of acquisition of skills and facts, from basic to more advanced (Knapp 1995a; Darling-Hammond 1997). When the basics do not come easily to children, they are separated from others to work on these basic skills. This sorting, or ability grouping, usually places students in permanent tracks with students of similar ability. Anna's and Richard's schools are examples of this practice. Anna is among a small number of students who, because they mastered basic skills easily, have the opportunity to develop more advanced skills. Prior to enrollment in the "accelerated fifth" class, Richard, like other students in the lower-ability groups, received a heavy dose of instruction that many feel is appropriate:

> [Children] need more control and structuring from their teachers: more active instruction and feedback, more redundancy, and smaller steps with higher success rates. This will mean more review, drill and practice, and thus more lower-level questions. Across the school year, it will mean exposure to less material, but with emphasis on mastery of the material that is taught and on moving students through the curriculum as briskly as they are able to progress. (Brophy and Good 1986: 365, in Knapp, Shields, and Turnbull 1995: 183)

Students lose interest in school when they are separated into classes that emphasize basic skills. This is especially damaging to students as they mature. Lounsbury and Clark note that an emphasis on rote memorization of basic skills is especially deadening in middle schools, since by the eighth grade most students can consider alternative solutions to problems and imagine consequences of a variety of actions. They can make plans and think ahead, and they understand multiple perspectives and consider different points of view (Lounsbury and Clark 1990, in Wheelock 1992: 11).

In addition to focusing on the acquisition of basic skills, subjects are typically taught in isolation from each other. Even in elementary schools where students remain with the same teacher all day, there are rarely connections drawn between what is learned in each subject area. Thematic units and efforts to integrate the curriculum are often discouraged because this form of teaching is seen as less effective in preparing students for standardized tests. Middle and high school teachers rarely attempt to integrate curriculum. Studies of high schools typically describe a student's day as a patchwork of unrelated classes. Students move from topic to topic, teaching style to teaching style; they are expected to make the connections and find relevance in what is being taught (Sizer 1992a; Phelan, Davidson, and Cao 1992; McQuillan 1998).

Teaching is an act of transmission of knowledge from teacher to student. In schools that discourage acceleration the administration rewards transmission teaching and maintenance of order. Transmission teaching involves a teacher in front of the room transmitting information to a group of students. The students are in various states of attention, or lack of attention. Some listen attentively; some are clearly in another world, while others are actively engaged in other activities (e.g., completing homework for another class, writing notes, talking to friends). Teachers are often aware that this mode of teaching does not reach all students, but everyone in their school expects them to engage in this kind of teaching, and few teachers resist for the following reasons:

> Transmission teaching is much simpler. Teachers can "get through" texts and workbooks. Classroom routines are straightforward; controls are easier to enforce. There is a sense of certainty and accomplishment when a lecture has been given, a list of facts covered, or a chapter finished, even if the result is little learning for students. When a teacher has transmitted information, it is easy to say "I taught that"–even when students have not learned it. Active learning situations infuse more uncertainty into the teaching process. (Darling-Hammond 1997: 13)

The pattern of providing whole group, direct instruction followed by individual seatwork consisting of worksheets and review of textbook chapters has a long history and a loyal following in the United States. In some cases, when lectures are stimulating and seatwork is well planned and challenging, this form of instruction is powerful (Hirsch 1996), but most often students find it dull, irrelevant, and repetitious. Students are unable to become engaged in the material and ideas because their role in the learning is passive. They are unable to build on their natural inclination toward group or collaborative learning (a skill found to be in demand in industry) (Secretary's Commission on Achieving Necessary Skills 1991; Darling-Hammond 1997).

When it is assumed that the teacher is solely responsible for the transmission of knowledge, classroom management emphasizes maintenance of quiet and order, often to the point of creating an oppressive environment (McCollum 1995). In these classes, little joy in learning is evident, and the balance between teacher talk and student talk largely favors the teacher (McCollum 1995). To retain the attention of twenty to thirty students, teachers often find themselves devoting a great deal of time to quelling disruptive behavior and to bringing students who have "lost focus" back to the topic.

Assumptions That Encourage Acceleration

The school structure gives all students access to challenging learning environments. In schools that accelerate learning, students are placed in classes according to what they can contribute to the class, not because of a label that has been applied to them. As Wheelock writes, "students are sorted by collective strength not by weakness" (1992: 16). Heterogeneous grouping and detracking is not merely a mechanical task of randomly assigning students to classes. In schools that accelerate learning, administration and teachers are careful to group students for "productive diversity" and to provide teachers and students the support they need to make heterogeneous grouping successful. All teachers in these schools are provided the professional development, assistance from resource or mentor teachers, peer support teams, or other interventions needed to reach all students.

Large schools determined to accelerate the learning of students often create smaller units within the school. In this way teachers can work productively with each other, and students develop a sense of community with each other and with their teachers. Structures of this kind can be found in schools associated with the Coalition of Essential Schools (Sizer 1992a), the AVID program (Mehan, Villanueva, Hubbard, and Lintz 1996), and in Philadelphia as part of the Philadelphia Schools Collaborative (Fine 1994). Efforts to reduce the size of the units, provide common curriculum for all students, and build close working relations among faculty reflect the extensive literature on the positive effect of small schools. In particular, student achievement (especially for low-income and minority students) improves when students learn in smaller, more intimate environments (see Lee, Bryk, and Smith 1993 for a review of the literature).

The kind of educational strategies that accelerate learning require flexibility in the use of time and resources (Newmann et al. 1996; Knapp, Shields, and Padilla 1995; Sizer 1992b). Students and teachers need time to engage in inquiry, discussion, and reflection. Rigid forty-minute blocks are not amenable to fostering deep, sustained thought and discussion. Schools that accelerate learning have developed structures that allow this flexibility. Darling-Hammond and colleagues, in a study of resource allocation, found that the most productive schools follow three organizational principles: elimination of the division between planners and doers; organization of teams of staff (including classroom teachers, specialists, special education teachers, teaching assistants) who are responsible for a group of students; and development of a calendar allowing students and teachers to spend more time in fewer classes each day (Darling-Hammond 1997: 179–180).

Teaching results in understanding, not in skills acquisition. Since these beliefs are primarily manifested in the classroom, these issues will be discussed in more depth in Chapter 7. However, school-level assumptions shape what happens in classrooms. Everyone in most schools that accelerate learning share a "culture of inquiry" encouraging all school community members to engage in ongoing research or inquiry into improving student learning. Collective inquiry is a key feature of school reform projects such as the Accelerated Schools Project (Hopfenberg et al. 1993; Finnan, St. John, McCarthy, and Slovacek 1996), the Coalition of Essential Schools (Sizer 1992b), and the School Development Project (Comer 1988). In the Accelerated Schools Project, school community members form cadres (small working groups) designed to conduct inquiry into problems in student achievement. Through cadre work, teachers become familiar with researching the cause of problems and the most effective solutions rather than jumping at convenient solutions. As teachers become more familiar with the process, they often adapt it for use in their classrooms. As inquiry takes hold, these schools truly become "communities of inquiry" (St. John, Meza, Allen-Haynes, and Davidson 1996).

Without a governance structure and decisionmaking process such as this in place, it is difficult for people to make the deep changes in conceptualizing the teaching and learning process required to accelerate the learning of all students (Elmore, Peterson, and McCarthey 1996). As Darling-Hammond writes, "complementary goals and supports must be present throughout the entire school environment—and, ideally, understood and supported in the home—if the habit of understanding is to be developed across domains and disciplines. Lone ranger teaching cannot enable students to become competent thinkers and decision makers as well as constructive human beings" (1997: 107). Knapp, Shields, and Padilla reach the same conclusion in their study of teaching for meaning in high-poverty classrooms. They conclude that collegial, supportive staffs encourage teaching for meaning by providing advice, consultation, materials, trouble-shooting, and curriculum direction to each other (1995: 166).

Darling-Hammond (1997) delineates nine key features of school environments that she found in schools that teach for understanding. These features are consistent with those found by Knapp et al. (1995) in their study of teaching for meaning and by Newmann et al. (1996) in their study of authentic achievement. Darling-Hammond's key features are summarized in Box 6.1.

BOX 6.1   Environmental Features of Schools That Teach for Meaning

- *active in-depth learning.* School cultures encourage a focus on core concepts so that students can engage in in-depth inquiry into subjects and can demonstrate their knowledge of the subject in a meaningful way. Teachers are evaluated on their ability to skillfully manage activity-based learning rather than content coverage. In addition, time is structured to allow for meaningful work.

- *emphasis on authentic performance.* Students throughout the school are expected to demonstrate their knowledge in authentic performances that account for the audience and are judged through multiple criteria. The school community supports efforts to move from norm-referenced multiple-choice standardized tests to criterion-referenced tests that allow students to demonstrate how they think as well as what they know.

- *appreciation for diversity.* The school provides ongoing support for teachers to learn to use diversity to their advantage in structuring the learning environment, in selecting instructional strategies, and in selecting the curriculum. The school also demonstrates a commitment to keeping all students in the regular classroom.

- *attention to development.* The school culture focuses on making the school "user friendly" by building on students' normal development and using their energy to learn what is developmentally appropriate for them. This involves ongoing discussion of child and adolescent development and making curricular decisions that respect the wide variety in normal development.

- *opportunities for collaborative learning.* The school culture values classrooms that are a buzz of productive talk and reciprocal teaching. These schools encourage all teachers to be skilled in establishing collaborative groups in classrooms and to engage in collaborative work outside of the classroom.

- *a collective perspective across the school.* Schools develop shared goals, standards, and assessments, which are enacted collectively. Teachers are given the opportunity to make important decisions about how and what to teach and are also held responsible for the outcomes of these decisions. To make these decisions effectively, schools have a governance structure and decisionmaking process in place that involves all school community members.

- *structures for caring.* Schools have in place processes that promote trusting and respectful relationships between and among adults and students. They design structures to provide the most personalized learning experiences possible, and they encourage the use of curriculum that develops respect and empathy.

- *support for democratic learning.* Schools model democratic learning by including all school community members in decisionmaking. Community members' ideas and beliefs are heard and valued, and multiple avenues for involving the entire community in shared activities are maintained.

- *connections to family and community.* Schools create true partnerships with families and communities and involve family members in the students' learning process. Family members and teachers develop shared goals for each student that are consistent with the standards set at the school level and the norms and expectations held in the home. (Darling-Hammond 1997: 107–146)

Assumptions About the Value of Change

Chapter 5 discusses broad issues of culture change. The following discussion concentrates on the impact that assumptions about the value of change have on schoolwide efforts to accelerate the learning of all students.

Assumptions That Discourage Acceleration

Resist all change.   A large body of literature on school reform describes failed attempts to change schools (Cuban 1990, 1992; Tyack and Tobin 1994; Tyack and Cuban 1995; Sarason 1996; Fullan and Hargreaves 1996). These efforts fail for many reasons (i.e., failure to involve school-level personnel in their design, neglecting to examine the fit between the reform initiative and the existing school culture, and a lack of resources follow-up support). Even when schools want to implement the reform, they often shape it in ways that render it unrecognizable to the reform designer (Berman and McLaughlin 1977; Jennings and Spillane 1996).

In addition, school culture plays a conservative role in maintaining the status quo. Tradition plays a large role in schools, and teachers and administrators often continue practices that are ineffective because they are familiar and because there are few rewards for taking risks (Tyack and Cuban 1995; Sarason 1996). Change and risk taking require time, reflection, and open discussion, commodities that are rare in most schools (Fullan and Hargreaves 1996). Given the conservative nature of culture and the lack of opportunities for collegial discussion, schools rarely change in any significant ways solely from their own initiative (Tyack and Cuban 1995; Sarason 1996).

Even when teachers or administrators initiate change, factions within the school often engage in overt or covert actions to thwart the change. For example, Datnow (1998) describes how a group of self-described "good old boys" used gender politics to stop efforts to detrack a high school. The combination of resistance to change from outside, internal micropolitics, and limited opportunity and incentive to change from within keep many schools mired in mediocrity.

Systemic change is impossible.   Given that school cultures tend to resist changes proposed from outside and legitimate the status quo, major systemic changes are rare. Tyack and Tobin (1994) and Tyack and Cuban (1995) describe what they call the "grammar of schooling" or the persistence of practices. Tyack and Cuban write:

> Once established, the grammar of schooling persisted in part because it enabled teachers to discharge their duties in a predictable fashion and to cope

with the everyday tasks that school boards, principals, and parents expected them to perform: controlling student behavior, instructing heterogeneous pupils, and sorting people for future roles in school and later life. Habitual institutional patterns can be labor-saving devices, ways to organize complex duties. Teachers and students socialized to such routines often find it difficult to adapt to different structures and rules. Established institutional forms come to be understood by educators, students, and the public as necessary features of a "real school." They become fixed in place by everyday custom in schools and by outside forces, both legal mandates and cultural beliefs, until they are barely noticed. They become just the way schools are. (1995: 86)

Deep, systemic change is difficult because it calls for change in what we accept as "real school." Efforts to make changes of this kind rarely succeed. It is much safer and easier to "tinker" with the current system, settling for smaller changes. Some school reform advocates, in fact, suggest that these smaller changes are preferable to fostering systemic changes.

Student achievement would improve if other people changed.   Most people are reluctant to change even though they want to improve and grow. As the adage states, "People want to go to heaven but they don't want to die." We want to see improvements, to grow, to make schools better for students, but we resist changing routines and comfortable practices (Evans 1996). When students do not learn, too often the circle of blame begins. Parents point their fingers at teachers; teachers have a wide range of people to blame—parents, other teachers, administrators, and central office. Administrators blame parents, teachers, teacher preparation institutions, and state and district policymakers. Rarely do we collectively look at our own role in poor student achievement and examine what everyone could do to make schools better for all students (Schlechty 1997).

There are many reasons why teachers resist personal change. Many veteran teachers have been involved in prior change efforts that failed. Those who supported the changes became disillusioned, and those who resisted felt justified in their resistance (Tyack and Cuban 1995). Teachers may also resist change for reasons that have nothing to do with the value of the proposed change. Most veteran teachers are middle-aged, a period of life when change is not as welcome as in earlier years. Middle-aged teachers are dealing with changes outside of work (e.g., aging parents, children leaving home) and find solace in the sense of competency they have in their work (Evans 1996; Fullan and Hargreaves 1996). To suggest that they need to change destroys their sense of competence and diminishes their sense of professionalism.

Assumptions That Encourage Acceleration

Change will lead to improved achievement for all students. Underlying the culture of all schools that accelerate learning is hope and optimism that change can lead to improvement. Michael Fullan writes that school reform is possible if we build on emotion and hope. Hope, he explains, is not a "naive, sunny view of life. It is the capacity not to panic in tight situations, to find ways and resources to address difficult problems" (1997: 221). People who are hopeful or optimistic tend to see problems as challenges and are energized by the opportunity to find creative solutions to problems.

Fullan couples hope with emotion, recognizing that change is an emotional process—negatively emotional if there is no hope, positively if there is. When the emotional side of change is recognized, productive roles are available to all actors, from the enthusiasts to the resisters. Resisters represent emotional energy that when acknowledged and seriously considered provides beneficial critical scrutiny of change proposals. Fullan continues, "Finding a way to reconcile positive and negative emotion is the key to releasing energy for change" (1997: 223). By using change to keep hope alive and recognizing the emotions involved in change, schools can truly make change their friend (Finnan 1996).

Positive changes are possible when they are supported internally and externally. As described above, school cultures are by nature conservative. Cultures protect and justify traditional behavior and attitudes. For this reason, it is very difficult for a school community to sustain systemic change that originates solely from within the school, and it is easy to resist change that is imposed from outside. Schools that embrace change as a positive force successfully combine influences from the outside into the culture that exists within the school. As Tyack and Cuban write, "Rather than starting from scratch in reinventing schools, it makes most sense to us to graft thoughtful reforms onto what is healthy in the present system" (1995: 133). Successful school reform initiatives such as the Accelerated Schools Project, the Coalition of Essential Schools, and the School Development Project provide a philosophy of school improvement and a structure for enacting this philosophy, but this philosophy and structure is permeable enough that each school can shape it to its existing culture.

Personal change is challenging and invigorating. Schools that accelerate the learning of all students encourage all community members to see change as an invigorating challenge. Rather than avoiding change and clinging to the familiar, people in schools that accelerate learning welcome opportunities to learn, grow, and change. A schoolwide climate of trust is essential in fostering this attitude. People are willing to take risks and experiment with new ways of thinking and doing if they can trust their colleagues to support their efforts (Knapp, Shields, and Padilla 1995; Fullan and Hargreaves 1996; Evans 1996). Collegial support entails an open exchange of ideas, questions, and concerns; a collegial environment encourages constructive critique as well as support and assistance (Fullan and Hargreaves 1996).

In addition, people who willingly participate in changing a school's culture find a fulfilling balance between their work and the rest of their life. Those who devote all of their time and energy to school are apt to burn out and become either cynical or apathetic. With a healthy balance between work and outside interests, they retain their energy and enthusiasm (Fullan and Hargreaves 1996; Fullan 1997). In a truly collegial environment, school community members move in and out of leadership roles in response to changing demands outside of work and to allow for renewal, reflection, and rededication (Evans 1996).

Moving School Culture Toward Acceleration

The preceding describes sets of assumptions that shape a school's ability and willingness to accelerate learning for all students. In some schools, the assumptions have a powerful hindering effect, negating any individual effort teachers, principals, or parents initiate to make accelerated learning available to all children. Conversely, in other schools, different assumptions support and facilitate efforts to change educational practice, attitudes, and beliefs.

What do schools do to create a culture that supports such change? Chapter 8 provides a more detailed description of what individuals can do to change school cultures, but the following are some collective actions a school can take. First, the school community members can make explicit their commitment to accelerating the learning of all children. By doing so, they take seriously the process of setting a vision and standards that will challenge all children. In addition, they can establish a governance structure and decisionmaking process that facilitates open communication, reflection, risk taking, and inquiry. As described above, some schools have done this independently. Many others have found that involvement in reform projects such as the Accelerated Schools Project, Coalition of Essential Schools, and the School Development Project provide both philosophical support for their commitment to raising the bar for all students and a process for making this happen.

Second, schools that accelerate learning must carefully tend to the changes they initiate. To return to the analogy introduced in Chapter 5, to successfully change school culture, the change must be cultured or cultivated. This involves ensuring a rich growth medium. Change will never "take root" in schools without a shared commitment to the change and proper supports for it (e.g., professional development, time, flexibility). Careful tending of the change involves years of support and nurturing. Change initiatives can begin in a rich growth medium, but without ongoing coaching, mentoring, and other support, they are likely to die. Finally, tending change can also involve strategic "pruning." Schools that accelerate the learning of all students constantly evaluate the effectiveness of the actions they initiate. If these actions lose their effectiveness, the school community understands that it is time for some pruning. Although this process is not easy, a school culture committed to accelerating the learning of all students can make it happen.

7   Cultivating Acceleration Within Classroom Cultures

Westview Elementary School's theme for the term is cooperation. All classrooms integrate instruction around this theme. Sara's fourth grade classroom has been reading James and the Giant Peach, *and they want to illustrate to the school how James and his compatriots had to cooperate to safely travel across the ocean. The classroom has been transformed into a giant peach. The room is tented in orange, and large insects are attached to the walls.*

Groups of students are busily at work on several projects. Some students are preparing a newspaper with articles on the importance of cooperation written from the perspective of each of the travelers. Other students have chosen to focus on how nature cooperated with James. They are plotting the course of the peach across the ocean, taking into account the influence of wind currents, hailstorms, and rain. Another group of students was impressed with the helpfulness of people when the peach arrived, and they are studying other examples of how Americans have cooperated to find homes for other refugees. Sara is part of a group working with the music teacher to write and perform an opera describing cooperation during the peach journey. Parents come and go; several mothers are planning a peach party complete with peach nectar, peach pie, and peach ice cream, The party coincides with a health unit on nutrition and the importance of a balanced diet.

A hum of active student voices fills the room. All students, from those who love to read to those who struggle with reading, are engaged in the projects and enthusiastically reading the novel. The teacher moves from group to group asking students to explain their projects, challenging them to make links to other things they have learned, and to do their personal best. From time to time she consults the state content standards guiding the fourth grade curriculum to be sure students are focused on important content and are learning needed skills. Students are assessed continuously on reading comprehension, clarity of writing, and persuasive speaking. Knowledge gained related to math, science, and social studies is tied into other lessons and assessments. Sara's teacher and the music teacher collaborate daily on the peach opera. Other teachers visit the room looking for ideas and offering suggestions; after school Sara's teacher joins a peer support team to research additional resources for their focus on cooperation.

The argument for making deeper changes in the school culture is supported by research on the limited success of many school restructuring efforts. This research (Tyack and Cuban 1995; Elmore, Peterson, and McCarthey 1996; Sarason 1996) supports two conclusions. The first, dealt with in the preceding chapter, is that *restructuring* does not extend deeply enough into the school culture; deeper cultural change must occur. The second, the focus of this chapter and the logical extension of the first conclusion, is that cultural change cannot exist only at the school level but must occur at the classroom level.

As the above example illustrates, Westview Elementary School supports accelerated learning, but it is in classrooms such as Sara's where "the rubber meets the road." The bulk of student learning in any school takes place in a classroom. Whether referred to as powerful learning (Hopfenberg et al. 1993; Keller and Huebner 1997), authentic achievement (Newmann, Secada, and Wehlage 1995; Newmann et al. 1996) teaching for understanding (Cohen, McLaughlin, and Talbert 1993; Darling-Hammond 1997), teaching for meaning (Knapp et al. 1995), or culturally relevant teaching (Ladson-Billings 1994), it is the nature of the interaction between teachers, students, and academic content that creates a classroom culture.

Classroom cultures share the three characteristics that were already presented as defining characteristics of school culture. First, there are aspects of every classroom culture that are simultaneously universal and unique. Just as you can walk into almost any school and recognize that it is a school, classrooms share common features that are undeniably those of classrooms. For example, classrooms are typically about the same size and are shaped so that the teacher can always see all of the students. They have desks or tables and chairs. Students always outnumber adults, typically by a ratio of between 15–35 students to 1 teacher. As is the case with schools, each classroom is unique, reflecting the teaching style and interaction patterns negotiated between the teacher and the students.

Second, classroom cultures, like school cultures, are both stable and ever changing. Patterns of interaction between the teacher and students are predictable; a basic scope and sequence in teaching varies little from year to year. Within this bubble of stability, however, classroom cultures change—as the student population changes, as teachers learn new content and instructional and management strategies, and as curriculum, policies, and mandates from the state and district change.

Finally, classroom cultures exist as worlds unto themselves, but they also exist within the wider culture of the school and society. The classroom becomes its own world as soon as the door closes. Behind this closed door magic or disaster can happen. But influences from outside the classroom walls do invade this closed world. The school culture is a primary influence. Depending on the compatibility between the classroom and school culture, one teacher may feel under siege by the school culture, while another may feel supported and nurtured. For example, Richard's teachers feel unsupported in their middle school because they are working with low-achieving students in a way many teachers do not understand or support. They know that when their grant money is gone they will probably be unable to continue this program. Anna's teacher chooses to isolate herself from the other teachers since she believes her colleagues have no use for the kind of teaching she does with her gifted students. In contrast, Sara's teacher feels supported and nurtured by her colleagues. Many of the ideas for her unit on *James and the Giant Peach* came from her colleagues. In addition, influences from the wider society (e.g., influences from the students' and teacher's homes and communities; the social and political climate in the community, state, and nation; and media influences, etc.) enter the classroom door every day.

Classroom and school cultures differ in the degree to which they are closed or bounded. The school is a relatively open unit in which many people and influences, both inside and outside of the school, mingle to create a school culture. The classroom is a relatively closed unit. Largely the teacher determines the boundaries of the classroom culture, with some influence from students and other adults (e.g., teaching assistants, resource teachers, student teachers, and parents). The classroom can be considered a negotiated space in which the teacher sets the tone and, with his/her students, creates a community. Obviously, the school culture and societal norms, values, and assumptions have a profound influence on classroom culture, but the teacher and, to a more limited extent, the students and other adults create a classroom culture.

Because the classroom can be a relatively closed entity, the teacher's ability to determine the culture of his or her classroom is greater than the principal's ability to create the school culture. A teacher's classroom culture remains relatively stable as generations of students and as a succession of principals and superintendents move through the classroom, school, and district. Teachers are quick to point out that each of their classes is different, that each group of students negotiates a culture that differs from others. This is undeniable, but the influence of students on the classroom culture does not negate the control teachers exert in their domain—the classroom.

The teacher's influence is evident in the tangible and visible aspects of the classroom. For example, the teacher determines how to embellish the room, deciding if the classroom is a showcase for student work, a kaleidoscope of colors and textures, or a minimalist room with a few commercially published posters on the wall. The teacher also determines the affective climate in the classroom. Can the classroom be described as caring; do students feel respected; is control of behavior a primary concern? Although more open for negotiation than the above, the teacher also has tremendous influence on the assumptions that shape the classroom culture in which he or she works.

In Chapter 6 we examined five assumptions that underlie school culture. These assumptions act to encourage or discourage efforts at the *school level* to accelerate the learning of all students. Assumptions have a similar effect at the classroom level. Assumptions held by the teacher and the students determine the success or failure of efforts to accelerate the learning of all students in a classroom. The following discussion parallels that presented in Chapter 6. We identify categories of assumptions that shape classroom culture and describe specific assumptions that encourage and discourage efforts to accelerate learning within the classroom.

Basic Assumptions Shaping Classroom Culture

As a negotiated environment, the teacher, students, and selected other adults shape a classroom culture.[1] The teacher has complete control of the tangible, visible aspects of the classroom culture and near complete control of the affective climate. Negotiations between the teacher and students occur over the assumptions that underlie the classroom culture. The following are critical components of classroom culture:

- Assumptions shaping expectations for student learning and appropriate behavior
- Assumptions shaping communication and discourse
- Assumptions shaping expectations of appropriate adult behavior
- Assumptions shaping conceptions of appropriate educational practices

These assumptions and how they serve to discourage or encourage efforts to accelerate the learning of all students are summarized in Table 7.1.

Assumptions Shaping Expectations for Student Learning and Appropriate Behavior

Assumptions That Discourage Acceleration

Students cannot learn challenging material and lack self-control.   Patricia Hilliard, a teacher in a predominantly African American school, notes: "You want to see intelligence walking around on two legs? Just go into a kindergarten class. They come to school with fresh faces, full of wonder.

TABLE 7.1   Cultural Assumptions: Classroom Level

Discourage Acceleration	*Encourage Acceleration*
Assumptions Shaping Expectations for Student Learning and Appropriate Behavior	
• Students cannot learn challenging material and lack self-control.	• All students have strengths that can be built upon.
• Students who are different are deficient or a problem.	• A positive learning environment is negotiated between the teacher and students.
• Students assume that they have "won" when they negotiate for less-challenging curriculum.	• Teachers develop a deep understanding of their students.
• Students are expected to be passive recipients of knowledge.	
Assumptions Related to Appropriate Communication and Discourse	
• The teacher directs all discourse.	• Discourse is communally developed.
• Diversity of communication modes is discouraged.	• Language is used to demonstrate understanding and thought processes.
	• Diversity of communication is built upon as a strength.
Assumptions Related to Appropriate Adult Behavior	
• The teacher expects to work alone.	• The classroom invites involvement of other educators, parents, and community members.
• Control of the classroom rests solely with either the teacher or the students.	• The teacher facilitates creation of a positive learning environment.
• The teacher controls what is learned and how it is learned.	• The teacher ensures that the classroom is known as a center of expertise.
• The classroom reflects little ongoing adult learning.	• The teacher is a "learning leader" in the classroom, transmitting passion for ongoing learning.
Assumptions Related to Appropriate Educational Practices	
• Memorization of facts and drill are the focus of teaching.	• All students engage in active exploration of relevant material.
• Emphasis is placed on order; students work alone in their seats.	• All students have the opportunity to develop basic skills and higher-order thinking skills.
• Emphasis is placed on acquisition of basic skills.	• Students learn to work productively with each other.

But by third grade you can see how badly school has beaten them down. You can really see it in the boys. I sometimes ask myself just what is it we're doing to these children" (Ladson-Billings 1994: 89).

What are we doing indeed? Assumptions that students cannot learn challenging material and lack self-control are manifested in many ways in classrooms. In some cases, students of color can do nothing to convince teachers that they are intelligent. Gloria Ladson-Billings reflects on her own school experience and writes:

> I had graduated from a junior high school that I hated with straight A's. I had had a report card of straight A's and I was miserable. I had not earned those A's because I was smart. I had not earned them because I wanted to be an outstanding student. I had earned them because my teachers did not think I could earn them and I had vowed right then and there to live up to my own standards of excellence (1994: 101).

Too few students have Ladson-Billings's self-confidence and perseverance. They assume that their teachers are right, that they are not as capable as other students (Oakes 1985; Oakes, Wells, Jones, and Datnow 1997; Jennings 1998). When many of these students fail, teachers feel justified in their assumptions that "those kids can't learn" (Shields 1995). Some teachers raise the bar higher and higher until students fail (as illustrated by Ladson-Billings's example); others set the bar for low-income and/or minority students so low that they are required to make little effort. They may do this out of a misplaced compassion, laziness, or from a belief that these students are unable to meet higher standards. Whatever the reason for not challenging students, there are gatekeepers later in life who hold high standards (e.g., college admissions offices, personnel directors), and students who have never failed before will be in a position to fail (Delpit 1988; Ladson-Billings 1994).

Coupled with low expectations for academic ability, many teachers assume that some children (typically those unlike themselves) lack self-control and must be controlled with a rigid system of rewards and punishments. Despite considerable research on the negative effects of extrinsic rewards and punishments on student motivation and self-discipline (Deci 1976; Lepper and Greene 1978; Lepper 1981; Kohn 1993, cited in Darling-Hammond 1997: 138), many teachers escalate what becomes a power struggle between themselves and a few students. They become *authoritarian* rather than *authoritative* (Florio-Ruane 1989). As Haberman writes, this escalation is the result of faulty assumptions about what motivates students:

> Children begin school intrinsically motivated to learn as much as possible, because they sense in their bones that learning is synonymous with living and growing. It is only after children begin school and are forced to respond to teachers whose major objective is class discipline, and whose strongest emotion is fear that they might lose control of the class, that children are taught to do things for extrinsic rewards: stars, stickers, longer recess, certificates for pizza, etc. (1995: 17)

Students who are different are deficient or a problem. Many teachers assume that all students learn in the same way. They do not know what to do with those who learn differently other than to label them and try to remove them from their classrooms. They explain students' poor performance by citing problems in the home and the community. These teachers rarely reflect on the influence of their own assumptions or their practice on student learning. As they continue to sort students, it becomes evident that "the children we teach best are those who need us least" (Haberman 1995: 81) and that those who will truly benefit from being taught are seen as a problem (Ladson-Billings 1994).

Students labeled as problems are often different in social class and/or ethnicity from their teacher. Since George Spindler's classic study of Roger Harker in the 1950s (Spindler and Spindler 1982),[2] research has consistently shown that teachers favor students like themselves, however unconscious this behavior is (Cornbleth and Korth 1980; Hale 1994; Ladson-Billings 1994). Well-meaning white teachers often claim to not "see color"; in saying this, they are reassuring themselves that they are not prejudiced. However, given that children of color are usually culturally different from their white teachers, such a statement rules out any effort to understand and build upon students' culture (Ladson-Billings 1994; Shields 1995).

Students assume that they have "won" when they negotiate for less-challenging curriculum.   As stated above, the teacher and the students negotiate the classroom culture. The teacher has considerable control over the classroom, but student assumptions have a powerful influence as well. This is especially true for middle school and high school students who are accustomed to exerting minimal effort in unchallenging classrooms. Once challenged, these students often resist and negotiate for the comfort of low expectations (McQuillan 1998). Wasley, Hampel, and Clark, in a study of five Coalition of Essential Schools high schools, found that

> Students in the five schools had little quarrel with the caring extended to them; it was the high expectations that they often ignored, resisted, or misunderstood. Many students began high school with the notion that learning means sitting still, working alone, memorizing, and recalling facts. That is a pervasive view of education, which millions of freshmen hold even if they have done some group work or finished a few comprehensive projects before entering high school. They think: teaching is telling, learning is listening, knowledge is in the textbook, the desks are in neat rows. (1997: 80)

One of the difficulties teachers have in negotiating high expectations for students is that students act collectively rather than individually on their sense of what learning should be. McQuillan writes:

> And when they resisted their teachers, they often did so in a collective fashion, building on one another's ideas, taking turns challenging their teachers, and providing moral support for each other. In so doing, students enacted their informal power so as to implicate themselves in their own educational

failure—in terms of the grades they received, the skills they never developed, and how their actions reinforced faculty perceptions of student indif-
ference (Willis 1977; McDermott 1987; Chandler 1992)." (1998: 24)

How are students able to achieve failure when many of them express a
desire to do well in school (Fine 1991; Solomon 1992) and teachers work
hard on their behalf? The teacher has the responsibility to create a positive balance between students' individual desires to learn and the collective meaning making and behavior that exists in the classroom. In the
case of many students who have little experience with high expectations
and little confidence in their own ability, the meaning they make collectively discourages efforts to accelerate learning. This is often done
through a collective agreement to use non-Standard English (e.g., street
language, dialect) in the classroom (Fordham 1999).

Students are expected to be passive recipients of knowledge.   Student involvement in acquiring knowledge is also negotiated between the teacher and
the students. Students become passive when teachers assume that they
cannot learn challenging material and lack self-control, and students assume that they have succeeded when they slide through class with little
effort. This insidious negotiation leads to classroom behavior that encourages conformity and compliance and discourages deliberation, critical thinking, and active engagement in ideas (Goodlad 1984; Oakes 1985;
Darling-Hammond 1997). Observations in high school classes indicate
that student comments and questions that could stimulate discussion are
ignored more often in schools serving low-income students than in more
schools serving more affluent students (Metz 1998).
   A classroom culture of student passivity provides few opportunities
for discourse, thought, reflection, and learning. In addition, students
have little opportunity to practice democracy. Darling-Hammond
maintains that the classroom should provide students an opportunity
to practice democracy, or the free exchange and blending of ideas and
knowledge (1997: 84). She draws upon John Dewey (1916), who writes,
"There must be a large variety of shared undertakings and experiences.
Otherwise the influences which educate some into masters educate others into slaves. And the experience of each party loses in meaning,
when the free interchange of varying modes of life experiences is
arrested" (in Darling-Hammond 1997: 84). When students passively
receive knowledge, their own experiences, ideas, and interests are
ignored.

Assumptions That Encourage Acceleration

All students have strengths that can be built upon.   Teachers that accelerate
the learning of all students assume that all students come to school with

strengths (Levin 1986, 1987, 1988, 1998; Hopfenberg et al. 1993; Finnan et al. 1996). They create classroom cultures based on this assumption. These teachers are uninterested in labeling and sorting children. They assume that children will learn material at different speeds and in different ways and that it is their job to find appropriate strategies for each child (Haberman 1995; Spear-Swerling and Sternberg 1996). Rather than assuming that some students can learn and others cannot, these teachers seek excellence in themselves and in students. This can either be done alone, like an orchestra conductor or in collaboration with others, like a coach (Ladson-Billings 1994).

Regardless of how teachers accomplish this, they do not allow societal notions of success and failure to undercut what their students can do (McDermott 1974, 1997). Teachers who accelerate the learning of all students do not accept the notion that we benefit from winners and losers. As McDermott writes:

> Fifty years ago, it was not possible to be learning disabled, although now it defines the school experience for one of every seven children in the United States: Japan and Denmark, on the other hand, have highly successful school systems with no learning disabilities. Similarly, whole countries get by without too much attention to school failure. In January 1942, there was no school failure problem in the United States (Berg 1969). Some people knew more than others, and some had gone to school more than others, but everyone was needed. The game had changed. Failure was not an option. (1997: 122–123)

Teachers that accelerate the learning of all students care enough for their students to expect more from students than students expect from themselves (Wasley, Hampel, and Clark 1997: 76). This is accomplished by consistently assuring students of their potential and worth and by persisting even when students are ready to give up.

A positive learning environment is negotiated between the teacher and students. Highly effective teachers use their authority to negotiate a positive learning environment. Neither permissive nor authoritarian, teachers that accelerate learning set limits and consequences that make possible whole class discussion, disagreement, and the exchange of ideas (Darling-Hammond 1997). This environment allows students to develop the ability to see the world as others might, thus developing "unsentimental compassion and . . . intellectual skepticism and empathy" (Meier 1995: 63).

When a class negotiates a positive learning environment, all students feel needed, wanted, and known (Ladson-Billings 1994; Haberman 1995). Discipline is not an issue separate from teaching since the class as a group sets the norms for appropriate behavior, and everyone knows that they cannot do their best when disrupted (Haberman 1995; Marks, Doane, and Secada 1996). These classrooms can function with very few rules because the teachers build strong personal relationships with children around learning tasks. Teachers get to know each child before a problem arises (Haberman 1995), and "they demonstrate a connectedness with all of their students and encourage that same connectedness between the students" (Ladson-Billings 1994: 25).

Teachers develop a deep understanding of their students. A deep understanding of students involves two kinds of knowledge. The first is knowledge of development, culture and community, and learning (e.g., learning styles, multiple intelligences). Teachers who successfully accelerate learning know "how children and adolescents think and behave, what they are trying to accomplish, what they find interesting, what they already know, and what concepts they might have trouble with in particular domains at particular ages" (Darling-Hammond 1997: 295). They also need to know how culture, social class, language, community, gender, and other factors influence learning and development (Delpit 1988, 1995; Florio-Ruane 1989; Sleeter 1993; Ladson-Billings 1994; Greenfield 1994; Darling-Hammond 1997; Jennings 1998; Ogbu and Simons 1998; Payne 1998). Effective teachers also take into account the wide range of aptitude in multiple intelligences (Gardner 1983; 1999) and the varied learning styles that exist in every class.

The second kind of knowledge is personal knowledge of the student. Students' sense of worth is connected to the degree to which they are known. As one student lamented, "I had to introduce myself to my math teacher at back-to-school night" (McLaughlin 1994: 9). Phelan, Davidson and Cao, in a study of high school factors that foster positive learning experiences, found the following:

> Most important, students say that they like classrooms where they feel they know the teacher and the other students. While students appreciate a well-organized and orderly environment, they do not like one in which the teacher is detached and treats the classroom as a whole rather than as a roomful of individuals. (1992: 696)

When teachers are able to combine both kinds of knowledge, students are more apt to try to meet teachers' high expectations and are less interested in negotiating lower ones. Such knowledge of students also helps teachers internalize key principles behind school reform initiatives, such as the Coalition of Essential Schools' principle of unanxious expectation (I won't threaten you, but I expect a lot from you) (Sizer 1992a; Wasley, Hampel, and Clark 1997) and the Accelerated Schools Project's principle of "building on strengths" (Hopfenberg et al. 1993).

Respecting cultural and social class differences while maintaining high expectations for all students is a difficult challenge for all teachers. Those who are most effective are very knowledgeable of the cultures in their classroom and are able to "tailor instruction to overcome potentially constraining background factors and make it clear that their [students'] culture is valued" (Shields 1995: 39). They also understand that class, race or ethnicity, and gender combine to shape students' reactions to learning (Cousins 1999). Teachers gain this knowledge through immersion in the students' communities (Delpit 1988; Ladson-Billings 1994), by listening carefully to students, and through gaining the trust and respect of families (Jennings 1998). Teachers who choose not to immerse themselves in the community must learn to differentiate between learning deficits (an individual student's unique learning problems) and cultural and class differences (collective differences that do not constitute deficits) (Jennings 1998: 32).

Acquiring a deep knowledge of students requires a reconceptualization of equity for many teachers. As Ladson-Billings writes:

> The notion of equity as sameness only makes sense when all students *are* exactly the same. But even within the nuclear family children born from the same parents are not exactly the same. Different children have different needs, and addressing those different needs is the best way to deal with them equitably. The same is true in the classroom. If teachers pretend not to see students' racial and ethnic differences, they really do not see the students at all and are limited in their ability to meet their educational needs. (1994: 33)

Assumptions Related to Appropriate Communication and Discourse

Assumptions That Discourage Acceleration

The teacher directs all discourse. The way in which the teacher organizes communication within the classroom greatly determines the learning that occurs (Florio-Ruane 1989: 168). In most classrooms, the teacher dominates all communication, leading to student passivity, limited understanding of content, and dismissal of student ideas (Florio-Ruane 1989, 1994; McLaughlin and Talbert 1993). Studies of many classrooms document a common pattern in which the teacher controls both what is talked about and who does the talking. Typical instructional discourse involves a three-part turn in which the teacher initiates a question (with an answer known to the teacher); students bid for the opportunity to respond, and the teacher evaluates the accuracy of the responses (Mehan 1979; Cazden 1988; Florio-Ruane 1994). Teachers discourage deviations from this pattern and rarely seek student responses that go beyond factual recall. Students quickly learn that there is usually only one right answer—the teacher's—and that their task is to parrot back an answer the teacher already told them. If a student provides the "right" answer, the teacher assumes that he or she understands the material.

Teacher-dominated discourse creates order and predictability but often results in disengagement and resistance on the part of students (Florio-Ruane 1994). Students' experiences and perspectives are not valued when only one perspective—the teacher's—is at the core of the communication. John Dewey writes, "Not only is social life identical with communication, but all communication (and hence all genuine social life) is educative. To be a recipient of a communication is to have an enlarged and changed experience. One shares in what another has thought and felt and in so far, meagerly or amply, has his own attitude modified (Dewey 1916: 6, in Darling-Hammond 1997: 143). Teacher learning, as well as student learning, suffers when all discourse is shaped by the teacher. Everyone in the classroom develops a belief that questions have only one right answer and that the goal of learning is factual recall, not conceptual understanding.

Teachers are often unprepared to change the discourse patterns in their classrooms and are not rewarded when they do. Even when teachers recognize that this discourse pattern is ineffective with many students, they continue because "managing these new student roles [active involvement in making meaning] presents a daunting challenge for many teachers and contradicts principles of practice conveyed in teacher education programs and assessed in teacher evaluation schemes" (McLaughlin and Talbert 1993: 3).

Teacher educators may talk about practices such as cooperative learning that encourage collective discourse, but they and other higher education faculty rarely model such practices. In addition, teacher evaluation tools are usually designed for teacher-dominated classroom experiences. Teachers report that evaluators will leave the room when students are engaged in cooperative groups or projects, saying that they will return when the teacher is "really teaching."

Diversity of communication modes is discouraged. Many teachers do not realize that considerable miscommunication exists in their classrooms. Most teachers recognize that children with limited English fluency require special attention, but they often do not recognize that English language communication patterns differ cross-culturally. When a child does not respond to questions as expected, teachers assume there is something wrong with the child. Teachers label these children as "language deprived" or "slow learners." Shirley Brice Heath, in a study of questioning at home and at school, found that white teachers asked questions designed to elicit factual recall (e.g., "What color is the ball?") that were unfamiliar to their African American students. African American students were accustomed to questions that asked for comparisons and analogies (e.g., "What does this ball look like?") (Heath 1982, 1983). Other researchers relate similar discontinuities between home and school that negatively affect the learning of many students whose culture differs from that of their teacher.

Teachers have been able to modify their language patterns to accommodate the speech patterns students bring to school (Delpit 1988; Erickson and Mohatt 1982; Heath 1983), but some of them go too far when students are not expected to learn Standard English (Delpit 1988, 1995). Teachers who allow students to rely solely on non-Standard English do these students no favor because they need to know Standard English to succeed. They also do not realize that students often use non-Standard English as a means of exerting power over their teachers (Fordham 1999). Teachers severely limit students' future opportunities when they do not use comfortable home language patterns as a vehicle to teach students Standard English. Unfortunately, few teachers understand the structures of non-Standard English, and they do not have the training to build from these structures to competency in Standard English (Delpit 1988, 1995).

Assumptions That Encourage Acceleration

Discourse is communally developed. Teachers who accelerate learning know that learning *is* communication and that it cannot be dominated by the teacher. These teachers recognize that language is the vehicle used to negotiate the classroom culture and that students' voices must be continuously heard in this negotiation. The teaching and learning connection in these classrooms looks very different from traditional classrooms, dramatically changing the teacher's role (Florio-Ruane 1989; Newmann, Secada, and Wehlage 1995; Jennings 1998). The teacher becomes less of a performer, a sage, or the "font of all knowledge" and more of a facilitator, negotiator, or conductor (Ladson-Billings 1994). Although discourse is communally developed, teachers retain a strong voice. Their authority, gained through acquisition of more extensive knowledge, not through authoritarian control, is demonstrated in their ability to make students think deeply, seek supporting evidence for ideas and beliefs, and challenge conventional wisdom (Florio-Ruane 1989; McLaughlin and Talbert 1993; Newmann, Secada, and Wehlage 1995; Darling-Hammond 1997).

Open discussion of ideas in the classroom requires special skills since students influence the direction of the discourse. For example, in an examination of two exemplary teachers of low-income urban students, Nancy Jennings describes a situation in which a teacher, in seeking to make a story relevant to her classroom of low-income white and African American second graders, asked the children to give examples of when someone or something they loved died. A child related her story in racially prejudiced terms, a version of the story that she obviously learned at home. As the faces of white and African American children looked to the teacher to make this situation comfortable, the teacher looked at Jennings and said, "No one ever tells you how to deal with *that* in those workshops" (1998: 27). This teacher is highly skilled, but even she lacked the resources to think quickly enough on her feet to turn a negative experience into a powerful one for her students.

Teachers who encourage collaborative discourse are skilled listeners as well as communicators. They have skill in listening to the ideas and comments made by students. Additionally, they analyze them not just for content but as an assessment of the student's understanding. For example, in the study cited above, Jennings observed a fifth grade teacher who, in teaching a lesson on probability, was surprised that students responded as if they did not understand the concept. By questioning the children and listening deeply to their responses, she found that the problem lay in the questions she asked, not in the students' understanding. Jennings concluded:

> So opening up classrooms to student voice can be key to helping teachers to change practice and teach effectively in schools of poverty, but teachers will need to learn to be careful listeners and observers in their classrooms. Student voice can serve as a catalyst for change only if it is heard and taken seriously by teachers. (1998: 31)

Language is used to demonstrate understanding and thought processes. The use of collaborative discourse in the classroom enables teachers to assess student understanding and to develop students' thinking processes. As the preceding example illustrates, students need to have a chance to explain their understanding of concepts and their thought processes in reaching conclusions. Most pencil and paper tests and the typical question/answer sequence used in most classrooms are limited in their capacity to assess student knowledge because they often test only at the level of factual recall. To return to Jennings's example, the fifth grade students did not do well on a written assessment of their understanding of probability. The teacher could have assumed that the test was a good assessment tool and retaught the material. Instead, she allowed students an opportunity to explain their thinking and discovered that they held a sophisticated understanding of the concept. Because of this questioning, the teacher realized that the question she had asked to assess the students' knowledge was unclear and did not allow students a valid opportunity to demonstrate their knowledge.

Teachers committed to promoting understanding and developing students' thinking and analytic skills understand the link between language and thinking (Darling-Hammond 1997). How many teachers have said,

"I never truly understood [a subject] until I taught it"? What they are re-ally saying is that through the process of verbalizing their understanding of a topic and making the topic understandable to others, they developed and refined their own thinking processes.

What is the role of the teacher when children are encouraged to demonstrate their understanding and thinking processes through dis-course? It is obviously not that of a "sage on the stage." The relationship between teacher talk and student talk shifts radically. The focus for teach-ers is not so much how to communicate material clearly (although clear communication remains important) but how to listen deeply and analyti-cally to student responses. Deborah Meier states that "teaching is mostly listening and learning is mostly telling" (1995: xi). The teacher's chal-lenge is to build the knowledge and expertise of a diverse group of stu-dents so that they can all benefit from the input of each other and build toward learning goals set by the teacher.

Diversity of communication modes is built upon as a strength.   Teachers who successfully accelerate student learning encourage language diversity but ensure that students' learning is not limited by their fluency. They find the balance between respecting and building on students' home lan-guage and providing all students an opportunity to develop oral and written fluency in the language of instruction (e.g., Standard English in the United States) and in the specific language of the discipline (Tharp and Gallimore 1988; Delpit 1988, 1995; Blake and Van Sickle 1997).

Effective teachers recognize two important differences between Eng-lish spoken by middle-class families and that spoken in working-class families. The first, mentioned earlier, is the use of questions. Middle-class parents communicate with their young children through a series of "What is that?" questions designed to help the child learn vocabu-lary and labels. This form of questioning is not used in all cultures and across social class lines, and it is foreign to many children when they encounter it in school (Florio-Ruane 1989; Heath 1982, 1983). These chil-dren may be more familiar with relational questions, such as "What is that like?"

The second difference relates to the use of directives and questions. Whereas middle-class parents tell their children to do something through the use of a question (e.g., "Johnny, would you please feed the dog?"), working-class parents are more likely to use a directive (e.g., "Johnny, go feed that dog."). When working-class children encounter questions masking a directive, they often respond incorrectly (Delpit 1988). The ef-fective teacher knows his or her children well enough to know when to alter speech patterns and is willing to work with the students so that they will understand how questions and directives are used in mainstream so-ciety. They also take the time to build on students' home language as a base for fluency in the standard language (Erickson and Mohatt 1982; Delpit 1988, 1995).

Stereotyping is a challenge for teachers striving to be sensitive to language and cultural differences. Effective teachers know that they cannot assume that all children within one ethnic or racial group come from homes with the same language and cultural patterns. Even if this were true, many teachers work with students from a wide variety of cultural, class, and language backgrounds. They cannot adequately adapt to multiple home environments. Rather, they learn about their students, and they learn to make their own cultural beliefs, assumptions, and values explicit. George and Louise Spindler (1994) suggest reflective strategies or "cultural therapy" to encourage teachers, counselors, and principals to better understand themselves as culture bearers so that they will better understand their students as culture bearers, whereas Liston and Zeichner (1996) offer case studies to stimulate such reflection.

Assumptions Related to Appropriate Adult Behavior

Assumptions That Discourage Acceleration

The teacher expects to work alone.   Teaching is described as a lonely profession (Lortie 1975; Kidder 1989). The structure of school buildings, the allocation of time within the day, the assignment of students to teachers, and even the design of typical professional development activities allow for little opportunity for teachers to work collaboratively. Within the classroom, teachers typically have little more than fleeting involvement with other adults.

Not only does school structure discourage professional interaction, teacher assumptions about their work and the value of interaction with colleagues and administrators contributes to professional isolation. In many schools, the only time that another adult spends any significant time in a teacher's classroom is when the teacher is being observed for evaluation purposes. As McLaughlin and Talbert (1993) write, "lack of support from one's colleagues or from administrators places fundamental restrictions on practice, will, and spirit. Teaching for understanding departs from the kinds of teaching and learning activities administrators are accustomed to evaluating and overseeing" (p. 5). Isolated teachers' classrooms rarely change because they are not apt to seek out innovative strategies, especially when they are evaluated on their proficiency in traditional teaching methods. On the rare occurrences when teachers are released from their classrooms to observe each other, their feedback is usually limited because they are unaccustomed and unprepared to give and receive constructive criticism. Many teachers prefer to work alone rather than risk looking bad in front of colleagues and administrators.

Control of the classroom rests solely with either the teacher or the students. Considerable time and energy is consumed when teachers and students battle over who will control the classroom. Rather than assuming that student engagement flows from involvement in learning (Haberman 1995), many teachers develop elaborate systems to control students. Hale graphically describes such a system:

> I have had an opportunity to observe in schools in several large American cities what I call *incarceration education.* In such schools, the teachers should receive certification for "lining up and walking down the halls," because a great deal of time is being spent on perfecting those activities. There are elaborate rituals and record-keeping around who lines up first and last and the facial expressions and body language that are appropriate. It seems to me that as much energy is used for that ritual as is used for instruction. (1994: 205)

When control of behavior is separated from engagement in learning and when "getting the teacher's definition of the situation accepted by the students" is the primary goal, a battle of wills between students and the teacher ensues (Waller 1932, in Florio-Ruane 1989: 166). Usually both parties in the battle lose.

In a study of the relationship between teaching for meaning and classroom management, Heather McCollum (1995) finds that less effective classrooms exist at two extremes. They are either "orderly to the point of being slightly oppressive, with little spontaneity evident" (p. 14) or disorderly with an "apparently capricious system of cues for punishment" (p. 13). Throughout the day, the teacher and students, either the whole class or a group of students, lose focus on instruction and are pulled into the battle of wills. Studies of lower-track classrooms document considerable time spent on noninstructional interactions, indicating that the students and the teacher have agreed to accept low expectations (Oakes 1985; Page 1987; Delpit 1988; McQuillan 1998; Metz 1998).

The teacher controls what is learned and how it is learned. The mantra for any inexperienced teacher is to be well prepared for each class. This is a worthy goal, but "well prepared" too often translates into inflexibility, rigidity, and lack of creativity. Inexperienced teachers often spend hours delineating discrete behavioral objectives and detailing lesson plans. However, as Florio-Ruane (1989) points out, "beginning teachers often write detailed lesson plans which they use as scripts, inventories, or procedural guides. These initial plans, however, bear little resemblance to the intellectual work of curriculum and instructional design undertaken by experienced teachers" (p. 165).

Unfortunately, experienced teachers who fear loss of control or who have limited content and pedagogical knowledge can also be rigid in their planning and execution of lessons, allowing little flexibility and adaptability to meet students' needs (Darling-Hammond 1997). These teachers often "freeze" when students do not respond to lessons in predicted ways and cannot build on students' ideas and experience (Peterson and Clark 1978).

The tendency to control through rigid planning is better than no planning, but both extremes typically indicate a lack of content and pedagogical knowledge. Although many excellent teachers choose to work with low-achieving students and in low-income schools, some teachers who work with slower students and in low-income schools are weaker in subject matter and pedagogical knowledge than other teachers (Oakes 1985; McLaughlin and Talbert 1993; Darling-Hammond 1997; Metz 1998). Fear of revealing this lack of knowledge makes it much more difficult for these teachers to be responsive to student input. Teachers with limited subject matter knowledge find comfort in following the textbook and discourage questions and discussion that stray from the text. As McLaughlin and Talbert (1993) write, "teachers with only superficial knowledge of their subject matter will have little flexibility in their pedagogical choices and preferences and thus be effectively constrained to teach 'just the facts,' or to leave learning up to the students" (p. 2).

Teachers who use a set curriculum and prescribed materials rarely vary their routine and instructional strategies. This leads to a sameness in the class that puts even motivated students in a stupor. Teachers complain that they have to "entertain" students, that they cannot compete with television, MTV, the Internet, and video games. In fact, most students merely seek some stimulation and engagement. Wasley, Hampel, and Clark (1997), in a study of students and school reform, found that students do not find school routines to be a problem, but they do grow tired of the overwhelming sameness of school. "The sameness of some routines made the kids feel dull, and, as if enveloped by a kind of numbing narcotic, they expended less energy, attended less closely, slipped toward minimal effort. Kids did not like this feeling. They preferred to feel stimulated, awakened, challenged, as if their time was well invested" (p. 40).

The classroom reflects little ongoing adult learning. In classrooms that discourage acceleration, the teacher does not expect to grow professionally. One reason many teachers "shut down" as learners is that their experience with professional development has been poor (Darling-Hammond 1997). Too often teachers sit through one-shot presentations on how to use prepackaged materials and then are left to put the materials into practice without any on-site guidance (Elmore, Peterson, and McCarthey 1996). Given that they begin professional development with little interest in the materials, they have limited motivation to make the materials work. In addition, teachers often have little choice in shaping the direction of their professional growth. The district or the principal decides what is best for teachers, whether they need the knowledge or not.

Many teacher assessment tools also discourage ongoing professional learning. As McLaughlin and Talbert (1993) point out, teachers may know that they need professional development to stay current and to grow but may be reluctant to identify areas that could be perceived as weaknesses.

Finally, many teachers become comfortable in their teaching styles and do not look for ways to add complexity to their job (Evans 1996; Elmore, Peterson, and McCarthey 1996). Given that they are usually the only adult critic of their teaching, teachers can retreat into the comfort that they are good teachers (as defined by themselves). Principals who are intent on maintaining a smoothly run school accept this assessment for fear of disrupting the school's routine. The closed nature and isolation of the classroom culture encourages many teachers to shut out influences that might complicate their image of themselves as competent professionals.

Assumptions That Encourage Acceleration

The classroom invites involvement of other educators, parents, and community members. Classrooms in which student learning is accelerated are less bounded and closed than those described above. The classroom door is usually open, and other adults are encouraged to participate. The teacher and students are still the primary forces in negotiating the classroom culture, but influences from outside the classroom are welcomed and incorporated. Teachers assume that anyone interested in being involved in their classrooms have the students' best interests at heart. These teachers keep an open mind to ideas, opinions, and suggestions from colleagues and parents.

In classrooms that accelerate learning, teachers assume that families care about their children, and they know that family involvement takes many often unanticipated forms—forms that are shaped by language, culture, class, and community/workplace obstacles (Cook and Fine 1995; Mehan et al. 1996). Study after study of Latino and African American parents show that these parents hold the same high expectations for their students as white and Asian parents (Diaz, Moll, and Mehan 1986; Delgado-Gaitan and Trueba 1991; Fine 1991; Delgado-Gaitan 1992; Daubner and Epstein 1993; Chavkin 1993; Swadener and Lubeck 1995; Arnold

1995; Mehan et al. 1996). As collaborators, teachers learn to work with these differences, and they stop seeing some behaviors, such as the lack of attendance at events or meetings, as a sign of not caring.

Teachers welcome the opportunity to collaborate with school-based and university- or district-based colleagues, understanding the value of multiple perspectives. Interaction with these educators provides the teacher an opportunity to verbalize thoughts and ideas and to see alternative approaches to engaging children (Elmore, Peterson, and Mc-Carthey 1996). Teachers engaged in collaborative teaching comment on its effectiveness in changing practice and assumptions, but also on its difficulty (Ball and Rundquist 1993; Heaton and Lampert 1993). For example, a teacher/university professor team comment on their experience:

> It is scary and unnerving to try to change your teaching, your curriculum, your assessment, your role and responsibilities, your students' assumptions and habits of mind (as well as their parents'). It must be equally frightening for students to define and identify their own problems in mathematics, or history, or biology. It is frightening to try to do that in front of other people—as teachers working collaboratively or as students talking openly. (Wilson, Miller, and Yerkes 1993: 122)

In addition, effective teachers take the positive aspects of their classroom culture and make them part of the school culture. They know that they must help other teachers cultivate acceleration in their classrooms; otherwise student gains made in their classes will not be maintained. Collaboration, mentoring, building on the strengths of others, and other interactive processes become a part of the school culture as well as the classroom culture; it becomes part of the air they breathe (Elmore, Peterson, and McCarthey 1996; Reese and Ahlas 1999).

The teacher facilitates creation of a positive learning environment. Teachers that accelerate learning understand that they negotiate a classroom culture with their students. By realizing that learning is socially constructed (Erickson 1986; Florio-Ruane 1989), teachers are able to engage students in the creation of a positive learning environment. When teachers understand that they control the *negotiation* of the classroom culture, rather than controlling behavior and discourse, they are freed to focus on student learning. These teachers understand that they form a partnership with each student that is dedicated to ensuring that the student learns the material, that they protect each student from extraneous influences, that they make learning engaging and relevant to all students (Haberman 1995).

A positive learning environment grows when teachers demonstrate care, respect, and high expectations for students and help students develop these same dispositions (Marks, Doane, and Secada 1996; Phelan,

Davidson, and Yu 1998; Wasley, Hampel, and Clark 1997). Students interviewed in all of these studies echo the words reported by Marks, Doane, and Secada:

> In supportive classrooms, students reported that interactions with teachers and peers were respectful and purposeful and that their teachers conveyed expectations that all students would try hard and master challenging work. The most positive classroom social environments were those where teachers helped students learn but students also assisted each other and where students felt encouraged to try hard, participate, and take intellectual risks. (1996: 210)

A positive learning environment results from culturally relevant teaching (Ladson-Billings 1994; Hale 1994; Delpit 1995). The following plea from an African American educator could be repeated in reference to many other students. The point is that teachers must know their students and must encourage students to know each other:

> If it is plausible that there is an African American preaching style, then it is equally plausible that there could be an African American teaching style, which would connect with the culture of African American children, inspire them, motivate them, and capture their imagination. This statement in no way implies that only an African American could utilize such a style. Just as southern white evangelists have approximated the African American preaching style and use it in their ministries, and as white rhythm-and-blues musicians and white artists like the New Kids on the Block have utilized African American musical styles, so European American teachers can utilize African American culture when it is in the interest of their students to do so. (Hale 1994: 204)

The teacher ensures that the classroom is known as a center of expertise. Classrooms in which learning is accelerated are known in the school as centers of expertise. They are known for their deep, focused learning, the teacher for his or her content expertise, and the students for their budding content expertise. Visitors to the school are always directed to these classrooms, and students know these rooms as hubs of knowledge.

The teacher plays a pivotal role in creating this center of expertise. These teachers understand that knowledge of students, content, and pedagogy are intertwined and deep. They are knowledgeable and passionate about their subject area (Ladson-Billings 1994; Haberman 1995; Elmore, Peterson, and McCarthey 1996; Darling-Hammond 1997; Wasley, Hampel, and Clark 1997). They enjoy creating their own curriculum, taking mandated curriculum and varying it to meet their students' needs, and devising innovative ways of teaching the particular content. Linda Darling-Hammond (1997) writes that effective teachers understand subject matter thoroughly enough to organize it so that students can create useful cognitive maps of the terrain they are studying. Teachers need more than formulaic or procedural understanding of the core ideas in a discipline and how these help to structure knowledge. . . . Teachers also need to be able to use subject matter knowledge flexibly to address ideas as they come up in the course of learning. They need to understand how inquiry in a field is conducted and what reasoning entails. . . . And they need to see ways that ideas connect across fields and to everyday life, so that they can select and use meaningful examples, problems, and applications. (p. 294)

These teachers also have an extensive "bag of tricks" that will stimulate a diverse group of students. These strategies are not merely "fun and cute"; their purpose is to challenge, not entertain, all students. The combination of deep content knowledge and effective teaching strategies combines into "pedagogical content knowledge." Lee Shulman (1987) defines this as representing

the blending of content and pedagogy into an understanding of how particular topics, problems, or issues are organized, represented, and adapted to the diverse interests and abilities of learners and presented for instruction. Pedagogical content knowledge is the category most likely to distinguish the understanding of the content specialist from that of the pedagogue."(p. 8)

Most teachers who accelerate learning create a center of expertise in the classroom not only to showcase their own knowledge and passions but those of their students as well. Many of these teachers consider themselves "constructivist" teachers (Levin 1986; Darling-Hammond 1997). They build on students' prior knowledge and interests so that students can internalize new knowledge and demonstrate expertise. This requires considerable knowledge of students (especially their prior knowledge and interests), content, and pedagogy. In constructivist classrooms, teachers have such a thorough knowledge of the subject matter that they can anticipate where students will take a subject or an issue and use this interest to meet the lesson, unit, or course objectives. The teacher understands where students' ideas originate and the direction these ideas may take the class. This knowledge gives the teacher the capacity to anticipate productive and nonproductive lines of inquiry.

Finally, classrooms become centers of expertise because the teachers have deep knowledge *about* children and youth (e.g., child development, learning issues, cultural and economic influences) and *of* the individual students in their care, and they can mesh this knowledge with externally mandated standards, goals, and expectations. These teachers understand that planning begins with knowledge of and about students and builds toward goals set by the teacher, the school, the district, and the state. Teachers with a thorough knowledge of students, both individually and collectively, know what they must do to help students meet standards and master challenging curriculum (Darling-Hammond 1997).

The teacher is the "learning leader" in the classroom, transmitting passion for ongoing learning. Maintenance of a center of expertise requires ongoing learning on the part of all members of the classroom culture, including the teacher. Those teachers with a passion for their work, their subject, and their students constantly seek opportunities to expand and deepen their knowledge and expertise. This deep knowledge and passion is continuously developed and refined through reading, professional development, interaction with others, and reflection. Teachers enliven their classrooms with their excitement of discovery, new knowledge, and new skills. Teachers' passion for learning is infectious; students in such classrooms catch this passion and enthusiasm, realizing that the subject area is interesting and engaging. Because these teachers believe that all students can learn, they focus on improving their own ability to motivate students rather than identifying weaknesses in their students (Ladson-Billings 1994; Haberman 1995; Darling-Hammond 1997).

To optimize the classroom's development as a center of expertise, teachers actively engage in professional communities at their school and beyond (McCarthey and Peterson 1993; Lewis, Kruse, and Marks 1996; St. John, Meza, Allen-Haynes, Davidson 1996; Darling-Hammond 1997). At the school level, teachers use peer support teams (Reese and Ahlas 1999), study groups, cadres (Hopfenberg et al. 1993; St. John, Meza, Allen-Haynes, Davidson 1996), and action research teams (Calhoun 1994) to grow, both individually and collectively. Beyond the school, teachers expand their expertise by pursuing accreditation from the National Board for Professional Teaching Standards (National Commission on Teaching and America's Future 1996; Darling-Hammond 1997), engaging in professional development classes, graduate programs, or by taking an active role in professional organizations. If they teach in a professional development school, they become active participants in such partnerships (Goodlad 1990; McCarthey and Peterson 1993).

Foremost, teachers who create centers of expertise realize that their learning must be deep and reflective. To create a center of expertise or to teach for understanding involves more than teaching differently; it involves developing a different relationship with knowledgeable people in the field, being willing to have practice scrutinized, and being willing to scrutinize others. Successful teachers change not only their view of how to teach but also their "view of how knowledge about teaching is developed, understood, and communicated to others" (Elmore, Peterson, and McCarthey 1996: 243). In addition, they are able to "translate the 'big ideas' of ambitious teaching into familiar practices" (Elmore, Peterson, and McCarthey 1996: 230). Teachers are more apt to hold these views and classrooms are more apt to become centers of expertise when they exist within a supportive school culture.

Assumptions Related to Appropriate Educational Practices

Assumptions That Discourage Acceleration

Memorization of facts and drill are the focus of teaching. Many teachers rely on seatwork and drill because they assume these are the most appropriate strategies for many students. Students, although they dread the monotony of these classrooms (Wasley, Hampel, and Clark 1997; Phelan, Davidson, and Yu 1998), come to expect, and by the time they reach high school even negotiate for, this low-level cognitive work (McQuillan 1998). As described by Janice Hale (1994), this routine, even as early as elementary school, becomes deadening:

> The children do dittoed sheets, workbook sheets, and chalkboard work. Then the teacher goes over the dittoed sheets, the workbook sheets, and the chalkboard work. In the morning, the teacher writes on the chalkboard the pages in the textbook the children should read and the questions at the end of the chapter that they should complete. In essence, the children teach themselves. (p. 205)

Memorization of facts, drill, and seatwork lead to little discussion and exploration of ideas. Students have no opportunity to grapple with the meaning of the material they are learning; they are merely expected to memorize facts, formulas, and procedures—to learn the "basics." Most of the work students accomplish is disconnected from their own experience and from the skills and knowledge the teacher expects them to gain (Metz 1978; Oakes 1985; Hale 1994; Ladson-Billings 1994; Darling-Hammond 1997).

Why are so many classrooms characterized by a heavy reliance on seatwork, dittoes, lecture, memorization, and textbook questions? Two explanations have already been offered in preceding sections. The first relates to expectations for students. When everyone in the classroom (the teacher and students) holds low expectations for learning, undemanding instructional strategies are tolerated (Ladson-Billings 1994; Shields 1995; Darling-Hammond 1997). With a focus on what students lack, teachers assume they can eliminate weaknesses one discrete skill at a time.

The second explanation relates to expectations for teachers, specifically to expectations for ongoing learning and subject matter expertise. Research points to the connection between lack of teacher expertise and reliance on tasks with limited challenge (Knapp 1995; Elmore, Peterson, and McCarthey 1996; Darling-Hammond 1997). Teachers lacking a deep knowledge of the subject and a willingness to take risks, often avoid teaching strategies that might unveil the limits of their knowledge. Those who have ventured into more engaging teaching often pull back to the safety of traditional practices when they realize the "thicket of intellectual and practical questions" that arise when they open up the classroom discourse (Elmore, Peterson, and McCarthey 1996: 234).

Emphasis is placed on order; students work alone in their seats. Hand in hand with an emphasis on memorization, seatwork, and drill is a belief that strict order must be maintained at all times. In many classrooms, students are rarely allowed to leave their seats, and the penalty for unauthorized movement is the elimination of recess (Hale 1994), more repetitive seatwork, or isolation for the rest of the class. A vicious cycle begins in these classrooms because the more the teacher attempts to control the class, the more disruptive or withdrawn students become. In her study of the relationship between classroom management and teaching for meaning, Heather McCollum (1995) found an interesting correlation:

> Thus, in classrooms in which there was a great deal of seatwork that was unconnected (in the students' minds) to anything important or interesting, teachers had a more difficult time establishing order. This is ironic, because some of these teachers emphasized seatwork precisely because they wanted to control the class. In contrast, classrooms with an interesting and varied diet of academic work were more likely to display a higher degree of order. (p. 31)

The situation is even worse in middle and high schools because teachers fear the students and administrators value order over learning (Cusick 1983; Oakes 1985; Page 1987; McQuillan 1998).

Maintenance of order and severely restricted student movement reflect an emphasis on management of *behavior* rather than management of *learning*. These teachers build a classroom culture around two assumptions that prove to be problematic in many classrooms (McQuillan 1998). The first is that students, as individuals, understand what is in their best interest and are motivated by rewards and punishments. This ignores peer influence, the collective creation of meaning in the classroom (Page 1987; McQuillan 1998), and the dynamic of student subgroup expectations for "appropriate classroom behavior" (Lee 1994, 1996; Phelan, Davidson, and Yu 1998). The second problematic assumption is that rewards and punishments are applied consistently (McQuillan 1998). Students quickly realize that social status, gender, ethnicity, and perceived academic ability influence teachers' use of rewards and punishments (Spindler and Spindler 1982; McQuillan 1998). Early adolescents, with their heightened sense of justice and fairness, rebel when they see inconsistencies in rewards and punishments. Students withdraw or actively oppose such systems seeing that they are arbitrary and that their peer group finds little value in the rewards and punishments.

Many of these classrooms are harsh environments that promote individualism and competition (Dreeben 1967; Florio-Ruane 1989) over collaboration and common goals. They ignore the interdependence stressed in many families and communities (Greenfield 1994). For example, research among Native American, Hispanic, African American, and Asian communities points to an emphasis on the development of a sense of self as a part of a social group (e.g., typically the family) rather than as an individual. Such interdependence promotes cooperation rather than competition (Phillips 1983; Ladson-Billings 1994; Greenfield 1994) and is at odds with classrooms in which students are expected to work alone and to compete against their classmates for grades and attention.

Emphasis is placed on acquisition of basic skills.   Classroom cultures that discourage acceleration adhere to the "conventional wisdom [that] focuses on what children lack (e.g., print awareness, grasp of Standard English syntax, a supportive home environment) and seeks to remedy these deficiencies by teaching discrete skills (e.g., decoding skills, language mechanics, arithmetic computation)" (Knapp 1995a: 6). A teacher interviewed by Spillane and Jennings (1997) illustrates this conventional wisdom:

> So we did a lot more critical thinking type activities [at an elite private school] because they already knew the basics. I didn't have to go back and backtrack to try to get them to where they needed to be. Whereas here [in a low-income urban public school] I feel like I'm constantly trying to play catch up. . . . I repeat myself a lot more here. I do a lot more vocabulary because their vocabulary is more limited. I have to do, you know, some more basic things as opposed to what I was doing before [critical thinking]. (pp. 20–21)

Despite research that challenges the sequential view of learning (e.g., that basic skills must be mastered prior to the introduction of higher-order skills) (McLaughlin and Talbert 1993), classroom instruction from kindergarten through twelfth grade is dominated by an emphasis on acquisition of basic skills. Not only is there extensive research showing that students disengage when classroom routines become monotonous (Darling-Hammond 1997; Wasley, Hampel, and Clark 1997), but cognitive psychologists have found that "'basic' and 'higher-order' instructional tasks each have their own inherent demands. Mastery of one type of task does not necessarily lead to proficiency on the other type of task" (McLaughlin and Talbert 1993: 178).

This belief in the sequential nature of learning is complicated at the high school level by the script of the "Real School" (Metz 1998). To be a

Real School, all high schools offer the same classes despite vast differences in student preparation and without special training for teachers to simultaneously teach basic and higher-order skills. Mary Haywood Metz concludes that "the curriculum was a symbolic statement of their equality and their worth" (p. 5); a curriculum that mirrors those offered in more affluent communities makes the school a Real School, the teachers Real Teachers, and the students, Real Students. The effect of enacting Real School on the classroom is a wide divergence in what is taught under the same course title, not a challenging opportunity for low-income students. For example, students enrolled in advanced English classes might be learning elementary-level grammar skills while being expected to write papers on Dante's *Inferno*; students in mandatory physics classes spend time reviewing basic arithmetic skills and may never touch on half of the physics course objectives. In both cases, the students' transcripts will indicate successful completion of a course that should be challenging.

Assumptions That Encourage Acceleration

All students engage in active exploration of relevant material. Many classrooms are active places in which knowledge is constructed or produced rather than reproduced (Newmann, Secada, Wehlage 1995). The kind of teaching and learning demonstrated in these classrooms has been variously described as powerful learning (Hopfenberg et al. 1993; Keller and Huebner 1997), authentic instruction or authentic achievement (Newmann, Secada, and Wehlage 1995; Newmann et al. 1996), teaching for meaning (Knapp et al. 1995), and teaching for understanding (Cohen, McLaughlin, and Talbert 1993; Darling-Hammond 1997). These approaches represent constructivist beliefs that the teaching and learning process is one of transaction, not transmission, that learning is constructed, not acquired by the learner. These classrooms resemble those usually reserved only for students identified as gifted or talented (Tomlinson 1996).

Classrooms nestled in school cultures that encourage this kind of teaching and learning have the advantage of a well-defined and shared understanding of how to encourage acceleration in all students. For example, teachers in schools engaged in the Accelerated Schools Project bring the concept of "powerful learning" alive in their classrooms (Hopfenberg et al. 1993; Keller and Huebner 1997). They ensure that learning is authentic, interactive, student-centered, inclusive, and continuous and that lessons and units build on the interaction between content, pedagogy, and the learning context (Keller and Huebner 1997). In schools engaged in the Coalition of Essential Schools, teachers are encouraged to create classrooms in which civil discourse prevails, student learning is targeted and in-depth (e.g., the adage "less is more" prevails), and students take responsibility for their learning while teachers guide rather than deliver knowledge acquisition (Sizer 1992b; Wasley, Hampel, and Clark 1997). As the following quote from a high school boy illustrates, students appreciate this kind of classroom environment:

> I like hands-on stuff. Especially in my new English class. It's different from all of my other classes where I can expect the same thing every day. Whenever we go into English, anything can break out. One day we are reading something. The next day we are acting something. The next day we have something to research. . . . It's a challenge. The teacher always has us doing something different. (Wasley, Hampel, and Clark 1997: 42)

This kind of learning is culturally and developmentally relevant as well as academically rigorous. All students are provided an opportunity to learn relevant subject matter and appropriate and significant skills and dispositions; the content they learn is accurate, and they acquire knowledge through disciplined inquiry that has value and meaning beyond school (Newmann, Secada, and Wehlage 1995: 3–4). Students also learn in an environment that is culturally relevant, in which the teacher's notion of knowledge is created through deep understanding of students' backgrounds. In such classrooms, knowledge is

> continuously re-created, recycled, and shared by teachers and students alike. They [teachers] view the content of the curriculum critically and are passionate about it. Rather than expecting students to demonstrate prior knowledge and skills, they help students develop that knowledge by building bridges and scaffolding for learning. (Ladson-Billings 1994: 25)

All students have the opportunity to develop basic skills and higher-order thinking skills. As described above, instruction in many classrooms is based on a belief in a sequential learning process, beginning with basic skills and building toward more advanced, higher-order skills (Knapp 1995a; Spillane and Jennings 1997; Jennings 1998). Classrooms in which acceleration occurs are exceptions. In these classrooms, teachers expect all students to engage in higher-order thinking tasks while they are learning and refining basic skills (Tomlinson 1996). These teachers recognize that their students may not possess expected basic skills, but they see this as one of the primary reasons why students need opportunities to develop higher-order skills. A fifth grade teacher explains why she emphasizes challenging, conceptually oriented instruction:

> One of the things I do in this class that I think is vital is to ask them what they did and why they did it. I try to prize everyone's thoughts because too many times—and not just in school—they've not been allowed to express

anything but the right answer which they don't often think they know so they shut down. They quit. They have no confidence in their own abilities to think. And that is the big deal for me. I want them to learn that they can use their brains and work things out for themselves. That doesn't happen in many places in their lives so it has to happen here. (Jennings 1998: 16)

Many of these teachers work with children culturally different from themselves, and while they value students' ideas, prior knowledge, and cultural heritage, they also expect students to gain skills needed to function effectively in mainstream society. Lisa Delpit (1988) argues that students of color learn best when their voice and language are valued. However, they also need to be taught

the codes needed to participate fully in the mainstream of American life, not by being forced to attend to hollow, inane, de-contextualized sub-skills, but rather within the context of meaningful communicative endeavors; that they be allowed the resources of the teacher's expert knowledge, while being helped to acknowledge their own "expertness" as well." (p. 296)

Students learn to work productively with each other. The kind of learning environment described above requires active engagement of students in their own learning. To be actively engaged, they are often working or engaged in discourse together. In these classrooms, everyone values trust and decency (e.g., fairness, generosity, and tolerance) and holds high expectations of each other (Sizer 1992b; Wasley, Hampel, and Clark 1997). Teachers skilled at developing positive interactions among students often frame assignments in terms of a shared challenge rather than as knowledge to acquire (Marks, Doane, and Secada 1996). In working toward a shared challenge, students are encouraged by their peers to take responsibility for learning and to recognize and build on each others' strengths. Competition between students is reduced since they are working toward common goals.

Collaborative work brings together students with different experiences, ideas, and expertise. As students work together they are encouraged to verbalize their knowledge. As described above, verbalizing ideas and knowledge serves two purposes. First, it helps students internalize and refine their thought processes. Second, it exposes other students to ideas and knowledge they otherwise might not have considered. These encounters stretch students' "zones of proximal development" or their current level of competence (Palincsar and Brown 1984).

Students take collaborative learning seriously when they know that they are working toward increasing their knowledge of a subject or solving a relevant problem. They find group work contrived when the goals and the direction of the learning are closely controlled by the teacher

(Ladson-Billings 1994). Teachers who use student group work effectively provide students with the skills to work in groups, the expectation that their work is valuable, and the freedom to take the assignment in directions they choose.

Moving Classroom Culture Toward Acceleration

Because of the isolation of most classrooms, changing their culture is typically more difficult than changing school culture. In this chapter we describe how classrooms are bounded, existing as separate entities within a school culture. One of the most important steps in changing classroom culture is to initiate activities or establish systems to reduce isolation, to open classroom doors. Teachers who accelerate learning engage in constant communication with each other. They visit each other's rooms, discuss student learning, research effective practices, and jointly plan units and lessons.

This kind of exchange often happens informally between like-minded teachers; to encourage it on a broader scale requires more formal vehicles. Communication among teachers can be encouraged through establishing peer support teams to provide an opportunity to observe, reflect on, and analyze each others' teaching (Showers and Joyce 1996). Peer support teams work best when regular opportunities to observe teaching and reflect on the observations are built into the school calendar.[3] Isolation is also reduced when teachers are involved in ongoing research and discussion of curriculum and instruction. Many schools encourage this through action research projects, study groups, or through involvement in teams, committees, or cadres devoted to a systematic examination of student learning, curriculum, and instruction.

In addition, classroom cultures are more likely to encourage accelerated learning when everyone in the school is committed to a shared vision and all members of the school community are held responsible for making the vision a reality in the classroom. This involves considerable reflection on assumptions and practices on the part of all teachers and other instructional staff. This point is discussed in more depth in Chapter 8.

Teachers who nurture classrooms that accelerate learning are active lifelong learners. They are eager to learn, and their learning goes beyond adding more techniques to their "bag of tricks." They seek professional development opportunities that provide more depth of knowledge about content and about student learning (Stein, Smith, and Silver 1999). They are not afraid to admit that they do not know something, and they model a love of learning for their students.

Another point stressed in this chapter is that classroom culture is negotiated between the teacher and students. Because students are participants in shaping the classroom culture, they are part of the process of changing it to accelerate learning. The teacher and students negotiate a classroom culture through communication and discourse and, in so doing, define expectations for students, the teacher, other adults, and for appropriate educational practices.

Teachers who effectively guide this negotiation are analogous to conductors or coaches (Ladson-Billings 1994). They assume responsibility and act with authority, but the players (e.g., musicians, athletes, students) are the performers. They are ultimately responsible for the outcomes. The orchestra conductor holds the baton; the coach calls the plays and sets the strategy; the teacher determines how students will meet learning goals, but in all cases, the players make the music, run the ball, or learn the material. Ultimately, students are responsible members of a learning community.

The classroom is not a concert hall or a playing field, and the dynamics negotiated within the classroom are more varied and complex than those of a concert or game, but in each case, one person acts with authority for the sake of the group. In the classroom, the teacher has the authority to ensure that students take responsibility for their learning. This is best done by giving them a voice in the classroom, encouraging active dialogue and open communication, and providing learning experiences that are relevant.

In the preceding chapter we concluded that efforts to accelerate learning within school cultures can be sustained through careful cultivation. This involves holding high expectations for what will grow, providing a "rich growth medium," tending to the change once it has begun, and pruning away activities that are no longer effective. Creating a classroom culture that accelerates learning also involves a cultivation process; everyone must be committed to acceleration for it to take root. To keep this commitment growing, it must be tended and receive periodic pruning. The cultivation process in classrooms is different from that in a school because it is a more personal, individual process. School culture change is a group endeavor, and the energy and momentum of the group dictates the direction change takes. Classroom culture change benefits from a supportive school culture, but it ultimately rests with the individual teacher's commitment to making changes in his or her own assumptions and behavior and with the students' commitment to making learning a high priority.

Notes

1. The emphasis of the discussion will be on the negotiation between the teacher and students. Although teaching assistants, resource teachers, and parents can have a profound effect on classroom culture, most classrooms are the do-

main of a single teacher and a group of students. The influence of other adults on the classroom culture will be described only where appropriate.

2. In the 1950s George Spindler observed in the classroom of an ambitious white middle-class teacher who was well regarded in the school. Spindler found that Harker attributed positive attributes to white, middle-class students (intelligence, popularity) while denying these attributes to minority students. In fact, some of the white students he labeled as popular had few friends in the classroom.

3. Within the Accelerated Schools Project a number of schools have initiated peer support teams. Typically ten to twelve days are scheduled throughout the school year for these teams. Teams of three to four teachers observe one team member for forty-five minutes, then the observers and the observed teacher meet for another forty-five minutes to reflect on the lesson. Substitutes rotate through the school, covering classes of all teachers interested in being on peer support teams (Accelerated Schools Project Newsletter 1999).

8 Individuals as Cultivators: Acting on Changed Assumptions Within and Beyond the School

After four years as an accelerated school, Westview Elementary School decided to reexamine its vision statement. The school had made many changes in curriculum and instruction, but members of the school community knew they could still improve the school. Through the process of revising the vision, the whole school community realized that increasing everyone's awareness of personal responsibility toward student learning was a key to reaching Westview's vision. They decided to host a community forum to discuss responsibilities for learning at the school. Invitations to the forum were sent to everyone in the community, including politicians, the news media, businesses, and teacher educators at the local state college.

The meeting was well attended; the mayor, school board members, school of education faculty, newspaper and television reporters, the district superintendent, president of the button factory, middle and high school teachers, parents (both English-speaking and Spanish-speaking), all Westview teachers, the principal, students, bus drivers, and cafeteria workers attended. They brainstormed ways for all members of the community to take responsibility for student learning. A subcommittee formed to draft a Proclamation of Responsibility, and all participants agreed to continue to meet throughout the year to reinforce their commitment to student learning. The following are examples of immediate actions groups agreed to take:

- Middle and high school teachers agreed to involve their students in working with individual elementary students in the after-school program.
- The news reporters agreed to consider whether a story was likely to encourage efforts to accelerate learning before covering it.

- Teachers agreed to remain active learners and to encourage communication, reflection, and discussion with colleagues.
- Students agreed to do their personal best and to encourage peers to do the same.
- The superintendent and school board chair agreed to accept well-researched proposals for change and to attempt to find resources to support them.

In the preceding chapters we identify sets of assumptions that have the potential to bring about change in school and classroom culture to accelerate the learning of all students.* This discussion highlights how assumptions held by diverse people form the collective culture in schools and classrooms. Change in the collective culture does not occur without change occurring in the individuals who come together to make the collective culture. This chapter, as illustrated by the example of Westview Elementary School, moves from the collective assumptions that make up school and classroom cultures to the actions individuals can take to make the school experience rewarding and challenging for all students. The chapter then returns to collective actions that will encourage and sustain the actions of individuals.

The kind of change proposed below involves both change in assumptions and change in behavior. One might ask which should come first. As in many "chicken and egg" situations, this depends. In some cases, changed behavior follows changed assumptions; in others, changes in assumptions result from changes in behavior. Which comes first is dependent on multiple factors, such as the interpersonal dynamics, context, leadership, and administrative mandates in a particular setting. In any case, it does not take massive school reform to begin to cultivate change. It can begin as simply as an individual doing something differently or several people engaging in meaningful dialogue. Change also begins when effective teachers talk about the assumptions from which their classroom or school behaviors stem.

Assumptions, Beliefs, and Actions

As discussed in Chapter 5, assumptions form a set of beliefs that shape what we value and what we do. Deeply seated and seldom examined, assumptions are our conjectures, theories, and speculations regarding all facets of life. They shape our values, which, in turn, shape our actions. For example, based on the assumption that "you only live once," a person forms a set of values that suggests how to behave in this one lifetime.

---

*This chapter was written by Diane C. Cudahy and Christine Finnan.

The values are put into operation by the manner in which the person lives. People have gotten themselves into considerable trouble acting on the assumption, "it won't happen to me." These assumptions, values, and actions can change, as exemplified by the assumptions held about women and education. As late as 1859, most people assumed that higher education was harmful to women's reproduction systems, so higher education for women was not valued. This belief was expressed in statements, such as "women don't need more schooling," and in actions, such as barring women from many universities. Although assumptions may be slow to change, this example illustrates that even deeply held assumptions can change.

So it is with assumptions regarding students and learning. The assumptions held by both those inside and those outside schools lead to actions, decisions, and policies, all of which come together to frame and influence school and classroom culture. These actions, when purposefully directed toward improving schools and classrooms, are seen by everyone as a set of responsibilities. Some assumptions lead to unintended and unfortunate consequences for students; others support accelerating learning of all students. In the following discussion, the assumptions that can facilitate accelerated learning are translated into tangible, observable actions and eventually into a set of responsibilities taken by people or groups of people.

Changing school and classroom culture to accelerate the learning of all students does not occur by changing *things*. Although new buildings, technological support, and safe school buses are important, they are not cultural changes; they do not represent changes in people's assumptions. Extending the school year or day, detracking, blocking classes, and other modifications in structure indicate change, but these changes are significant only if they are a reflection of, or lead to, assumptions that encourage accelerated learning for all students. Change begins within individuals—since assumptions are held by and acted upon by *individuals*. True change occurs when a teacher *acts* on the assumption that every child, even the one who comes from the poorest home, comes to class with strengths. This change becomes a part of the culture when the teacher assumes that these actions are his or her responsibility.

Responsibilities of Individuals Within Schools and Classrooms

Chapters 6 and 7 identify groups of people internal to a school and within a classroom who are the keys to changing school and classroom culture. At the school level they include principals, teachers, students, and staff. Parents and district office administrators, although not in the school building all of the time, can also be considered key players within schools. Their collective assumptions about students, adults, appropriate educational practice, the value of change, and communication within the classroom create and maintain the positive school and classroom cultures described above. At the classroom level, all of the above people have an influence, but the key actors in changing classroom culture are the teacher and students. Below are some of the actions each of these sets of individuals inside schools can take to accelerate the learning of all students. The responsibilities assumed by these individuals are summarized in Table 8.1 and are generated in response to the statement: If I am truly committed to acting in the best interest of *all* students and wish to accelerate their learning, then it is my job, my responsibility, to do the following.

Actions of School-Level Administrators
That Support Accelerated Learning

When viewed collectively, administrators who are committed to the acceleration of learning act very differently than traditional hierarchical, authoritarian administrators (Deal and Peterson 1998; Christensen 1996; Evans 1996). These administrators build on the strengths of everyone in the school, promoting a unity that fosters a sense of "we," not "I" and "them." Their focus is shifted from designing controls to developing capacity in their staff (Darling-Hammond 1997), their students, and themselves. They operate the school on democratic principles. Leaders who sustain school reform of this type solicit the input of many people. Parents, community members, teachers, staff, and students are encouraged to make their opinions known. Administrators who accelerate learning promote learning among all members of the school community; they are active learners and expect the same of everyone else. In addition, they distribute both authority and responsibility throughout the community (United States Department of Education 1996).

Administrators take their role as keeper of the dream very seriously (Deal and Peterson 1998). They encourage celebrations, actively promote the school, and hold everyone to the high standards set in the school's vision. At the same time, they create and maintain many avenues for reaching the vision, which build on the diverse skills, personalities, and experiences of their staff and community. They keep a wide-angled lens focused on the whole vision as they deal with individual staff, student, and community concerns (United States Department of Education 1996).

The administrator serves as the buffer, a sort of "traffic cop" who protects teachers and students from distractions and interruptions. The intercom remains silent except in emergency situations, and administrative business is handled before or after school. Instructional time is guarded for all students so that learning does not become fragmented. The admin-

TABLE 8.1   Responsibilities of Individuals Inside Schools

Responsibilities of School-Level Administrators
- Actively encourage, expect, provide for, and reward high standards of achievement by all students.
- Establish an environment of care and trust in the school.
- Assemble a high-quality staff who share commitment to accelerating the learning of all students.
- Facilitate open and frequent communication among and between all members of the school community.
- Foster partnerships with parents and between parents and teachers.
- Support teachers' decisions about appropriate educational practice.
- Share decisionmaking, authority, and leadership.
- Provide for continual development of expertise of myself and all other staff members.
- Actively participate in the education profession through modeling high professional standards, mentoring, and disseminating best practice knowledge.
- Advocate for a high-quality education for all students.

Responsibilities of Teachers and School-Based Professionals
- Promote a climate of care and trust in the classroom and school.
- Create a learning environment for students in which they are all actively engaged with challenging material.
- Maintain and continuously develop content and pedagogical expertise and share this passion for lifelong learning with students.
- View and plan for each student as an individual (i.e., take into account a student's developmental level, learning style, strengths, interests, prior knowledge, culture, community, "dreams").
- Lead courageously, in children's best interests, based on knowledge and expertise.
- Give students an active voice and listen to them.
- Allow and encourage students to take an active role in the negotiation of learning.
- Be an active participant in the education profession through modeling high professional standards, mentoring, and disseminating best practice knowledge.
- Work with colleagues, administrators, parents, and students to build and maintain a school culture that promotes accelerated learning for all students.

Responsibilities of Students
- Care about myself and my peers.
- Take learning seriously for myself and others.
- Actively engage in classroom activity.
- Hold visions of the future in which my peers and I are productive, contributing members of society.
- Work productively, both independently and with others.
- Live by the rules negotiated by everyone in the school.
- Reciprocate the trust and care offered to me by adults.

(continues)

TABLE 8.1   *(continued)*

Responsibilities of Parents
- Hold high expectations for my own children and all children.
- Communicate openly with my children.
- Advocate for my own children and all children.
- Support the work of teachers.
- Share expertise and time with school.
- Have children present and ready for school each day.
- Reciprocate the care and trust that teachers and administrators offer me.

Responsibilities of Staff Members
- Model respectful behavior and modes of communication.
- Promote a climate of care and trust in the school.
- Hold high expectations for the behavior and achievement of all students.
- Support teachers as educational leaders.
- Participate in decisionmaking of the school.

Responsibilities of District Office Administrators
- Work as partners with teachers, administrators, and other school-based professionals to support their efforts to accelerate the learning of all students.
- Provide specialized support for special needs students.
- Recognize that people closest to the students make the best decisions for their students.
- Serve as a buffer between schools and directives from outside of the school.
- Ensure that schools are adequately funded and staffed with high-quality professionals.

istrator takes control of the schedule and seeks ways to make "time" an ally of learning, not the enemy (Armeta and Darwin 1998). As administrators buffer classrooms from interruption, they also scrutinize the teaching and learning that occurs in each classroom to be sure that isolated examples of poor teaching, little learning, and low expectations do not exist in the school. Mediocrity in any classroom is not accepted.

Administrators who cultivate acceleration take deliberate action to build competency and efficacy in their staff. They do not send down edicts for change; these are determined in dialogue with their staff. They are willing to question new programs and policies of their supervisors and boards in light of the competency and opinions of their instructional staff and what is best for all students. They are adept negotiators of policy, knowing when to push supervisors and board members and when to wait for a more auspicious time to question decisions.

Students learn best in an environment of high expectations and praise and celebration of individual accomplishments (Stocklinski and Miller-Colbert 1991). Administrators make sure this happens by keeping the educational achievement of students squarely in the center of all considerations. They hold their teaching staff accountable for every student's achievement. They hold their support staff and volunteers responsible for contributing positively to the learning of all students. They ensure that the school sends a message of high expectations for every student, and they work with parents to realize dreams and, in some cases, to broaden dreams for their children.

Actions of Teachers and School-Based Professionals That Support Accelerated Learning

Just as the actions of the principal or assistant principal model the assumptions and values for which the school stands (Deal and Peterson 1998) so too do the actions of the classroom teacher and other professionals (e.g., guidance counselors, psychologists, media specialists, behavior interventionists, therapists, etc.). All decisions and actions, whether they are examined or unexamined, purposeful or habitual, convey subtly and not so subtly the assumptions of the teacher.

Although the administrators set the tone for schoolwide reform, there cannot be any significant innovation in education that does not have at its center the assumptions of teachers and other school-based professionals. Indeed it is an illusion to think otherwise (Postman and Weingartner 1979). Day in and day out, teachers' actions convey to students the purpose of school and the students' role in it. The craft of teaching is essentially the actualization of a teacher's assumptions and value system and the transmission of this to students (Ayers 1994; Swadener and Kessler 1991). The same is true for school-based professionals. Guidance counselors work from their assumptions about students and families as they guide students to make good decisions. They are quick to encourage students to push for more, while they provide support when students struggle. Psychologists and therapists bring to their work assumptions about student weaknesses and appropriate interventions. They learn to look for strengths of students even when their training typically prepares them to identify weaknesses.

Teachers who accelerate the learning of all students reject the assumption that poverty precludes academic success (Ascher 1993; Payne 1998) and accept students as they are. Most importantly, they take responsibility to ensure that all students learn (Haberman 1995; Darling-Hammond 1997). To ensure that all students learn, teachers turn first to an examination of their own teaching and the curriculum before looking at factors outside of the classroom. They do not readjust their sense of responsibility for student learning in a downward manner and lower goals due to a child's background (Metz 1993). They refuse to blame the students and their parents for low achievement (Haberman 1995; Cook and Fine 1995), although they make students and parents aware of their own responsibilities for learning.

Because these teachers assume that students will actively engage in learning if given the opportunity, they create environments conducive to learning. Their classrooms are inviting learning environments that build on students' diversity and strengths. They build close, caring, trusting relationships with students and their families. They listen to their students and create an environment that encourages dialogue, debate, reflection, and active listening. These teachers are not easy; they do not coddle students. They provide continuous assessment of student progress and understand what students know at the beginning of each unit and encourage constant growth toward meeting standards.

Teachers who accelerate learning base their instructional decisions on sound, proven pedagogical knowledge, a pedagogy that combines theoretical knowledge, applied research, and "best practice" knowledge (Shulman 1987). Their teaching is student-centered, structured, and rigorous. It stresses higher-order thinking skills and is eclectic. Finally, it is integrally related to the reality of students' lives, experiences, and cultures, and it is conducted in an atmosphere of mutual respect and enthusiasm (Ladson-Billings and Henry 1990; Brookhart and Rusnak 1993; Ladson-Billings 1994; Newmann, Secada, and Wehlage 1995). These teachers find the appropriate and necessary ways of making the school "fit" the child instead of making the child "fit" the school (Cudahy 1996).

Teachers and other school-based professionals are active in their profession. They work with colleagues in their school for schoolwide improvement and with colleagues in professional organizations to improve their profession. They serve as advocates for students in their school and community. They recognize that they, too, must be lifelong learners. They transmit their passion for learning to students and experiment constantly with new ideas. When afforded the opportunity to study or participate in a workshop on a new methodology, they embrace the opportunity. They understand that high-achieving students are taught by high-achieving teachers (Darling-Hammond 1997).

Actions of Students That Support Accelerated Learning

Students' actions related to learning are developed in the classroom, home and community. Creating an environment in which students take responsibility for their actions falls primarily on teachers, school staff, and parents. Students do have responsibilities related to accelerating learning, but adults have the responsibility to guide them and set an environment in which they are encouraged to take responsibility. Students very quickly learn what behavior is expected of them. By the age of eight most children have already internalized the purpose of school. As most schools are currently structured, elementary-aged students list the following as expectations: to learn, stick to tasks, do their work, raise their hands, volunteer answers, remember facts for tests, listen, stay out of trouble, go to school even when it is boring, and put up with school so that they can be with friends (Gleaves 1994).

In schools that accelerate the learning of all students, students learn that they are expected to be actively engaged in their learning, take responsibility for learning, and resist the temptation to negotiate with teachers for less-challenging assignments (Sizer 1992b; Wasley, Hampel, and Clark 1997; Schlechty 1997; McQuillan 1998). In addition, students actively engage in productive classroom discourse. They complete assignments and participate in whole class and small group work. They are willing to express ideas and to listen openly to the ideas expressed by their peers and teachers. In this context, they allow a democratic exchange of ideas to flourish (Florio-Ruane 1989; Phelan, Davidson, and Yu 1998; McQuillan 1998). Coupled with these expectations for students is an expectation that they will be taught in classrooms that provide opportunities for active exploration of content and ideas, engage them in relevant and interesting assignments, and provide an atmosphere conducive to an open exchange of ideas.

To be active participants in accelerating their own learning and that of their peers, students learn about power and who has it, praise and who gets it, and authority and how and when to challenge it (Apple 1979). Rather than resisting school and classroom culture, they work collaboratively with adults to ensure that everyone in the school is challenged and that adults exert authority based on knowledge rather than on a hidden curriculum (Jordan, Methna, and Webb 1996). Students take these actions in an environment in which their opinions are valued and everyone is striving for the same learning goals.

In addition, students take responsibility for interacting with their peers in a supportive, caring manner (Phelan, Davidson, and Yu 1998). They seek to understand culture and class differences and resist the temptation to assume that their values, beliefs, and behaviors are right or more valid than those of other students. They view school as an opportunity to not only learn the official curriculum taught in class but to learn about other students, especially those different from themselves.

Within schools committed to accelerating the learning of all students, students also serve as change agents. Their enthusiasm for learning makes teachers quick to accept new programs, methodologies, or procedures, especially when teachers find they increase the learning of their students (Guskey 1986). In this way student success can lead to changes in assumptions and beliefs in teachers.

Actions of Parents That Support Accelerated Learning

The relationship between parental involvement and academic success of students is well documented (White, Taylor, and Moss 1992; Henderson 1988). Too often teachers and principals assume that parents must be in-

volved *in* the school for students to be successful.[1] Although students of
parents heavily committed to school are likely to succeed, Nieto's (1992)
studies show that home activities and intangibles such as consistent communication, high expectations, pride, understanding, and enthusiasm for
their children's school experiences contribute to their children's success
in school. In this way parents demonstrate their commitment to accelerating the learning of their own children.

It is through involvement *at* the school that parents move from supporting the learning of their own children to supporting the learning of
all students. Most parents initially become involved in the school or
classroom to support their own children. Upon realizing that their own
children thrive in an environment in which all students are challenged,
they move from being advocates for their own children to becoming advocates for all students. In a school environment that encourages success
for all students, parents do not need to look out for their own children at
the expense of other children. In this context, parents become powerful
advocates for school change.

Parents have significant influence on educational policies and practices. Through connections in the community, informal grapevine discussions, financial contributions, and threats to withhold support of elected
officials, parents can promote the success of change initiatives or easily
derail them (Wells and Serna 1996; Konzal 1997).

Actions of Staff That Support Accelerated Learning

Often overlooked, but vitally important to developing and then articulat-
ing a school culture, are the actions of staff. This includes office workers,
teacher aides, cafeteria workers, security staff, the custodial department,
and bus drivers. Teaching assistants have a profound effect on the culture
of the classrooms in which they work. They join the teacher and students
in negotiating a classroom culture. The ways parents and children are
greeted at the front office of the school send messages. Am I welcome?
Am I a nuisance? Do I have any role here? Is this a kind and caring place?
All these questions are answered in how staff members interact with students, parents, and teachers.

Members of the community in which a school is located often fill staff
positions. Often parents are recruited to fill staff positions, formalizing
their relationship with the school. Because of their role as staff and
community members, staff members serve as conduits of information
and support between community, parents, and the school. In schools
that accelerate learning for all students, staff members exhibit behavior
similar to that described for teachers and parents. Along with other
members of the school community, they explore their assumptions
about students and the work of teachers, administrators, and staff.

Through this process they become essential contributors to the culture of school.

Actions of District Office Administrators That Support Accelerated Learning

District office administrators serve as both internal and external influences on efforts to accelerate the learning of all students. Within the school, they serve as partners with teachers and administrators, assisting with professional development, curriculum development, and instructional innovations. They work with special needs students to be sure these students receive needed services. District administrators recognize that people at the school level make the best decisions for their students and provide them support to carry out these decisions (Driver 1995).

Outside of the school, district administrators perform other services to support schools. They serve as a buffer between schools and district, state, and federal directives, shielding schools from some of these directives and providing support to implement others. They maintain relationships with professional organizations, textbook publishers, technology providers, teachers' unions, colleges and universities, and other sources of support for schools. They stay current on curricular and pedagogical innovations, sharing this expertise freely with teachers, administrators, and other school-based professionals.

The superintendent and other district administrators ensure that funds are used fairly and take care that schools serving low-income students receive funding that at least equals that of other schools. These administrators make difficult decisions with students' best interests in mind. For example, they may remove inadequate teachers or principals, or they may eliminate programs that are no longer serving students even when these decisions may be unpopular in the short term.

Responsibilities of Individuals Outside of Schools

The preceding chapters describe the assumptions held by people within schools that form school and classroom cultures. Important as teachers, administrators (building and district office), students, staff members, and parents are in changing schools and classrooms, they cannot do the job alone. People inside schools are the critical cultivators of culture change, but their efforts may be in vain if they clash with assumptions held by individuals outside of the school. Classrooms and schools can be rather closed, but they do not exist in isolation from external influences. Opinions expressed by members of the local communities surrounding or feeding schools, decisions made by policymakers and

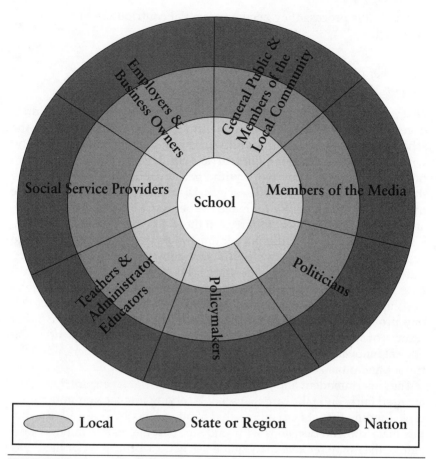

FIGURE 8.1   External Influences on School and Classroom Cultures

politicians, the manner in which the news media chooses to cover stories about schools all influence the culture created in schools and to a lesser degree in classrooms.

The individuals and groups that influence schools from the outside fall into many categories, and their influence varies depending on whether they reside in local communities or the wider society. Figure 8.1 describes the key groups of people in local communities, the state or region, and the nation that influence efforts to accelerate learning.

Chapter 5 presents a set of assumptions held by members of local communities and the wider society that influence school communities' and individual teachers' efforts to accelerate learning. The following discussion provides examples of what individuals outside of the school can do to support schools and classroom teachers. Table 8.2 summarizes the responsibilities that people outside of schools must assume to promote accelerated learning for all students.

TABLE 8.2   Responsibilities of Individuals Outside of Schools

Responsibilities of the General Public and Members of Local Communities
- Spend time in schools to better understand their dynamics.
- Listen to diverse voices in the community.
- Advocate for all children, not just those most like me.
- Vote with care and knowledge.

Responsibilities of Members of the Media
- Provide accurate and complete information.
- Avoid sensationalism and focus on what will best serve all students.
- Advocate for all students.
- Serve as a resource and partner to schools.

Responsibilities of Politicians
- Avoid using schools and educational issues to better own position.
- Be careful to work from accurate data.
- Listen to all constituents.
- Do not compromise if students might suffer.

Responsibilities of Policymakers
- Understand that policy implementation is a teaching/learning process.
- Engage in dialogue with teachers, administrators, and parents.
- Avoid political pressure and make policy based on the best interests of students.
- Understand the need to mesh policy with school's existing culture.
- Determine the policies that are best made at the local, state, and national levels.
- Be aware of the human and monetary costs of implementing policies.

Responsibilities of Teacher and Administrator Educators
- Provide programs that develop teachers' and administrators' skills and dispositions to work effectively with all students.
- Remain or become actively engaged in K–12 schools to bridge the gap between theory and practice.
- Support partnerships with K–12 schools to build on the expertise of teachers.
- Stay current with research, policies, and practice.
- Provide exposure to different schools, classrooms, and diverse students.

Responsibilities of Social Service Providers
- Reach out to public schools and be creative in designing easy access to services.
- Avoid "turf" battles with other service agencies.
- Make good use of limited resources.

Responsibilities of Employers and Business Owners
- Truly understand the skills needed by workers and work with schools to be sure students acquire them.
- Become partners with schools and provide mentors and tutors for students and opportunities for teachers to work with employers.
- Recognize that schools, students, and teachers are different from businesses, products, and employees.

Actions of the General Public and Members of
Local Communities That Support Accelerated Learning

The general public and members of local communities speak often, loudly, and influentially about their perceptions of schools. Other than expressing their opinions about schools, there are a number of ways community members can encourage schools to accelerate the learning of all students. First, they can support schools by spending time in them (Mathews 1996). As people gain a deeper and broader understanding of the challenges and excitement that exist in schools, their assumptions about schools and students change. Religious and community groups can take the lead in organizing mentoring programs, tutoring opportunities, fundraising events, and volunteer programs. The understanding of school cultures gained through such involvement cannot be achieved at a distance.

Additionally, members of the general public need to listen to the voices of all members of their community to understand the necessity of providing a challenging education to all students in the community and nation, not just their own children or the children in their neighborhood. To better understand the dynamics of most schools, people benefit from working with and listening to diverse people to understand multiple perspectives on issues. This involves keeping an open mind, actively listening to diverse views, and challenging opinions and actions that may not serve the best interests of all students.

At a minimum, the general public and members of the local communities need to be actively engaged in the electoral process and to vote with care and knowledge of issues and candidates' platforms regarding education. They can identify their own assumptions regarding school and question the assumptions of others. Change in the culture of schooling can begin in the ballot box.

Actions of Members of the Media That Support Accelerated Learning

Schools have increasingly become the focus of media attention. Newscasters and reporters flock to schools when tragedies occur and when controversies arise. These stories are repeated again and again. To act responsibly, members of the media need to be careful to publish or broadcast accurate information that provides a complete picture of educational practices and issues. Coverage must avoid sensationalism and bias. The headlines broadcast hour after hour are what stick in people's minds, not the in-depth analysis that may come at 11:00 P.M. Too often, even the "story that follows" is superficial and sensationalized.

The media is absent from schools most of the time. It rarely covers the day-to-day triumphs and challenges that occur within schools. Its definition of "a good story" is based more on anticipating viewers' or readers' interests than on covering issues of importance to students. Because of its reach into every home in the community and nation, the media has a responsibility to be an advocate for children—all children—and can choose to become a vital partner as a teaching resource.

Actions of Politicians That Support Accelerated Learning

In recent years, education has become a "hot" political issue (Education Commission of the States 1997). Candidates, whether running for school board, mayor, governor, or senator, build on citizens' concerns about schools to promote themselves and to distinguish themselves from their opponents. To act responsibly, politicians, both as candidates and as elected officials, must be careful not to use schools and educational issues for their own advantage. They need to check facts before making public statements to ensure accuracy. Schools should not get caught in the cross fire of opposing political forces. Politicians need to build relationships of trust and honesty and listen to the voices of all of their constituents. While doing so, they have the responsibility to keep the needs of all children in mind, not just a few whose parents are most vocal or influential.

Actions of Policymakers That Support Accelerated Learning

Policymakers and those who influence and design plans to carry out policy at the local, state, and national levels have a profound effect on efforts to accelerate learning for all students. At the local level this includes school board members, district office administrators, and local union officials; at the state level, members of the legislature, state school board, board of regents, state departments of education, state and regional professional organizations, and unions are very influential. At the national level, members of Congress, staff of the U.S. Department of Education, staff of national professional organizations, and unions have a profound influence on school communities' and teachers' efforts to accelerate the learning of all students. It is true that teachers and principals are the ultimate policy implementers and shape the policies take in schools and classrooms (Knapp 1997; Berman and McLaughlin 1977), but policymakers remain very influential. To more effectively make policy, they need to learn from past failures to ensure that policies are constructive, value the interests of all students, are funded, and are properly implemented.

Policymakers are often subject to political pressures to further the agendas of key constituents, lobbyists, and special interest groups. Although it is tempting to accommodate all of these groups, policymakers have to make difficult decisions that reflect a shared goal and always put the best interests of student learning at the front.

Policymakers need to understand the process of policy implementation. They cannot make a policy, write up an implementation plan, disseminate the plan to schools, and expect principals and teachers to implement it as written. Policy implementation needs to be viewed as a part of the teaching and learning process (Knapp 1997; Jennings and Spillane 1996). It should begin with building a conversation between policymakers and school community members about the reason for the policy, prior assumptions and experience with similar policies, and the ultimate goals of the policy. Through ongoing dialogue, the likelihood of reaching a collective, realistic goal is heightened, and students benefit. This dialogue begins as policies are designed jointly with teachers, administrators, and parents and continues through the implementation and evaluation process. It recognizes the collective culture shared by schools and the individual culture that makes each school unique.

Policymakers should work from an understanding of local conditions and know when policies are best set at the local, state, or national level. Given the diversity of local conditions across the country, it is difficult to develop national policies that are responsive to local needs. Some federal policies and mandates have played an important role in providing access to school and programs for all students (e.g., *Brown v. Board of Education,* P.L. 94-142, Title IX). Others have placed undue burden on schools and districts when the policies become too prescriptive in how they are to be carried out. Policymakers must trust the individual schools or districts to implement policy mandates within their school or district culture.

Finally, policymakers must be aware of the costs, both financial and human of policies and mandates. They need to provide the financial and human resources needed to implement policies and be sure these funds reach schools that have historically been underfunded (Darling-Hammond 1997; Levin 1992). Unfunded mandates and underfunded policies place an overwhelming burden on the limited resources of most schools and lead to great frustration and resentment. Such mandates and policies require that schools and districts redirect millions of dollars from their educational plan to "other" ideas. This leads to incomplete implementation of new programs or even abandonment of existing sound, successful programs due to the diversion of funds to implement the new policy (Hartman 1992).

Actions of Teacher and Administrator Educators That
Support Accelerated Learning

Schools, colleges, and departments of education, state credentialing boards, and national professional organizations are responsible for the preparation and professional development of teachers, principals, and other instructional staff (e.g., media specialists, guidance counselors, school psychologists). Faculty members in teacher preparation departments and in the arts and sciences have the responsibility to provide programs for preservice and in-service teachers that will give them the academic content and pedagogical skills to teach effectively. In addition, they must recognize their responsibility to help build the dispositions needed to effectively teach all students.

Teacher and administrator educators must remain (or become) actively involved in K–12 schools. As individuals, they must spend considerable time in schools working with students, teachers, and administrators in order to stay current on issues and to broaden their experience with schools and students. This leads to a narrowing of the gap between theory and practice and provides for a coherent teacher and administrator educational experience (Holmes Group 1995; National Commission on Teaching and America's Future 1996).

Institutions of higher education acknowledge that they alone do not train the next generation of teachers and administrators; this is done in schools and by the practitioners through intensive, well-planned, well-supervised field experiences. The expertise of effective teachers and principals in the field is recognized and valued. Formal and informal partnerships that share mutual goals exist between K–12 schools and colleges and universities (see Teitle 1999 for a review of the literature on professional development schools). Some teacher educators teach classes in local schools. Others team teach with local teachers (Goodlad 1984; Ball and Rundquist 1993; Wilson, Miller, and Yerkes 1993). This exchange of ideas between schools and higher education provides opportunities for teachers, professors, administrators, and students to learn.

Effective teacher/administrator educators stay current in curricular, pedagogical, and school organization issues. Through involvement in research and development, they stay abreast of methodologies that have proven to accelerate the learning of all students. Not only do they teach from a philosophical position that encourages the acceleration of all students, but they ensure that their students know academic content and can demonstrate knowledge of practices that accelerate learning and their underlying assumptions. In order to do this, teacher educators know their content and model best practice, meaning that their classrooms accelerate the learning of the college or university students. In other words, they practice what they preach.

Finally, teacher educators ensure that students receive considerable exposure to different schools, classrooms, and students. To this end, students become skillful observers of school and classroom culture and develop an understanding of the role of teachers, administrators, staff, students, and parents in shaping these cultures. They also grow to see diversity as a strength and learn the skills needed to work productively with culturally different students. Difference is valued; diversity is celebrated.

Actions of Social Service Providers That Support Accelerated Learning

Social service providers, such as police, social workers, health providers, and public housing administrators have an influence on students and schools. In most communities, social service providers and schools work together only when a crisis occurs. In highly effective communities, these providers and schools work jointly to provide services to schools and students. Across the country, "full-service schools" provide health care, adult education, and help with public assistance and legal counsel so that the total child's needs are met (Comer 1988; Dryfoss 1994). In these communities, agencies have overcome "turf" issues, realizing that the limited resources to serve the needs of people are best used in concert, not in opposition.

Actions of Employers and Business Owners That Support Accelerated Learning

Employers and business owners often drive discussions about the skills students need when they leave school. It is the responsibility of employers to truly understand the skills prospective workers must bring to the job and those that are best taught on the job (Rumberger, Darrah, Levin, and Finnan 1994; Secretary's Commission on Achieving Necessary Skills 1991). They need to become partners with schools so that students have opportunities to shadow workers, employees have the chance to mentor students, and principals, teachers, employers, and business leaders have the chance to work together to better link the world of work with schools (Black 1998).

In addition to working closely with schools, employers and business leaders need to realize that schools do not function the same as businesses. Students are not products. They are individuals who have lives outside of school that influence their performance in school. They cannot be rejected because they do not meet "industry standards." The same holds for teachers. Business leaders need to realize that people are attracted to teaching for reasons that differ greatly from what attracts people to other jobs. Most effective teachers enter teaching with "missionary zeal" and are not motivated by the same threats and incentives as workers in other jobs and professions.

So How Do We Do This?

Let's return to the three students we introduced in the beginning of the book. As described in earlier chapters, Anna, Richard, and Sara were well served in very different classrooms. Could they be as well served in the same classroom? Yes, if they were in Sara's class. Were all of the students well served in the three schools? No, many students in Anna's and Richard's schools were not challenged. For all students—whether gifted, low-achieving or average—to experience accelerated learning, a synergy between individual and collective action must exist at the school and within classrooms. This kind of synergy exists at Sara's school but is absent at Anna's and Richard's schools.

The above describes individual actions that facilitate accelerated learning. Individual actions are critical; it is the individual actions of strong teachers and caring parents that give Anna and Richard good school experiences. It is the individual action of many people in Sara's school that has led to increased student achievement. However, individual actions are not enough. All of the individuals described in this chapter could decide to act on their commitment to accelerate all students' learning and find themselves at cross-purposes with each other. For all students to experience accelerated learning, individual actions must meld into collective actions both in the school and in the classrooms. Westview Elementary School is an example of such a synergy between individual and collective actions. It illustrates that collective action of individuals committed to a shared goal is a powerful force for positive change.

How do we create situations in which students of very different ability are all provided accelerated learning experiences? It is most likely to begin at the school level through a shared commitment to accelerate learning for all students. As described at the beginning of Chapter 6, Westview Elementary School used the Accelerated Schools Project to guide their change process. For Westview, this national reform project provided a philosophy (providing all students with what we want for our own children) and a process compatible with the culture that already existed at Westview. Using the Accelerated Schools model, the school community created a shared vision that describes outcomes everyone can work toward. They then established a governance structure and began using ongoing decisionmaking process to ensure that decisions are research based and shared. For Westview Elementary School, this process has provided a voice to all members of the school community, a process to guide continuous change, and a shared commitment to improving achievement of all students. In other words, it facilitates continuous school culture change.

Other schools use different vehicles (whether homegrown or adopted), but they share several key elements. First, they focus on reaching consensus on a vision or goals. Although any vision or set of goals must be compatible with those set at the state or district level, it is important for a school community to collectively dream about what school *can* be like for all students. No school will change its culture by adopting someone else's vision.

Second, the school needs a governance structure or well-defined communication channels that allow all members a voice in decisionmaking. As the preceding chapters stress, culture is developed and passed on through discussion and dialogue. Without a voice, people are not true players. Giving voice to all members of the school community involves listening to dissenters as well as supporters of ideas and calling on everyone to explain why they support or oppose change efforts.

Third, the school needs to adopt a systematic, research- or inquiry-based decisionmaking process. The school community must be trained to thoroughly understand the nature and cause of problems and to seek solutions that best fit the problem and the school culture. Few teachers, parents, administrators, or students are comfortable with research- or inquiry-based decisionmaking at first, but as they develop competency in it, they recognize that this is one of the most powerful ways of guiding actions and changing assumptions.

Finally, efforts must be targeted to change classroom cultures as well as the school culture. Little change in student learning occurs when change efforts focus only at the school level. Changing classroom culture involves holding a vision of what an effective classroom is like but does not insist that all classrooms in the school be the same. Chapter 7 describes the assumptions underlying classrooms that accelerate learning and suggests some actions that will encourage efforts to accelerate learning. Change efforts at the classroom level have to begin with the teacher; where each teacher's journey begins is an individual matter. For one teacher it may begin through introspection, through an examination of deeply held assumptions, beliefs, and values. For another teacher, it may begin through involvement in a graduate course or workshop, where a spark may be kindled to approach the teaching and learning process differently. For another teacher, change may begin through interaction with colleagues, possibly through involvement in peer support teams, team teaching, or working with a mentor teacher. Finally, a teacher may change through involvement in preparation of new teachers or through collaboration with teacher educators.

The strength of building a synergy of change among individuals, classrooms, and the school is that no one has to make the journey alone. An individual teacher may feel he or she is fighting an uphill battle if students refuse to take responsibility for their learning or if the administration and other colleagues belittle their efforts. Principals may feel that they are leading a solo charge if classrooms remain the same despite efforts to change the school culture. Changing schools and classrooms to accelerate the learning of all students is a collective and individual process that requires nurturing and cultivation.

Actions that are cultivated differ significantly from those that happen randomly or out of habit. Cultivation has a purpose, a goal. When we cultivate, we look to our goal and do everything in our power to reach it. In this case, we are cultivating schools and classrooms that challenge and engage all students. Cultivation also goes beneath the surface; when we cultivate plants we dig deeply in the soil to be sure that the plants have every chance to grow. When we cultivate change in schools and classrooms we also dig deeply; in this case we go beyond surface change to an examination of deeply held assumptions, beliefs, and values. Deep cultivation results in a change in behavior that will be sustained.

As described above, this cultivation process is both a group effort (many people both inside and outside of the school are involved) and an individual responsibility. Although each group of individuals described above assumes a different set of responsibilities in making acceleration of all students possible, all individuals share a common responsibility for sustaining the following actions:

- being involved in productive, respectful dialogue that includes voicing opinions and listening to the voices of others.
- being involved in or passionate about learning.
- being trustworthy and willing to trust others.
- taking steps to make it possible for all students to learn. This includes the responsibility students take for their own learning.
- demonstrating care for everyone involved in educating all students.
- working collaboratively for shared goals, allowing everyone to build on their own expertise.
- demonstrating patience and perseverance.

This book illustrates that it is possible to create schools and classrooms that accelerate the learning of all students. We have provided examples of schools in which all students are challenged and where expectations for everyone are high. Examples are also available of classrooms in which teachers provide demanding and engaging learning environments and expect all students to take advantage of these opportunities. Currently these examples are limited to isolated cases of schools or classrooms; they are not widespread and do not describe school systems.

The next challenge is to build on what we have learned from the schools and classrooms that accelerate the learning of all students and to expect the same from all schools and all classrooms. It is not enough for a few schools and classrooms to challenge all students; all schools and classrooms must do so. How do we make such a radical transformation in classrooms, schools, and school systems? The following attitudes will facilitate the process.

First, the commitment to accelerate learning for all students must exist at the school level and be supported by external policies and actions. A district or state cannot mandate culture change. Change can be facilitated by policies that work with existing school and classroom cultures. For individuals to embrace change, they must feel that they have a voice in the change, can shape the direction of the change, and see the benefit of the change for students. For example, the current effort to hold all students to a common set of high standards is one of the few mandated change policies that has the potential to encourage school culture change. In many states, the standards are sufficiently conceptual to allow considerable flexibility in determining what and how students are taught. Once teachers become familiar with the standards, they see their value in guiding teaching and learning. In contrast, accountability legislation, which ties student promotion and teacher and administrator jobs to scores on standardized tests, is unlikely to significantly change school or classroom cultures because people at the school level are being told to change rather than voluntarily choosing to change. People at the school level do not see the benefit of accountability to students, and accountability legislation generally ignores the existence of school culture.

Second, each school needs to reach consensus that all students must be challenged. We cannot assume that some students (based on their family background) will be "winners," while others will be "losers." This is both a moral imperative and a practical one. Among the societal assumptions described earlier is one that provides the moral imperative—we believe in equal opportunity for all. Currently all students have access to education, but they do not have equal access to a high-quality education. Individuals within and outside of schools must agree that a poor or mediocre education is not okay for "those kids." The standards movement provides the first example in history of expecting all students to reach the same standards. Standards vary, and they certainly have their critics (Ohanian 1999), but if implemented with care they can result in equal opportunity being a reality for most, if not all, students.

The practical imperative to challenge all students lies in the societal assumption that people need skills for productive work and active citizenship. No one would deny that the skills needed to participate productively in today's economy and world are more demanding than those required in the past. If we want all people to be able to work and to contribute to society, then we must recognize that they need the skills to make this happen, skills that go beyond basic literacy and numeracy to include higher-order thinking, decisionmaking, and communication skills.

Third, people need a vehicle for making purposeful change possible. People need vehicles that help them create a living vision to guide school and classroom change, standards for what students will know and be able to do, and goals to work toward so that the vision and standards can be met. Purposeful change rarely happens without a systematic process in place. The process must encourage open dialogue, research into more effective ways of teaching, and exposure to new and different strategies and ideas. Change processes have to happen at the school level, with local, state, and national input.

Fourth, purposeful change takes time. It goes without saying that ambitious goals cannot be reached quickly. The kind of deep change required to change assumptions, values, actions, and responsibilities takes time. Too often we become impatient for change to happen quickly. This leads to superficial change and frustration. We need to keep in mind that although assumptions are hard to change, once they have changed, they are unlikely to revert.

Fifth, people must realize that the change process is complex and that simple solutions do not exist. Although purposeful change requires a shared vision and a commitment by everyone in the school to work toward it, the route to this vision is rarely linear or clear. Many people must be involved in cultivating change, and they each have their own sets of assumptions that shape their actions. Changing assumptions occurs one person at a time, and sometimes in a "two steps forward, one step backward" manner. When we become frustrated with people because they appear to resist change, we must remember that assumptions and values are at the core of who we are as people. When people are reluctant to change, it is possible that they realize that by changing assumptions, they will change their identity.

Finally, the cultivation process must be undertaken with a sense of hope and optimism no matter how negative a school or classroom culture may be. As Michael Fullan (1997) points out, the "lost causes" are often the ones worth fighting for. Without approaching each school, each classroom, and each individual as a starting place for change, as a potential source of nourishment for students, we settle for a society that is less than it can be. Every spring, cultivators across the country face their farms and gardens with hope and optimism; they look upon the soil and dream of what will grow. Every fall educators must face their schools and classrooms with the same dream of what will grow.

Note

1. The term "parent" is used to include all adults assuming a parental role for a child. This includes guardians, foster parents, grandparents, aunts or uncles, or adult siblings.

References

Accelerated Schools Project. 1999. *Newsletter* 8 (no. 1).

Aikin, W. M. 1942. *The Story of the Eight Year Study*. New York: Harper and Brothers.

Allington, R. L. 1994. "The Schools We Have. The Schools We Need." *Reading Teacher* 48 (no. 1): 14–27.

Allington, R. L., and S. Li. 1990. "Teacher Beliefs About Children Who Find Learning to Read Difficult." Paper presented at the National Reading Conference, Miami, Florida.

Apple, M. W. 1979. *Ideology and Curriculum*. Boston: Routledge & Kegan Paul.

Armeta, T., and E. Darwin. 1998. "Coping with Time-Robbers." *Principal* 78 (no. 1): 26–29.

Arnold, M. S. 1995. "Exploding the Myths: African American Families At Promise." In *Children and Families "At Promise": Deconstructing the Discourse of Risk*, edited by B. B. Swadener and S. Lubeck, 143–162. Albany: State University of New York Press.

Ascher, C. 1993. "Changing Schools for Urban Student: The School Development Program, Accelerated Schools and Success for All." *Trends and Issues* 18: 1–46.

Ayers, W. 1992. "Work That Is Real: Why Teachers Should Be Empowered." In *Empowering Teachers and Parents: School Restructuring Through the Eyes of Anthropologists*, edited by G. A. Hess, 13–28. Westport, CT: Bergin and Garvey.

———. 1994. "To Teach: The Journey of a Teacher." *Democracy & Education* 83: 9–12.

Ball, D. L., and S. S. Rundquist. 1993. "Collaboration as a Context for Joining Teacher Learning with Learning About Teaching." In *Teaching for Understanding: Challenges for Policy and Practice*, edited by D. K. Cohen, M. W. McLaughlin, and J. E. Talbert, 13–43. San Francisco: Jossey-Bass.

Banks, J. 1998. "The Lives and Values of Researchers: Implications for Educating Citizens in a Multicultural Society." *Educational Researcher* 27 (no. 7): 4–17.

Benbow, C. P. 1991. "Mathematically Talented Children: Can Acceleration Meet Their Educational Needs?" In *Handbook of Gifted Education*, edited by N. Colangelo and G. A. Davis, 154–165. Needham Heights, MA: Allyn and Bacon.

Berg, I. 1969. *Education and Jobs: The Great Training Robbery*. Boston: Beacon Press.

Berman, B., and M. W. McLaughlin. 1977. *Federal Programs Supporting Educational Change*. Vol. 7, *Factors Affecting Implementation and Continuation*. Santa Monica, CA: Rand.

Billingsley, A. 1968. *Black Families in White America*. Englewood Cliffs, NJ: Prentice Hall.

Bireley, M. 1992. "Conceptions of Intelligence and Giftedness." In *Challenges in Gifted Education: Developing Potential and Investing in Knowledge for the 21st Century,* edited by Ohio State Department of Education, 21–33. Columbus: Ohio State Department of Education.

Black, S. 1998. "Research: Learning to Work." *American School Board Journal* 185 (no. 3): 36–38.

Blake, M., and M. Van Sickle. 1997. *Language Diversity and the At-Risk Student.* Center of Excellence in Accelerating Learning: Research and Development Brief. September, College of Charleston, Charleston, South Carolina.

Bloom, B. S., ed. 1985. *Developing Talent in Young People.* New York: Ballantine Books.

Bourdieu, P. 1986. "The Forms of Capital." In *Handbook of Theory and Research for Sociology of Education,* edited by J. G. Richardson, 241–258. New York: Greenwood Press.

Bourdieu, P., and C. Passeron. 1977. *Reproduction in Education, Society, and Culture.* London: Sage.

Brody, L., and C. Benbow. 1987. "Accelerated Strategies: How Effective Are They for the Gifted?" *Gifted Child Quarterly* 31: 105–109.

Brookhart, S. M., and T. G. Rusnak. 1993. "A Pedagogy of Enrichment, Not Poverty: Successful Lessons of Exemplary Urban Teachers." *Journal of Teacher Education* 441: 17–37.

Brophy, J., and T. L. Good. 1986. "Teacher Behavior and Student Achievement." In *Handbook of Research on Teaching,* 3rd ed., edited by M. Wittrock, 328–375. New York: McMillan.

Calhoun, E. F. 1994. *How to Use Action Research in the Self-Renewing School.* Alexandria, VA: ASCD.

Carnegie Council on Adolescent Development. 1989. *Turning Points: Preparing Youth for the 21st Century.* New York: Carnegie Corporation of New York.

Carnegie Forum on Education and the Economy. 1986. *A Nation Prepared: Teachers for the 21st Century.* Washington, DC: Carnegie Forum on Education and the Economy.

Carter, L. F. 1984. "The Sustaining Effects Study of Compensatory and Elementary Education." *Educational Researcher* 13 (no. 7): 4–13.

Cazden, C. B. 1988. *Classroom Discourse.* Portsmouth, NH: Heinemann.

Cedoline, A. J. 1982. *Job Burnout in Public Education: Symptoms, Causes, and Survival Skills.* New York: Teachers College Press.

Chandler, S. 1992. "Learning for What Purpose? Questions When Viewing Classroom Learning from a Sociocultural Curriculum." In *Redefining Student Learning: Roots of Educational Change,* edited by H. Marshall, 33–38. Norwood, NJ: Ablex.

Chavkin, N. F. 1993. "Introduction: Families and the Schools." In *Families and Schools in a Pluralistic Society,* edited by N. Chavkin, 1–20. Albany: State University of New York Press.

Christensen, G. 1996. "Toward a New Leadership Paradigm: Behaviors of Accelerated School Principals." In *Accelerated Schools in Action: Lessons from the Field,* edited by C. Finnan, E. St. John, J. McCarthy, and S. Slovacek, 185–207. Thousand Oaks, CA: Corwin Press.

Clifford, J. 1986. "Introduction: Partial Truths." In *Writing Culture: The Poetics and Politics of Ethnography,* edited by J. Clifford and G. Marcus, 1–26. Berkeley: University of California Press.

Cohen, D. K., M. W. McLaughlin, and J. E. Talbert, eds. 1993. *Teaching for Understanding: Challenges for Policy and Practice*. San Francisco: Jossey-Bass.

Cohn, S. J. 1991. "Talent Searches." In *Handbook of Gifted Education*, edited by N. Colangelo and G. A. Davis, 166–177. Needham Heights, MA: Allyn and Bacon.

Colangelo, N., and G. A. Davis. 1991. "Introduction and Historical Overview." In *Handbook of Gifted Education*, edited by N. Colangelo and G. A. Davis, 3–13. Needham Heights, MA: Allyn and Bacon.

Comer, J. P. 1980. *School Power: Implications of an Intervention Project*. New York: Free Press.

———. 1988. "Educating Poor Minority Children." *Scientific American* 259 (no. 5): 42–48.

Comer, J. P., N. M. Haynes, and E. T. Joyner. 1996. "The School Development Program." In *Rallying the Whole Village: The Comer Process for Reforming Education*, edited by J. P. Comer, N. M. Haynes, E. T. Joyner, and M. Ben-Avie, 1–26. New York: Teacher's College Press.

Commission on the Skills of the American Workforce. 1990. *America's Choice: High Skills or Low Wages*. Washington, DC: National Center for Education and the Economy.

Conway, G. E. 1995. "Small Scale and School Culture: The Experience of Private Schools." *ERIC Digest* (On-Line): 3–4.

Cook, D. A., and M. Fine. 1995. "'Motherwit': Childrearing Lessons from African American Mothers of Low Income." In *Children and Families "At Promise": Deconstructing the Discourse of Risk*, edited by B. B. Swadener and S. Lubeck, 118–142. Albany: State University of New York Press.

Cornbleth, C., and W. Korth. 1980. "Teacher Perceptions and Teacher-Student Interaction in Integrated Classrooms." *Journal of Experimental Education* 48: 259–263.

Cousins, L. H. 1999. "'Playing Between Classes': America's Troubles with Class, Race, and Gender in a Black High School and Community." *Anthropology and Education Quarterly* 30 (no. 3): 272–294.

Cremin, L. A. 1961. *The Transformation of School*. New York: Vintage Books.

Cuban, L. 1990. "Reforming Again, Again, and Again." *Educational Researcher* 19: 3–13.

———. 1992. "What Happens to Reforms That Last? The Case of the Junior High School." *American Educational Research Journal* 29 (no. 2): 227–252.

Cudahy, D. 1996. "It Takes More Than Good Intentions: Teachers' Experience of Cross-Cultural Teaching." Unpublished Ph.D. dissertation., University of Tennessee, Knoxville.

Cusick, P. 1983. *The Egalitarian Ideal and the American High School*. New York: Longman.

Darling-Hammond, L. 1997. *The Right to Learn: A Blueprint for Creating Schools That Work*. San Francisco: Jossey-Bass.

Datnow, A. 1998. *The Gender Politics of Educational Change*. London: Falmer Press.

Daubner, S. L., and J. L. Epstein. 1993. "Parents' Attitudes and Practices of Involvement in Inner-City Elementary and Middle Schools." In *Families and Schools in a Pluralistic Society*, edited by N. L. Chavkin, 53–71. Albany: State University of New York Press.

Daurio, S. P. 1979. "Educational Enrichment vs. Acceleration: A Review of the Literature." In *Acceleration and Enrichment: Strategies for Educating the Gifted*, edited by W. C. George, S. J. Cohen, and J. C. Stanley, 13–63. Baltimore: Johns Hopkins Press.

Davis, G. A., and S. B. Rimm. 1998. *Education of the Gifted and Talented,* 4th ed. Needham Heights, MA: Allyn and Bacon.

Deal, T. E., and K. D. Peterson. 1998. *Shaping School Culture: The Heart of Leadership.* San Francisco: Jossey-Bass.

Deci, E. L. 1976. "The Hidden Costs of Rewards." *Organizational Dynamics* 43: 61–72.

Delgado-Gaitan, C. 1992. "School Matters in the Mexican-American Home: Socializing Children to Education." *American Educational Research Journal* 29: 495–513.

Delgado-Gaitan, C., and H. Trueba. 1991. *Crossing Cultural Borders: Education for Immigrant Families in America.* New York: Falmer.

Delpit, L. 1988. "The Silenced Dialogue: Power and Pedagogy in Educating Other People's Children." *Harvard Educational Review* 58 (no. 3): 280–298.

———. 1995. *Other People's Children: Cultural Conflict in the Classroom.* New York: The New Press.

Department of the Interior, Bureau of Education. National Education Association. 1918. *The Cardinal Principles of Secondary Education: A Report of the Commission on the Reorganization of Secondary Education.* Bulletin no. 35. Washington, DC.

Dewey, J. 1900. *The School and Society.* Chicago: University of Chicago Press.

———. 1902. *The Child and the Curriculum.* Chicago: University of Chicago Press.

———. 1916. *Democracy and Education.* Old Tappan, NJ: McMillan.

Diaz, S., L. C. Moll, and H. Mehan. 1986. *Sociocultural Resources in Instruction: A Context Specific Approach. Beyond Language.* Los Angeles: California State University Evaluation, Dissemination, and Assessment Center.

Diener, C., and C. Dweck. 1978. "An Analysis of Learned Helplessness: Continuous Changes in Performance, Strategy, and Achievement Cognitions Following Failure." *Journal of Personality and Social Psychology* 35: 451–462.

Dornbusch, S., and P. L. Ritter. 1988. "Parents of High School Students: A Neglected Resource." *Educational Horizons* 66: 75–77.

Dreeben, R. 1967. "The Contribution of Schooling to the Learning of Norms." *Harvard Educational Review* 37: 211–227.

Driver, C. 1995. "Accelerated Districts—The Next Step. A Summary of Research and Development." Paper presented at the American Educational Research Association, San Francisco, California.

Dryfoss, J. G. 1994. "Under One Roof." *American School Board Journal* 181 (no. 8): 28–31.

Education Commission of the States. 1997. *America's Public Schools Must Change . . . But Can They?* Denver.

Elmore, R. F., P.L. Peterson, and S. J. McCarthey. 1996. *Restructuring in the Classroom: Teaching, Learning, and School Organization.* San Francisco: Jossey-Bass.

Erickson, F. 1986. "Qualitative Research." In *Handbook of Research on Teaching,* 3rd ed., edited by M. C. Wittrock, 119–161. New York: Macmillan.

Erickson, F. and G. Mohatt. 1982. "Cultural Organization of Participation Structures in Two Classrooms of Indian Students." In *Doing the Ethnography of Schooling: Educational Anthropology in Action,* edited by G. Spindler, 102–132. New York: Holt, Rinehart and Winston.

Evans, R. 1996. *Human Side of School Change: Reform, Resistance, and the Real-Life Problems of Innovation.* San Francisco: Jossey-Bass.

Feldhusen, J. F. 1989. "Synthesis of Research on Gifted Youth." *Educational Leadership* 46 (no. 6): 6–11.

Feldhusen, J. F., T. B. Proctor, and K. N. Black. 1986. "Guidelines for Grade Advancement of Precocious Children." *Roeper Review* 9 (no. 1): 25–27.

Ferguson, R. F. 1991. "Paying for Public Education: New Evidence on How and Why Money Matters." *Harvard Journal on Legislation* 28 (no. 2): 465–498.

Fine, M. 1991. *Framing Dropouts: Notes on the Politics of an Urban Public High School.* Albany: State University of New York Press.

———. 1994. *Chartering Urban School Reform.* New York: National Center for Restructuring Education, Schools, and Teaching, Teachers College, Columbia University.

———. 1995. "The Politics of Who's 'At Risk.'" In *Children and Families "At Promise": Deconstructing the Discourse of Risk,* edited by B. B. Swadener and S. Lubeck, 76–96. Albany: State University of New York Press.

Finnan, C. 1996. "Making Change Our Friend." In *Accelerated Schools in Action: Lessons from the Field,* edited by C. Finnan, E. St. John, J. McCarthy, and S. Slovacek, 104–123. Thousand Oaks, CA: Corwin Press.

Finnan, C., and H. M. Levin. 1998. "Using School Culture to Bring Vision to Life." Paper presented at Annual Meeting of the American Educational Research Association Accelerated Schools Special Interest Group Conference, April, San Diego, California.

———. 2000. "Changing School Culture." In *Images of Educational Change,* edited by J. Elliott and H. Altrichter. Milton Keynes, UK: Open University Press.

Finnan, C., E. St. John, J. McCarthy, and S. Slovacek, eds. 1996. *Accelerated Schools in Action: Lessons from the Field.* Thousand Oaks, CA: Corwin Press.

Finnan, C., and J. Swanson. Forthcoming. "Changing School Culture: Rutledge Elementary as an Accelerated School." In *Transforming the Culture of Schools: Lessons Learned from Field Studies of Several Leading Reform Strategies,* edited by G. Noblit and W. Pink. Cresskill, NJ: Hampton Press.

Florio-Ruane, S. 1989. "Social Organization of Classes and Schools." In *Knowledge Base for the Beginning Teacher,* edited by M. Reynolds, 163–172. New York: Pergamon Press.

———. 1994. "Anthropological Study of Classroom Culture and Social Organization." In *International Encyclopedia of Education Research and Studies,* 2nd ed., edited by T. Husen and T. N. Postlethwaite, 796–803. Oxford: Pergamon.

Ford, D. Y. 1996. *Reversing Underachievement Among Gifted Black Students: Promising Practices and Programs.* New York: Teachers College Press.

Fordham, S. 1999. "Dissin' 'the Standard': Ebonics As Guerrilla Warfare at Capital High." *Anthropology and Education Quarterly* 30 (no. 3): 272–294.

Foster, H. 1974. *Ribbin' Jivin' and Playin' the Dozens: The Unrecognized Dilemma of Inner City Schools.* Cambridge, MA: Ballinger.

Franklin, B. M. 1994. *From "Backwardness" to "At-Risk": Childhood Learning Difficulties and the Contradictions of School Reform.* Albany: State University of New York Press.

Freire, P. 1970. *Pedagogy of the Oppressed.* New York: Herder and Herder.

Fullan, M. 1991. *The New Meaning of Educational Change.* New York: Teachers College Press.

———. 1993. *Change Forces.* London: Falmer Press.

————. 1997. "Emotions and Hope: Constructive Concepts for Complex Times." In *Rethinking Educational Change with Heart and Mind,* edited by A. Hargreaves, 216–223. Alexandria, VA: ASCD.

Fullan, M., and A. Hargreaves. 1996. *What's Worth Fighting for in Your School?* New York: Teachers College Press.

Gallagher, J. J. 1985. *Teaching the Gifted Child.* Newton, MA: Allyn and Bacon.

————. 1991. "Educational Reform, Values, and Gifted Students." *Gifted Child Quarterly* 35 (no. 1): 12–19.

Galton, F. 1869. *Hereditary Genius.* London: Macmillan.

Gardner, H. 1983. *Frames of Mind: The Theory of Multiple Intelligences.* New York: Basic Books.

————. 1999. *Intelligence Reframed: Multiple Intelligences for the 21st Century.* New York: Basic Books.

Gleaves, K. 1994. "Some Thoughts on the Purpose of School from a Group of Third Grade Students." *Democracy & Education* 7 (Spring): 28–32.

Gonzales, C. L. 1994. "A Study of the Effectiveness of a Middle Schools Humanities Program Used By Low-Achieving Readers." *Dissertational Abstracts International* 56 (no. 03A): University Microfilms no. AA [9520256].

Goodlad, J. I. 1984. *A Place Called School.* New York: McGraw-Hill.

————. 1990. *Teachers for Our Nation's Schools.* San Francisco: Jossey-Bass.

Greenfield, P. M. 1994. "Independence and Interdependence as Developmental Scripts: Implications for Theory, Research, and Practice." In *Cross-Cultural Roots of Minority Child Development,* edited by P. M. Greenfield and R. R. Cocking, 1–37. Hillsdale NJ: Lawrence Erlbaum.

Guskey, T. R. 1986. "Staff Development and the Process of Teacher Change." *Educational Researcher* 15 (no. 5): 5–12.

Haberman, M. 1995. *Star Teachers of Children in Poverty.* West Lafayette, IN: Kappa Delta Pi.

Hale, J. E. 1994. *Unbank the Fire: Visions for the Education of African American Children.* Baltimore: Johns Hopkins University Press.

Hartman, W. T. 1992. "State Funding Models for Special Education." *Remedial and Special Education* 13: 47–58.

Heath, S. B. 1982. "Questioning at Home and at School: A Comparative Study." In *Doing the Ethnography of Schooling: Educational Anthropology in Action,* edited by G. Spindler, 96–102. New York: Holt, Rinehart and Winston.

————. 1983. *Way with Words: Language, Life, and Work in Communities and Classrooms.* Cambridge: Cambridge University Press.

Heaton, R. M., and M. Lampert. 1993. "Learning to Hear Voices: Inventing a New Pedagogy of Teacher Education." In *Teaching for Understanding: Challenges for Policy and Practice,* edited by D. K. Cohen, M. W. McLaughlin, and J. E. Talbert, 43–84. San Francisco: Jossey-Bass.

Henderson, A. T. 1988. "Parents Are a School's Best Friends." *Phi Delta Kappan* 70: 148–153.

Henderson, A. T., ed. 1987. *The Evidence Continues to Grow: Parent Involvement Improves Student Achievement.* Columbia, MD: National Committee for Citizens in Education.

Hirsch Jr., E. D. 1996. *The Schools We Need and Why We Don't Have Them.* New York: Doubleday.

Hoff, D. J. 1999. "A Blueprint for Change." *Education Week* 17 (no. 32): 37–43.

Holmes Group. 1986. *Tomorrow's Teachers: A Report of the Holmes Group.* East Lansing, MI: Holmes Group.

———. 1995. *Tomorrow's Schools of Education.* East Lansing, MI: Holmes Group.

Hopfenberg, W., H. M. Levin, C. Chase, S. G. Christensen, M. Moore, P. Soler, I. Brunner, B. Keller, and G. Rodriquez. 1993. *The Accelerated Schools Resource Guide.* San Francisco: Jossey-Bass.

Horne, D. L., and P. J. Dupuy. 1981. "In Favor of Acceleration for Gifted Students." *Personnel and Guidelines Journal* 60: 103–106.

Hymes, D. 1972. "Introduction." In *Functions of Language in a Classroom,* edited by C. B. Cazden, V. P. John, and D. Hymes, xi-vii. New York: Teachers College Press.

———. 1974. *Foundations in Sociolinguistics: An Ethnographic Approach.* Philadelphia: University of Pennsylvania Press.

James, S., director. 1994. *Hoop Dreams.* (Film). Available from Kartemquin Films.

Jennings, N. E. 1998. "Reforming Practice in Urban Schools of Poverty: Lessons from the Field." Paper presented at the annual meeting of the American Educational Research Association, April, San Diego, California.

Jennings, N. E., and J. Spillane. 1996. "State Reform and Local Capacity: Encouraging Ambitious Instruction for All and Local Decision-Making." *Journal of Education Policy* 11 (no. 4): 465–482.

Johnson, D. L., N. Boyce, and J. Van Tassel-Baska. 1995. "Science Curriculum Review: Evaluating Materials for High-Ability Learners." *Gifted Child Quarterly* 39 (no. 1): 36–42.

Johnston, P. 1985. "The Congruence of Classroom and Remedial Reading Instruction." *Elementary School Journal* 85 (no. 4): 465–478.

Jordan, K. F., A. Methna, and A. Webb. 1996. *Foundations of American Education.* Upper Saddle River, NJ: Prentice-Hall.

Justman, J. 1959. "Academic Achievement of Intellectually Gifted Accelerants and Nonaccelerants in Junior High School." In *Educating Gifted Children: A Book of Readings,* edited by J. L. French, 480–489. New York: Rinehart & Winston.

Keller, B., and T. Huebner. 1997. "Powerful Learning in Accelerated Schools: Opportunities for and Impediments to Implementation." Paper presented at the annual meetings of the American Educational Research Association, March, Chicago, Illinois.

Kidder, T. 1989. *Among School Children.* Boston: Houghton Mifflin.

Kliebard, H. M. 1987. *The Struggle for the American Curriculum, 1893–1958.* New York: Routledge.

Kluckhohn, C. 1949. *Mirror for Man: The Relationship of Anthropology to Modern Life.* New York: Whittlesey House.

Knapp, M. S. 1995a. "Introduction: The Teaching Challenge in High-Poverty Classrooms." In *Teaching for Meaning in High-Poverty Classrooms,* edited by M. S. Knapp, N. E. Adelman, C. Marder, H. McCollum, M. C. Needels, C. Padilla, P. M. Shields, B. J Turnbull, A. A. Zucker, 1–11. New York: Teachers College Press.

———. 1995b. "Forces Inside the Classroom Linked with Teaching for Meaning." In *Teaching for Meaning in High-Poverty Classrooms,* edited by M. S. Knapp, N. E. Adelman, C. Marder, H. McCollum, M. C. Needels, C. Padilla, P. M. Shields, B. J. Turnbull, A. A. Zucker, 145–159. New York: Teachers College Press.

————. 1997. "Between Systemic Reforms and the Mathematics and Science Classroom: The Dynamics of Innovation, Implementation, and Professional Learning." *Review of Educational Research* 67 (no. 2): 227–267.

Knapp, M. S., P. M. Shields, and C. Padilla. 1995. "The School and District Environment for Meaning-Oriented Instruction." In *Teaching for Meaning in High-Poverty Classrooms,* edited by M. S. Knapp, N. E. Adelman, C. Marder, H. McCollum, M. C. Needels, C. Padilla, P. M. Shields, B. J Turnbull, A. A. Zucker, 160–183. New York: Teachers College Press.

Knapp, M., P. M. Shields, and B. J. Turnbull. 1995. "Conclusion: Teaching for Meaning in High-Poverty Classrooms." In *Teaching for Meaning in High-Poverty Classrooms,* edited by M. S. Knapp, N. E. Adelman, C. Marder, H. McCollum, M. C. Needels, C. Padilla, P. M. Shields, B. J Turnbull, A. A. Zucker, 183–204. New York: Teachers College Press.

Knapp, M. S., N. E. Adelman, C. Marder, H. McCollum, M. C. Needels, C. Padilla, P. M. Shields, B. J Turnbull, A. A. Zucker. 1995. *Teaching for Meaning in High-Poverty Classrooms.* New York: Teachers College Press.

Kohn, A. 1993. *Punished by Rewards.* Boston: Houghton Mifflin.

Konzal, J. L. 1997. "Attitudes: How Parental Attitudes May Influence Classroom Instructional Practices." Paper presented at the Annual Meeting of AERA, 24–28 March, Chicago, Illinois.

Ladson-Billings, G. 1994. *Dreamkeepers: The Successful Teachers of African American Children.* San Francisco: Jossey-Bass.

Ladson-Billings, G., and A. Henry. 1990. "Blurring the Borders: Voices of African Liberatory Pedagogy in the U.S. and Canada." *Journal of Negro Education* 613: 378–391.

Leakey, R. E., ed. 1979. *On the Origin of the Species: The Illustrated Origin of the Species by Charles Darwin.* New York: Hill and Wang.

LeCompte, M. D., and A. G. Dworkin. 1991. *Giving Up on School: Student Dropouts and Teacher Burnouts.* Newbury Park, CA: Corwin Press.

Lee, S. 1994. Behind the Model–Minority Stereotype: Voices of High- and Low-Achieving Asian American Students. *Anthropology and Education Quarterly* 25 (no. 4): 413–429.

————. 1996. *Unraveling the "Model Minority" Stereotype: Listening to Asian American Youth.* New York: Teachers College Press.

Lee, V. E., A. Bryk, and J. B. Smith. 1993. "The Organization of Effective Secondary Schools." *Review of Research in Education* 19: 171–267.

Lee, V. E., J. Smith, and R. Croninger. 1995. "Another Look at High School Restructuring: More Evidence That It Improves Student Achievement and More Insights into Why." *Issues in Restructuring Schools* 9: 1–9 (Center on Organization and Restructuring of Schools, University of Wisconsin).

Lepper, M. R. 1981. "Intrinsic and Extrinsic Motivation in Children: Detrimental Effects of Superfluous Social Controls. Aspects of the Development of Competence." *Minnesota Symposia on Child Psychology* 14: 155–214.

Lepper, M. R., and D. Greene. 1978. *The Costs of Reward: New Perspectives on the Psychology of Human Motivation.* Hillsdale, NJ: Erlbaum.

Levin, H. M. 1986. *Educational Reform for Disadvantaged Students: An Emerging Crisis.* Washington, DC: National Education Association.

————. 1987. "Accelerated Schools for Disadvantaged Students." *Educational Leadership* 44 (no. 6): 19–21.

———. 1988. "Accelerating Elementary Education for Disadvantaged Students." In *Council of Chief State School Officers, School Success for Students at Risk*, 209–226. Orlando, FL: Harcourt Brace Jovanovich.

———. 1992. "The Necessary and Sufficient Conditions for Achieving Educational Equity." Paper prepared for the Commissioner's Education Equity Study Group. Department of Education, New York.

———. 1996. "Accelerated Schools: The Background." In *Accelerated Schools in Action: Lessons from the Field*, edited by C. Finnan, E. P. St. John, J. McCarthy, and S. P. Slovacek, 3–23. Thousand Oaks, CA: Corwin Press.

———. 1998. "Accelerated Schools: A Decade of Evolution." In *International Handbook of Educational Change*, edited by A. Hargreaves, A. Lieberman, M. Fullan, and D. Hopkins, 807–830. Boston: Kluwer Academic.

Lewis, K. S., S. D. Kruse, and H. M. Marks. 1996. "Schoolwide Professional Community." In *Authentic Achievement: Restructuring Schools for Intellectual Quality*, edited by F. M. Newmann et al., 179–205. San Francisco: Jossey-Bass.

Liston, D. P., and K. M. Zeichner. 1996. *Culture and Teaching*. Mahwah, NJ: Lawrence Erlbaum Associates.

Lortie, D. C. 1975. *Schoolteacher: A Sociological Study*. Chicago: University of Chicago Press.

Lounsbury, J. H., and D. C. Clark. 1990. *Inside Grade Eight: From Apathy to Excitement*. Reston, VA: National Association of Secondary School Principals.

Lubeck, S. "Mothers At Risk." In *Children and Families "At Promise": Deconstructing the Discourse of Risk*, edited by B. B. Swadener and S. Lubeck, 50–75. Albany: State University of New York Press. 1995.

Lubeck, S., and P. Garrett. 1990. *Pre-Kindergarten Programs in North Carolina: Preferences of Superintendents and Principals*. Raleigh, NC: Report to the North Carolina General Assembly.

MacLeod, J. 1995. *Ain't No Makin' It: Aspirations and Attainment in a Low-Income Neighborhood*. Boulder: Westview Press.

Mahiri, J. 1998. *Shooting for Excellence: African American and Youth Culture in New Century Schools*. New York: Teachers College Press.

Marks, H. M., K. B. Doane, and W. G. Secada. 1996. "Support for Student Achievement." In *Authentic Achievement: Restructuring Schools for Intellectual Quality*, edited by F. M. Newmann et al., 209–228. San Francisco: Jossey-Bass.

Mathematical Association of America. 1998. *The Third International Mathematics and Science Study*. Washington, DC: Mathematical Association of America.

Mathews, D. 1996. *Is There a Public for Public Schools?* Dayton, OH: Kettering Foundation Press.

McCarthey, S. J., and P. L. Peterson. 1993. "Creating Practice Within the Context of a Restructured Professional Development School." In *Teaching for Understanding: Challenges for Policy and Practice*, edited by D. K. Cohen, M. W. McLaughlin, and J. E. Talbert, 130–166. San Francisco: Jossey-Bass.

McCollum, H. 1995. "Managing Academic Learning Environments." In *Teaching for Meaning in High-Poverty Classrooms*, edited by M. S. Knapp, N. E. Adelman, C. Marder, H. McCollum, M. C. Needels, C. Padilla, P. M. Shields, and B. J Turnbull, A. A. Zucker, 11–32. New York: Teachers College Press.

McDermott, R. P. 1974. "Achieving School Failure." In *Education and Cultural Process*, edited by G. D. Spindler, 82–118. New York: Holt, Rinehart and Winston.

———. 1987. "Achieving School Failure: An Anthropological Approach to Illiteracy and Social Stratification." In *Education and Cultural Process,* 2nd ed., edited by G. D. Spindler, 132–154. Prospect Heights, IL: Waveland Press.

———. 1989. "Discussant's Comments: Making Dropouts." In *What Do Anthropologists Have to Say About Dropouts? The First Centennial Conference on Children At Risk,* edited by H. T. Trueba, G. D Spindler, and L. Spindler, 16–26. New York: Falmer Press.

———. 1997. "Achieving School Failure, 1972–1997." In *Education and Cultural Process: Anthropological Approaches,* 3rd ed., edited by G. D. Spindler, 110–135. Prospect Heights, IL: Waveland Press.

McDermott, R. P., and H. Varenne. 1995. "Culture As Disability." *Anthropology and Education Quarterly* 26 (no. 3): 324–348.

McGill-Franzen, A. 1994. "Compensatory and Special Education: Is Their Accountability for Learning and Belief in Children's Potential?" In *Getting Reading Right from the Start: Effective Early Literacy Interventions,* edited by E. H. Hiebert and B. M. Taylor, 13–35. Boston, MA: Allyn and Bacon.

McGill-Franzen, A., and I. James. 1990. "Teacher Beliefs About Remedial and Learning Disabled Readers." Paper presented at the National Reading Conference, Miami, Florida.

McLaughlin, M. W. 1994. "Somebody Knows My Name. Issues in Restructuring Schools." *Newsletter, Center on Organization and Restructuring of Schools, University of Wisconsin* 7: 9–11.

McLaughlin, M. W., and J. E. Talbert. 1993. "Introduction: New Visions of Teaching." In *Teaching for Understanding: Challenges for Policy and Practice,* edited by D. K. Cohen, M. W. McLaughlin, and J. E. Talbert, 1–12, San Francisco: Jossey-Bass.

McNeil, L. 1986. *Contradictions of Control.* New York: Routledge.

McQuillan, P. J. 1998. *Educational Opportunity in an Urban American High School: A Cultural Analysis.* Albany: State University of New York Press.

Means, B., C. Chelemer, and M. S. Knapp. 1991. *Teaching Advanced Skills to At-Risk Students.* San Francisco: Jossey-Bass.

Mehan, H. 1979. *Learning Lessons: Social Organization in Classrooms.* Cambridge: Harvard University Press.

Mehan, H., I. Villanueva, L. Hubbard, and A. Lintz. 1996. *Constructing School Success: The Consequences of Untracking Low-Achieving Students.* New York: Cambridge University Press.

Meier, D. 1995. *The Power of Their Ideas: Lessons for America from a Small School in Harlem.* Boston: Beacon Press.

Metz, E. D. 1993. "The Camouflaged At-Risk Student: White and Wealthy." *Momentum* 24 (no. 2): 40–44.

Metz, M. H. 1978. *Classrooms and Corridors: The Crisis of Authority in Desegregated Secondary Schools.* Berkeley: University of California Press.

———. 1989. "Teachers' Pride in Craft, School Subcultures, and Societal Pressures." In *Crisis in Teaching: Perspectives on Current Reforms,* edited by L. Weis, P. G. Altbach, G. P. Kelly, H. G. Petrie, S. Slaughter, 205–225. Albany: State University of New York, Albany.

———. 1998. "Veiled Inequities: The Hidden Effects of Community Social Class on High School Teachers' Perspectives and Practices." Paper presented at the annual meeting of the American Educational Research Association, April, San Diego, California.

Mims, S. 1996. "Principals Speak Out on Their Evolving Leadership Roles." In *Accelerated Schools in Action: Lessons from the Field*, edited by C. Finnan, E. St. John, J. McCarthy, and S. Slovacek, 208–218. Thousand Oaks, CA: Corwin Press.

Moles, O. C. 1993. "Collaboration Between Schools and Disadvantaged Parents: Obstacles and Openings." In *Families and Schools in a Pluralistic Society*, edited by N. Chavkin, 21–52. Albany: State University of New York Press.

Murphy, J., and P. Hallinger. 1992. "The Principalship in an Era of Transformation." *Journal of Educational Administration* 30 (no. 3): 77–88.

National Center for Educational Statistics. 1991. *National Educational Longitudinal Survey, NELS 88*. NCES no. 91–460. Washington, DC: Office of Educational Research and Improvement.

National Commission on Excellence in Education. 1983. *A Nation At Risk: The Imperative for National Reform*. Washington, DC: United States Department of Education.

National Commission on Teaching and America's Future. 1996. *What Matters Most: Teaching for America's Future*. New York: Teacher's College Press.

National Education Association. 1893. *Report of the Committee of Ten on Secondary Schools*. Washington, DC.

Newman, J. W. 1990. *America's Teachers: An Introduction to Education*. London: Longman.

Newmann, F. M. 1996. "Introduction: The School Restructuring Study." In *Authentic Achievement: Restructuring Schools for Intellectual Quality*, edited by F. M. Newmann et al., 1–17. San Francisco: Jossey-Bass.

Newmann, F. M., et al. 1996. *Authentic Achievement: Restructuring Schools for Intellectual Quality*. San Francisco: Jossey-Bass.

Newmann, F. M., W. G. Secada, and G. G. Wehlage. 1995. *A Guide to Authentic Instruction and Assessment: Vision, Standards, and Scoring*. Madison: Wisconsin Center for Education Research.

Nieto, S. 1992. *Affirming Diversity: The Sociopolitical Context of Multicultural Education*. White Plains, NY: Longman.

Noblit, G. W. 1993. "Power and Caring." *American Educational Research Journal* 30 (no. 1): 23–38.

Noddings, N. 1984. *Caring*. Berkeley: University of California Press.

Oakes, J. 1985. *Keeping Track: How Schools Structure Inequality*. New Haven: Yale University Press.

Oakes, J., A. S. Wells, M. Jones, and A. Datnow. 1997. "Detracking: The Social Construction of Ability, Cultural Politics, and Resistance to Reform." *Teachers College Record* 98: 482–510.

Ogbu, J. U. 1987. "Variability in Minority School Performance: A Problem in Search of an Explanation." *Anthropology and Education Quarterly* 18: 321–334.

Ogbu, J. U., and H. D. Simons. 1998. "Voluntary and Involuntary Minorities: A Cultural-Ecological Theory of School Performance with Some Implications for Education." *Anthropology and Education Quarterly* 29: 155–188.

Ohanian, S. 1999. *One Size Fits Few: The Folly of Educational Standards*. Portsmouth, NH: Heinemann.

O'Laughlin, M. 1990. "Teachers' Ways of Knowing: A Journal Study of Teacher Learning in a Dialogical and Constructivist Learning Environment." Paper presented at the Annual Meeting of the American Educational Research Association, April, Boston, Massachusetts.

Page, R. 1987. "Lower-Track Classes at a College-Preparatory High School: A Caricature of Educational Encounters." In *Interpretive Ethnography of Education: At Home and Abroad*, edited by G. D. Spindler and L. Spindler, 447–472. Hillsdale, NJ: Lawrence Erlbaum Associates.

Palincsar, A. S., and A. L. Brown. 1984. "Reciprocal Teaching of Comprehension: Fostering and Monitoring Activities." *Cognition and Instruction* 12: 117–175.

Paul, R. 1992. "Critical Thinking: What Every Person Needs to Survive in a Rapidly Changing World." Santa Rosa, CA: Foundations for Critical Thinking.

Payne, R. K. 1998. *A Framework for Understanding Poverty*. Baytown, TX: RFT Publishing.

Peterson, J. M. 1989. "Remediation Is No Remedy." *Educational Researcher* (March): 24–25.

Peterson, K. D., and T. E. Deal. 1998. "How Leaders Influence the Culture of Schools." *Educational Leadership* 56 (no. 1): 28–30.

Peterson, P. L., and C. M. Clark. 1978. "Teachers' Reports of Their Cognitive Processes During Teaching." *American Educational Research Journal* 154: 555–565.

Phelan, P., A. L. Davidson, and H. T. Cao. 1992. "Speaking Up: Students' Perspectives on School." *Phi Delta Kappan* 73 (no. 9): 695–704.

Phelan, P., A. L. Davidson, and H. C. Yu. 1998. *Adolescents' Worlds: Negotiating Family, Peers, and School*. New York: Teachers College Press.

Phillips, S. U. 1983. *The Invisible Culture: Communication in Classroom and Community on the Warm Springs Indian Reservation*. New York: Longman.

Piaget, J. 1970. *Science of Education and the Psychology of the Child*. New York: Penguin Books.

Pogrow, S. 1990. "Challenging At-Risk Students: Findings from the HOTS Program." *Phi Delta Kappan* (January): 389–397.

Pollins, L. D. 1983. "The Effects of Acceleration on the Social and Emotional Development of Gifted Students." In *Academic Precocity : Aspects of Its Development*, edited by C. P. Benbow and J. C. Stanley, 160–179. Baltimore: Johns Hopkins University Press.

Postman, N., and C. Weingartner. 1979. *Teaching as a Subversive Activity*. New York: Delacorte Press.

Pressey, S. L. 1949. *Educational Acceleration: Appraisal of Basic Problems*. Bureau of Educational Research Monographs, no. 31. Columbus: Ohio State University Press.

Proctor, T. B., K. N. Black, and J. F. Feldhusen. 1986. "Early Admission of Selected Children to Elementary School: A Review of the Research Literature." *Journal of Educational Research* 80: 70–76.

Ramos-Ford, V., and H. Gardner. 1991. "Giftedness from a Multiple Intelligences Perspective." In *Handbook of Gifted Education*, edited by N. Colangelo and G. A. Davis, 55–64. Needham Heights, MA: Allyn and Bacon.

Reese, S., and G. Ahlas. 1999. "Powerful Learning Peer Support Teams." Presentation at the Second Accelerated Schools Project national conference, 19 January, New Orleans, Louisiana.

Reis, S. M., M. L. Gentry, and S. Park. 1995. *Extending the Pedagogy of Gifted Education to All Students.* Storrs: University of Connecticut, National Research Center on the Gifted and Talented.

Renzulli, J. S. 1986. "The Three-Ring Conception of Giftedness: A Developmental Model for Creative Productivity." In *Conceptions of Giftedness,* edited by R. Sternberg and J. Davidson, 53–92. Cambridge, MA: Cambridge University Press.

———. 1994a. *Executive Summary: Schools for Talent Development: A Practical Plan for Total School Improvement.* Mansfield Center, CT: Creative Learning Press.

———. 1994b. *Schools for Talent Development: A Practical Plan for Total School Improvement.* Mansfield Center, CT: Creative Learning Press.

Renzulli, J. S., and S. M. Reis. 1985. *The Schoolwide Enrichment Model.* Mansfield Center, CT: Creative Learning Press.

———. 1991. "The Schoolwide Enrichment Model: A Comprehensive Plan for the Development of Creativity Productivity." In *Handbook of Gifted Education,* edited by N. Colangelo and G. A. Davis, 111–141. Needham Heights, MA: Allyn and Bacon.

Robinson, H. B. 1983. "A Case for Radical Acceleration: Programs of the Johns Hopkins University and the University of Washington." In *Academic Precocity: Aspects of Its Development,* edited by C. P. Benbow and J. C. Stanley, 139–159. Baltimore: Johns Hopkins University Press.

Rogers, K. 1990. "Using Effect Size to Make Good Decisions About Acceleration." Paper presented at the Annual Meeting of the National Association for Gifted Children, November, Little Rock, Arkansas.

Ross, P. O. 1993. *National Excellence: A Case for Developing America's Talent.* Washington, DC: U.S. Department of Education.

Rotberg, I. C., and J. J. Harvey. 1993. *Federal Policy Options for Improving Education of Low-Income Students.* Vol. 1, *Findings and Recommendations.* Santa Monica, CA: Rand.

Rumberger, R., C. Darrah, H. M. Levin, and C. Finnan. 1994. "Assessing the Educational Requirements of Work: Two Views from the Shop Floor." Unpublished manuscript.

Russell, R. S., and J. Meikamp. 1994. "Creativity Training: A Practical Teaching Strategy." In *Rural Partnerships: Working Together,* edited by D. Montgomery, Proceedings of the Annual National Conference of the American Council on Rural Special Education, March, Austin, Texas.

Sarason, S. 1996. *Revisiting "The Culture of the School and the Problem of Change."* New York: Teachers College Press.

Schëin, E. 1992. *Organizational Culture and Leadership,* 2nd ed. San Francisco: Jossey-Bass.

Schiever, S. W., and C. J. Maker. 1991. "Enrichment and Acceleration: An Overview and New Directions." In *Handbook of Gifted Education,* edited by N. Colangelo and G. A. Davis, 99–110. Needham Heights, MA: Allyn and Bacon.

Schlechty, P. C. 1990. *Schools for the Twenty-First Century: Leadership Imperatives for Educational Reform.* San Francisco: Jossey-Bass.

———. 1997. *Inventing Better Schools: An Action Plan for Educational Reform.* San Francisco: Jossey-Bass.

Secretary's Commission on Achieving Necessary Skills (SCANS). 1991. *What Work Requires of Schools.* Washington, DC: U.S. Department of Labor.

Semel, S. F. 1999. "Introduction." In *Schools of Tomorrow, Schools of Today: What Happened to Progressive Education*, edited by S. F. Semel and A. R. Sadovnik, 1–20. New York: Peter Lang.

Shields, P. M. 1995. "Engaging Children of Diverse Backgrounds." In *Teaching for Meaning in High-Poverty Classrooms*, edited by M. S. Knapp et al., 33–46. New York: Teachers College Press.

Showers, B., and B. Joyce. 1996. "The Evolution of Peer Coaching." *Educational Leadership* (March): 12–16.

Shulman, L. S. 1987. "Knowledge and Teaching: Foundations of the New Reform." *Harvard Education Review* 57 (no. 1): 1–22.

Silverman, L. K. 1986. *Perfectionism*. Denver: Gifted Child Development Center.

Sizer, T. 1984. *Horace's Compromise: The Dilemma of the American High School*. Boston: Houghton Mifflin.

———. 1992a. *Horace's Compromise*, rev. ed. Boston: Houghton Mifflin.

———. 1992b. *Horace's School: Redesigning the American High School*. Boston: Houghton Mifflin.

Slavin, R. 1987. "Ability Grouping and Student Achievement in Elementary Schools: A Best-Evidence Synthesis." *Review of Educational Research* 573: 293–336.

Sleeter, C. E. 1993. "How White Teachers Construct Race." In *Race Identity and Representation in Education*, edited by C. McCarthy and W. Crichlow, 157–170. New York: Routledge Press.

Solomon, R. P. 1992. *Black Resistance in High School: Forging a Separatist Culture*. Albany: State University of New York Press.

Southern, W. T., and E. D. Jones. 1991. "Academic Acceleration: Background and Issues." In *The Academic Acceleration of Gifted Children*, edited by W. T. Southern and E. D. Jones, 1–28. New York: Teachers College Press.

Southern, W. T., E. D. Jones, and E. D. Fiscus. 1989. "Practitioner Objections to the Academic Acceleration of Young Gifted Children." *Gifted Child Quarterly* 33: 29–35.

Spear-Swerling, L., and R. J. Sternberg. 1996. *Off Track: When Poor Readers Become "Learning Disabled."* Boulder: Westview Press.

Spillane, J. P., and N. E. Jennings. 1997. "Constructing a Challenging Pedagogy for All Students: Contrasting the Rhetoric of Reform with Practice and the Rhetoric of Practitioners." Paper presented at the annual meeting of the American Educational Research Association, March, Chicago, Illinois.

Spindler, G. 1999. Personal communication. August 25.

Spindler, G., and L. Spindler. 1982. "Roger Harker and Schöenhausen: From the Familiar to the Strange and Back Again." In *Doing the Ethnography of Schooling: Educational Anthropology in Action*, edited by G. Spindler, 14–19. New York: Holt, Rinehart and Winston.

———. 1987. "Cultural Dialogue and Schooling in Schöenhausen and Roseville: A Comparative Analysis." *Anthropology and Education Quarterly* 18 (no. 1): 3–16.

———. 1989. "There Are No Dropouts Among the Arunta and Hutterites." In *What Do Anthropologists Have to Say About Dropouts? The First Centennial Conference on Children at Risk*, edited by H. T. Trueba, G. Spindler, and L. Spindler, 7–15. New York: Falmer Press.

————. 1993. "Cross-Cultural, Comparative, Reflective Interviewing in Schöenhausen and Roseville." In *Voices in Educational Research*, edited by M. Schratz, 150–175. New York: Falmer Press.

————. 1994. "What Is Cultural Therapy?" In *Pathways to Cultural Awareness: Cultural Therapy with Teachers and Students*, edited by G. Spindler and L. Spindler, 1–34. Thousand Oaks, CA: Corwin Press.

Stanley, J. C. 1977. "Rationale for the Study of Mathematically Precocious Youth (SMPY) During Its First Five Years of Promoting Educational Acceleration." In *The Gifted and Creative: A Fifty-Year Perspective*, edited by J. C. Stanley, W. C. George, and C. M. Solaro, 75–112. Baltimore: Johns Hopkins Press.

————. 1985. "Fostering Use of Mathematical Talent in the USA: SMPY's Rationale." Paper presented at Sixth World Conference on Gifted and Talented Children, August, in Hamburg, Germany.

Stanley, J. C., and C. P. Benbow. 1983. "SMPY's First Decade: Ten Years of Posing Problems and Solving Them." *Journal of Special Education* 17: 11–25.

Stanton-Salazar, R. 1997. "A Social Capital Framework for Understanding the Socialization of Racial Minority Children and Youth." *Harvard Educational Review* 67 (no. 1): 1–40.

Starko, A. J. 1986. *It's About Time: In-Service Strategies for Curriculum Compacting.* Mansfield Center, CT: Creative Learning Press.

Stein, M. K., M. S. Smith, and E. A. Silver. 1999. "The Development of Professional Developers: Learning to Assist Teachers in New Settings on New Ways." *Harvard Educational Review* 69 (no. 3): 238–269.

Sternberg, R. J. 1985. *Beyond IQ: A Triarchic Theory of Human Intelligence.* New York: Cambridge University Press.

————. 1986. *Intelligence Applied: Understanding and Increasing Your Intellectual Skills.* San Diego: Harcourt, Brace and Jovanovich.

St. John, E. P., J. Meza Jr., L. Allen-Haynes, and B. M. Davidson. 1996. "Building Communities of Inquiry: Linking Teacher Research and School Restructuring." In *Accelerated Schools in Action: Lessons from the Field*, edited by C. Finnan, E. St. John, J. McCarthy, and S. Slovacek, 124–138. Thousand Oaks, CA: Corwin Press.

Stocklinski, J., and J. Miller-Colbert. 1991. "The Comer Process: Moving from 'I' to 'We.'" *Principal* 70 (no. 3): 18–19.

Stringfield, S., L. Winfield, M. A. Milsap, M. J. Puma, B. Gamse, and B. Randall. 1994. *Urban and Suburban/Rural: Special Strategies for Educating Disadvantaged Children: First Year Report.* Washington, DC: U.S. Department of Education.

Swadener, B. B., and S. Kessler. 1991. "Introduction to the Special Issue: Reconceptualizing Early Childhood Education." *Early Education and Development* 2 (no. 2): 85–94.

Swadener, B. B., and S. Lubeck. 1995. "The Social Construction of Children and Families 'At Risk': An Introduction." In *Children and Families "At Promise": Deconstructing the Discourse of Risk*, edited by B. B. Swadener and S. Lubeck, 1–16. Albany: State University of New York Press.

Swanson, J. D. 1998. "Project Breakthrough: Application for Grant Under the Javits Gifted and Talented Students Education Program Grants." Unpublished document.

————. 1999. "Project Breakthrough: Performance Report for Year One." Unpublished document.

Taba, H. 1962. *Curriculum Development: Theory and Practice.* New York: Harcourt, Brace and World.

Tannenbaum, A. J. 1979. "Pre-Sputnik to Post-Watergate Concern About the Gifted." In *The Gifted and Talented,* edited by A. H. Passow, 5–27. Chicago: National Society for the Study of Education.

Teitle, L. 1999. "Professional Development Schools: A Literature Review." In *Designing Standards That Work for Professional Development Schools,* edited by M. Levine. Commissioned papers for the NCATE Professional Development Standards.

Terman, L. M., and M. H. Oden. 1947. *Genetic Studies of Genius.* Vol. 4, *The Gifted Child Grows Up: Twenty-Five Years' Follow-Up of a Superior Group.* Stanford: Stanford University Press.

Tharp, R., and R. Gallimore. 1988. *Rousing Minds to Life: Teaching, Learning, and Schooling in Social Context.* New York: Cambridge University.

Tomlinson, C. A. 1996. "Good Teaching for One and All: Does Gifted Education Have an Instructional Identity?" *Journal for the Education of the Gifted* 20 (no.2): 155–174.

Tomlinson, C. A., and C. M. Callahan. 1992. "Contributions of Gifted Education to General Education in a Time of Change." *Gifted Child Quarterly* 364: 183–189.

Treffinger, D. J., C. M. Callahan, and V. L. Vaughn. 1991. "Research on Enrichment Efforts in Gifted Education." In *Handbook of Special Education, Research, and Practice,* vol. 4., edited by M. C. Wang, N. C. Reynolds, and H. J. Wahlberg, 37–55. New York: Pergamon Press.

Tyack, D. 1974. *The One Best System: A History of American Urban Education.* Cambridge: Harvard University Press.

Tyack, D., and L. Cuban. 1995. *Tinkering Toward Utopia: A Century of Public School Reform.* Cambridge: Harvard University Press.

Tyack, D., and W. Tobin. 1994. "The Grammar of Schooling: why Has It Been So Hard to Change?" *American Research Journal* 31: 453–479.

United States Department of Education. 1996. *The Role of Leadership in Sustaining School Reform: Voices from the Field.* Washington, DC: United States Department of Education.

Van Tassel-Baska, J. 1981. "The Great Debates: For Acceleration." Paper presented at CEC/TAG National Topical Conference on Gifted and Talented Children, December, Orlando, Florida.

————. 1986. "Acceleration." In *Critical Issues in Gifted Education,* edited by C. J. Maker, 179–196. Rockville, MD: Aspen Publishers.

————. 1991. "Identification of Candidates for Acceleration: Issues and Concerns." In *The Academic Acceleration of Gifted Children,* edited by W. T. Southern and E. D. Jones, 148–161. New York: Teachers College Press.

Varenne, H. 1982. "Jocks and Freaks: The Symbolic Structure of the Expression of Social Interaction Among American Senior High School Students." In *Doing the Ethnography of Schooling: Educational Anthropology in Action,* edited by G. D. Spindler, 210–235. New York: Holt Rinehart and Winston.

Waller, W. 1932. *The Sociology of Teaching.* New York: Wiley.

Wasley, P. A., R. L. Hampel, and R. W. Clark. 1997. *Kids and School Reform*. San Francisco: Jossey-Bass.

Wax, M. L. 1993. "How Culture Misdirects Multiculturalism." *Anthropology and Education Quarterly* 24 (no. 2): 99–115.

Wehlage, G., G. Smith, and P. Lipman. 1992. "Restructuring Urban Schools: The New Futures Experience." *American Educational Research Journal* 29 (no. 1): 51–96.

Weissglass, J. 1999. Curriculum and Society. *Education Week* (April): 45–47.

Wells, A. S., and I. Serna. 1996. "The Politics of Culture: Understanding Local Political Resistance to Detracking in Racially Mixed Schools." *Harvard Educational Review* 66 (no. 1): 93–118.

Wheelock, A. 1992. *Crossing the Tracks: How "Untracking" Can Save America's Schools*. New York: New Press.

White, K. R., M. J. Taylor, and V. D. Moss. 1992. "Does Research Support Claims About the Benefits of Involving Parents in Early Intervention Programs?" *Review of Educational Research* 62 (no. 1): 91–125.

Willis, G., W. H. Schubert, R. V. Bullough Jr., C. Kridel, and J. T. Holton, eds. 1993. *The American Curriculum: A Documentary History*. Westport, CT: Greenwood Press.

Willis, P. 1977. *Learning to Labour*. Westmead, England: Saxon House.

Wilson, S. M., C. Miller, and C. Yerkes. 1993. "Deeply Rooted Change: A Tale of Learning to Teach Adventurously." In *Teaching for Understanding: Challenges for Policy and Practice*, edited by D. K. Cohen, M. W. McLaughlin, and J. E. Talbert, 84–130. San Francisco: Jossey-Bass.

Wong, B. Y. L. 1991. "The Relevance of Metacognition to Learning Disabilities." In *Learning About Learning Disabilities*, edited by B. Y. L. Wong, 231–258. San Diego: Academic Press.

Yao, E. L. 1993. "Strategies for Working Effectively with Asian Immigrant Parents." In *Families and Schools in a Pluralistic Society*, edited by N. F. Chavkin, 149–156. Albany: State University of New York Press.

Zilversmit, A. 1993. *Changing Schools: Progressive Education Theory and Practice, 1930–1960*. Chicago: University of Chicago Press.

Index